Diversity in Psychotherapy

DIVERSITY IN PSYCHOTHERAPY

The Politics of Race, Ethnicity, and Gender

Jean Lau Chin, Victor De La Cancela, and Yvonne M. Jenkins

Foreword by Stanley Sue

PRAEGER

Westport, Connecticut
London

Library of Congress Cataloging-in-Publication Data

Chin, Jean Lau.
   Diversity in psychotherapy : the politics of race, ethnicity, and
gender / Jean Lau Chin, Victor De La Cancela, and Yvonne M.
Jenkins ; foreword by Stanley Sue.
      p. cm.
   Includes bibliographical references and index.
   ISBN 0–275–94180–9 (alk. paper)
   1. Psychiatry, Transcultural.   2. Psychotherapy—Social aspects.
3. Intercultural communication.   4. Minorities—Mental health
services—Social aspects.   5. Psychiatry, Transcultural—United
States.   I. Cancela, Victor De La.   II. Jenkins, Yvonne M.
III. Title.
RC455.4.E8C55   1993
616.89'14—dc20   93–18240

British Library Cataloguing in Publication Data is available.

Library of Congress Catalog Card Number: 93–18240
ISBN: 0–275–94180–9

First published in 1993

Praeger Publishers, 88 Post Road West, Westport, CT 06881
An imprint of Greenwood Publishing Group, Inc.

Printed in the United States of America

The paper used in this book complies with the
Permanent Paper Standard issued by the National
Information Standards Organization (Z39.48–1984).

10 9 8 7 6 5 4 3 2 1

All names and most identifying characteristics of clients described have been changed
in order to protect their privacy.

CONTENTS

ACKNOWLEDGMENTS

There are many more people who have contributed to this book than it is possible to acknowledge. First and foremost, we would like to acknowledge the contributions from the cultures of our people—that is, the Asian, Latino, and African-American families with whom we identify and from which we gain our perspectives. Our struggles, our joys, our vision—shared but diverse—contributed greatly to our thinking. Second, we would like to mention a few who have contributed directly to the production of this book, whose guidance, wisdom, and thoughtfulness have made a positive difference: John T. Harney, Stanley Sue, Deborah R. Brome, and L. Philip Guzman. We would also like to thank Irís Závala-Martínez and Lillian Comas-Díaz for their critical input and guidance.

Each of us has had particular sources of support whom we would like to acknowledge.

I, Jean Lau Chin, would like to acknowledge my appreciation of my board of directors at South Cove Community Health Center for their support of my professional development. I owe special thanks to Michele Robichaud for her technical support. With love, I dedicate this to my family for their patience and sacrifice, to my parents for giving within their limits so that I could reach heights they never even dreamed, and to Scott for never letting me forget where my priorities should be.

I, Victor De La Cancela, would like to express my gratitude to all the people who have worked with me to enhance my understanding of different world views, therapy, and politics over the years. These collaborators include those who at different times have carried the identification of client, student, mentor, supervisor, professor, or colleague.

I also want to thank my parents, brother and sisters, extended and adopted family members, and friends who have provided support, insight, and encouragement. I am especially grateful for the administrative and office staff who have facilitated the editorial process over the years. My sincerest thanks also go out to my coauthors from whom I have learned much and by whom I have been enriched. Finally, I acknowledge all those unsung heroes and heroines, people of different ethnicities and class backgrounds whose suffering and lifelong struggles have provided people of color with opportunities and knowledge they otherwise would never have had.

I, Yvonne M. Jenkins, wish to express my gratitude to all those who have contributed to my appreciation of diversity, the interactive nature of cultural, sociopolitical processes and psychosocial development, and the practice of psychotherapy with pluralistic populations. I am especially grateful to the Center for Multicultural Training in Psychology and its professional network for having the vision and the courage to train culturally competent psychologists long before the necessity for this was widely embraced. I also thank those mentors, colleagues, and friends who have encouraged and supported me in this endeavor. With love and appreciation I acknowledge my family whose faith, love, and support have sustained me in all of my endeavors. To those clients that I have been privileged to work with over the years I am especially grateful. Finally, I wish to express my sincerest thanks and admiration to my coauthors who have taught me much and inspired me considerably since the inception of this project.

FOREWORD

Stanley Sue

Little did the founding forefathers know that by introducing African slavery into the United States, they were laying the seeds for centuries of racial and ethnic strife. While the nature of the strife has changed over time, it can be seen in all phases of life in the United States.

Diversity in Psychotherapy, written by Jean Lau Chin, Victor De La Cancela, and Yvonne M. Jenkins, is a vivid account of how ethnic and racial diversity issues, as well as other diversity issues such as gender and sexual orientation, are embedded in society in general and psychotherapy in particular. The perspective of the authors is that effective psychotherapy for culturally diverse populations is not simply a matter of finding a culturally specific technique to use or of understanding the cultural content of the client. Rather, a broad understanding of personal, professional, and political processes is needed. This is illustrated not only in the analysis of race/ethnic relations but also in the presentation of clinical cases. In addition, diversity needs to be respected and valued as an asset instead of a liability. To the authors, concepts involving "liberation," "empowerment," "capitalism," "oppression," and so on are germane. They will also provoke much controversy. Some readers who want to know how to conduct psychotherapy with pluralistic populations will not find simple and easy answers; those whose vision of issues in psychotherapy is limited to the disciplines of the helping professions—for example, psychology, psychiatry, social work, and psychiatric nursing—will more clearly see the difficulties in confining their analysis to these disciplines. Indeed, the book is as much a sociopolitical and historical statement as it is a mental health guide.

The fact of the matter is that as we approach the twenty-first century, our society is becoming increasingly diverse. Significant strides in addressing diversity issues in general and psychotherapy in particular cannot be achieved if we fail to recognize how these issues are woven throughout the fabric of society. The authors advocate self-knowledge, empowerment, and multicultural education as means of nurturing diversity. The challenge for those in the mental health profession is to gain self-knowledge, to help empower others, and to promote multicultural education. In doing so, psychotherapy as an institutional process in the mental health system will become more effective for diverse populations.

PART ONE

Deborah Ridley Brome

In his seminal work *The Structure of Scientific Revolutions*, Thomas Kuhn argues that what we know as scientifically based truth and accept as laws of nature are intricately linked to history and social context. He further suggests that history and context have and will continue to influence the emergence and acceptance of key paradigms of natural science and plant the seeds for paradigm shifts. Paradigm shifts occur when there is significant tension between paradigms that explain how we know and understand our world and our social/historical context. The authors of this volume join with other scholars in calling for a paradigmatic shift in the theory and practice of psychotherapy.

Drs. Chin, De La Cancela, and Jenkins document the inadequacy of "traditional" psychotherapy practices as effective frameworks of intervention with pluralistic populations. Traditional psychotherapy paradigms are minimally, if at all, effective in explaining and conceptualizing the world view and particular human dilemmas of a number of groups in the United States. In part one Chin, De La Cancela, and Jenkins significantly contribute to shaping the structure of diversity-inclusive frameworks by reformulating those constructs that will be central in defining culturally competent psychotherapy. The need for paradigms that are inclusive and accommodate diversity is essential. The parameters of culturally competent psychotherapy include diversity, race, gender, ethnicity, culture, and empathy as concepts which require reframing. In addition, the importance of acknowledging critical sociopolitical realities associated with these parameters is emphasized.

In chapter one, the authors discuss why a paradigmatic shift is needed. They begin to challenge several key assumptions and ways that we as psychotherapists have come to know and understand our roles and function as healers. Specifically, they challenge the idea that psychotherapy is objective and apolitical. These authors join others in advocating that the race, ethnicity, gender, and culture of both the client and the therapist are important attributes that should be explored and utilized in the therapeutic process. Their perspective is unique in that it describes these variables as contributing to concepts that assist us in maximizing empathy and transference in psychotherapy. They suggest that the same variables should be incorporated into the process of defining empathy.

In chapter two, the authors continue to build the case for a paradigmatic shift and to articulate a set of concepts that create a culturally competent framework. For them, a culturally competent paradigm has the capacity for cultural self-evaluation on the part of the therapist and client and promotes opportunities for bias-free service delivery that is responsive to the unique needs of each client. In this chapter they present an intriguing notion that a particular racial, ethnic, or cultural group's history significantly shapes how it defines or perceives these aspects of identity. This idea is a novel one and holds a wide range of implications for psychotherapy with pluralistic populations. To demonstrate the variety of meanings that these concepts have, the authors give historical summaries followed by a discussion of the saliency of race, ethnicity, gender, and culture for African-Americans, Chinese-Americans, and Puerto Ricans. Most therapists assume that clients from pluralistic populations have similar formulations of and attribute similar personal relevance to these concepts. Yet, this is not so. Therapists who are respectful of diversity and hope to build an empathic relationship with persons from different backgrounds need to recognize differences that exist between groups. In addition, the significance of these concepts to self-definition must also be recognized. The authors' reframing of these concepts also highlights the depth at which historical and cultural experiences color our understanding of ourselves and of self-other relationships. Furthermore, they challenge therapists who work with particular ethnocultural groups to study their historical, social, and political struggles.

The authors also provide examples of how racial, ethnic, and economic power differentials have historically affected social esteem and gender role expectations of those groups highlighted. Social esteem is the value that one holds for one's own group that can be evaluated on a positive-negative continuum. For pluralistic populations, social esteem is related to what extent their world views and perceptions of reality have been valued and embraced throughout history. Social esteem is significant to self-esteem.

In chapter three, Jenkins elaborates on the relationship between diversity and social esteem. In relation to the Racial and Cultural Identity Model (Atkinson, Morten, & Sue, 1989), she calls for the inclusion of social esteem as a central construct in working with people of color and others who have been "cut off" from empowering cultural legacies. Jenkins also discusses common ways that members of society and therapists inadvertently devalue diversity and suggests alternatives that nurture diversity.

The idea of social esteem as a pivotal concept in working with pluralistic populations is an innovative one. This notion recognizes the idea that most members of these groups understand themselves through their groups. Their world views are "we" oriented rather than "I" oriented, and the social esteem construct captures how the larger societies' historical treatment of their particular group is incorporated in the self-definition of the person of color.

In sum, part one documents the need for a culturally competent paradigmatic shift and begins to redefine and reframe key concepts that are needed in order to embrace diversity. The overarching objective is to provide therapists with a framework to increase empathy and assist with understanding transference.

REFERENCE

Atkinson, D., Morten, G., & Sue, D. W. (Eds.) (1989). *Counseling American minorities: A cross-cultural perspective*. Dubuque, IA: W. C. Brown.

CHAPTER ONE

DIVERSITY IN PSYCHOTHERAPY: EXAMINATION OF RACIAL, ETHNIC, GENDER, AND POLITICAL ISSUES

Victor De La Cancela, Yvonne M. Jenkins, and Jean Lau Chin

This is a book about psychotherapy with diverse populations. It is the result of our collaboration in developing a symposium presentation on gender and ethnicity in psychotherapy with persons of color for the American Psychological Association's ninety-seventh annual convention in New Orleans. As such, this is a jointly authored manuscript that reflects our struggle with the topic, the form and content of the text, and the commitment to produce a document that adequately presents similarities and differences in theory, practice, and racial and cultural perspectives over a three-year period. In many ways, this book is the outcome of diversity as a process in which we have been both subjects and objects. It reflects the clear differences among us in tone, language, and directness of communication. It reveals to the reader how spirited, provocative, personal, critical, and courageous each of us is at different points in our work with psychotherapy clients, toward our colleagues, and with ourselves as professionals of color.

This is a professional and personal book. Therefore it is also an extremely political book that critiques current professional practices in psychotherapy that carry a majority, mainstream, and dominant order perspective. It is our hope that this framework will lead to reexamination of the sociocultural and political factors that influence the practice of psychotherapy. It is also our intent to provide competent views on how to work with diversity in the practice of psychotherapy. We invite readers to review and critique how successful we have been in meeting our purpose and to share their responses and reactions with us and others toward promoting the acceptance of differences that is as important in psychotherapy as it is in society.

WHY DIVERSITY?

The concept of *diversity* is one that has gained prominence in the field of mental health. Increasingly, this term is used as a political, social, and professional statement of openness, forward thinking, and differences. What does diversity mean in the context of psychotherapy?

We define diversity in psychotherapy as an openness to new experiences and progressive ideas among practitioners and a more flexible and socially contextualized view of personal histories among clients. Thus diversity is the valorization of alternate lifestyles, biculturality, human differences, and uniqueness in individual and group life. Diversity promotes an informed connectedness to one's reference group, self-knowledge, empowering contact with those different from oneself, and an appreciation for the commonalities of our human condition. Diversity also requires an authentic exploration of the client's and practitioner's personal and reference group history. This exploration empowers the therapeutic dyad by providing a meaningful context for understanding present realities, problems of daily living, and available solutions. Chapter 2 expands on this definition in a historical context.

Just as the civil rights, indigenous, Latino, African, and Asian movements have demonstrated that events that celebrate a biased history (e.g., Columbus Day) must be replaced by events that speak to the perspectives of people of color, so must psychotherapy struggle to broaden western views of psychological health by respecting the cultural development of its diverse participants. Besides attending to fantasy, psychotherapy must attend to discrete realities and place them in the context of economic and political relationships. Progressive psychotherapy needs to respect and reflect diversified criteria for excellence, creativity, and mental health that are based on the different perspectives and standards of communities of color. The challenge then is to develop a practice that operationalizes cultural equity, parity, and the validity of all groups, focusing on the restructuring of personal resources and encouraging the redistribution of external resources to support the diversity of all members of society.[1]

WHO ARE WE TALKING ABOUT?

If diversity is understood as a positive, enriching perspective in psychotherapy, then differences are to be viewed as assets rather than as liabilities. This simple statement represents a profound departure from the pathological diagnosis bias of traditional psychotherapy toward almost all populations. Indeed the deficit-driven medical model of psychoanalytically oriented therapies has long been criticized from both within and outside of the profession for its emphasis on labelling and treating as character weakness, emotional disturbance, or mental illness those behaviors, beliefs, or cognitions that do not validate an idealized Caucasian, middle-class male, and western construction of reality. However, it has been the ethnoculturally diverse, particularly visible racial and ethnic groups, who have suffered the most at the hands of ethnocentric therapists and society as a whole.

Indeed the very terms used to describe these populations reflect a negation of reality. For example, "minority," used as a label to refer to populations of color, ignores the reality that it is the Caucasian race which is a numerical minority globally.[2] It also acknowledges what group is in a political majority (i.e., power elite) in the United States and generalizes this to the entire world. We see in this term oppressive connotations of disempoweredness and poverty that are inappropriate and offensive in the context of African, Latino, indigenous, and Asian ethnic groups who are becoming increasingly numerous, economically strong, and sociopolitically organized.[3]

For this reason, we use the terms "people of color," "visible racial ethnocultural groups of color," "pluralistic populations," "disenfranchised people," "culturally different,"and "diversified groups" in places where others who partake of a different ideology would use "minority." We have similarly attempted to be as specific as possible in the identification of subgroups within larger ethnic or racial categories (e.g., Chinese). And we have avoided using terms that are clearly thought to be discriminatory by some members of the group to which these terms are applied such as Hispanic or American. "Hispanic," a term coined by the U.S. Census Bureau, meaning Spanish-speaking, is not preferred since it does not connote the ethnic, racial origins of Latinos, who are people from Central and South America or the Caribbean region, or their descendants in the United States. "American" is often used in the United States to refer to U.S. citizens; however, most Latinos see themselves as Americans in the context of the Americas, which include North, Central, South, and Latin America.

We remind readers that how people are labeled by others and by themselves changes according to the racial, ethnic, legal, social, and political statements being made at a particular time. Thus, terms used by us now may be used differently in the future. We have also used several terms interchangeably for indigenous people, none of which are entirely accurate, though they are in current usage and accepted to varying degrees.[4] Indeed, the aboriginal people of North America bear the questionable distinction of having the U.S. Congress formulate a legal definition of their ethnic group.[5]

Though some might find such efforts faddish or deride them as attempts to be "politically correct," we feel that it is as important to avoid Eurocentric and anglocentric categorization of individuals and their reference groups as it is to learn to address men and women in a nonsexist and nonhomophobic manner. As La Due[6] and Tong[7] indicate, there is both a critical need to be mindful of avoiding sexist language and inappropriate designations of people, and a need for understanding the sociological and psychological implications of terminology within historical contexts. Within the context of psychotherapy, understanding people of color through the lenses of oppressive language and terminology (i.e., culturally disadvantaged or culturally deprived) serves to restrict psychological growth.

Our specific focus is on three of the visible racial ethnic groups in the United States. We have limited the main focus of our discussion to African-American, Asian/Chinese-American, and Latino/Puerto Rican populations because these are the groups we collectively and individually know best and therefore are competent to discuss. We feel, however, that the true practice of diversity in psychotherapy would lead to examination of how our current systems of service delivery also fail indigenous groups, other ethnic people, and disenfranchised members of U.S. society (e.g., children, the elderly, women, gay men and lesbians, the differently abled, and people with psychiatric labels).

McGoldrick, Pearce, and Giordano,[8] in their book on family therapy, capture some of the differences among European-American and non-European families as a descriptive context for diversity. Since the groups in their book are mostly Caucasian, we feel that our book provides a different focus because people of color are likely to identify themselves on the basis of race, as well as class, ethnicity, and gender. People of color are also more likely to become targets of oppression primarily on the basis of race. It is this legacy of oppression that translates into economic and political discrimination, which also leads to our view of psychotherapeutic diversity as including a social action approach.

WHERE DOES GENDER FIT IN?

In much the same way that we differentiate our book from McGoldrick, Pearce, and Giordano's, we also seek to build on and expand on the work of Sue, Richardson, Ruiz, and Smith[9] and Fulani,[10] whose contributions, though seminal, are somewhat incomplete in addressing the areas they set out to explore. First, we wish to do more with the issue of politics in therapy than Sue did within the counseling area. Second, we wish to broaden the discussion of gender issues to include men, which Fulani's work does very little with. We are particularly concerned about being male inclusive, given the "crisis of extinction" that African-American and Latino/Puerto Rican males increasingly are experiencing. The emasculation of Asian males or its polar opposite—their vilification—also concerns us greatly. If being a poor male of color translates into exposure to inadequate health care facilities, shorter average life expectancies, and higher overall homicide, drug use, and accident rates,[11] then it becomes an ethical responsibility for therapists to recognize the limitations of their art in enhancing the male's coping abilities to face this social milieu.

Too often, however, the extent of Euro-American understanding regarding men of color is limited to negative stereotypes related to sexist behavior. If we were to ask most anglocentric therapists to word-associate about Asian, African-American, and Latino men, chances are that most of the descriptors would be passive aggressive or aggressive, macho or "traditional," and "old country" chauvinist behavior. This exercise would reveal that as regards men and women of color, most therapists have little understanding of the specific positive and negative cultural and contradictory sociopolitical and economic forces impinging on their lives.[12]

Sadly, it is also true that many men and women of color are similarly disabled by an alienation from self that blinds them to the intersection of their personal and reference group history. Thus a necessary component of therapy with them becomes enhancing reality testing in this regard. This aspect of therapy could be and has been considered as consciousness-raising and profeminist, and, as such, political.

WHAT DOES POLITICS HAVE TO DO WITH IT?

We chose to focus on diversity involving the issues of race, ethnicity, and gender as it influences the theory and practice of psychotherapy and found that the principles and concepts derived from our clinical work with communities of color raise much broader concerns about the general practice of psychotherapy with other populations. These concerns can be adequately categorized as political since they relate to how psychotherapy as a profession supports the form or process of organized society, with its specific government and economic interests and power struggles. Support of the status quo occurs even when therapists choose not to be political because the fundamental connection to political affairs is often obscured by the western ideology of psychotherapy—that is, therapy is apolitical, scientifically neutral, and bias free. This ideology minimizes social inequities such as sexism, ethnocentrism, and classism inasmuch as it overlooks structural problems in our society and economy and places emphasis on psychological explanations. Thus it supports institutional racism by decontextualizing the experiences of people of color and eschewing more explicitly empowering and egalitarian therapy.

Our stance is that denial of sociopolitical factors in therapy is harmful to clients. Indeed, it leads to a noxious relationship and runs the risk of not making accessible to clients useful external resources and services. There is no such thing as neutral therapy. It either facilitates the client's integration into the "logic" of the status quo or it liberates by critically and creatively reality-testing as it encourages participation in transformation of the world.[13]

We are aware that such views of psychotherapy are not "mainstream" and therefore they might alienate or disturb some readers. Yet it is their very differentness that makes them an integral part of a discussion of diversity in the field. Indeed, it may be that our willingness as authors to see cultural, ideological, and political implications as key to practice and theory in psychotherapy is a reflection of our sharing similar backgrounds with psychologists in the so-called Third World or "developing" nations who are more likely to engage in such discussions.[14]

Psychologists in less industrialized societies often find western concepts and methods irrelevant to their social reality—a reality that is shared with many U.S. communities of color. This reality includes the negative conditions of exile, immigration, crowding, unemployment, poverty, disease, violence, undereducation, and malnutrition. Similar world views or cultural perspectives include such other realities as: group and family orientation rather than individualistic orientation; serving and collaborating with others instead of competition; and combating oppression and assimilation while adapting and building bridges between tradition and modern practices.

Sloan[15] indicates that western psychologists have ignored Third World or developing countries, seeing them only as objects of study for other fields. We would add that it is only in the very recent past that North American psychotherapy has attended to the needs of people of color residing on this continent, needs that have led some to categorizing the *barrios*, neighborhoods, and towns of people of color in the United States as "islands of Third World realities" in a "First World of affluence."[16] Sloan claims that the role of psychology in technologically "developed" countries has primarily been the adjustment and fine-tuning of individuals for education, work, and self-actualization within a high-tech society. These are the very roles that too often have been denied to visible ethnic and racial groups in the United States. Albee[17] adds that therapy provides privatized solutions and adjustment to societal problems rather than prevention of these problems. We see our efforts as a partial remedy to these failures and conceive of psychotherapeutic interventions as appropriately including prevention, health education, systemic approaches, community organization, and political consciousness raising.[18]

For diversity to flourish, therapists in our view ought to promote micro and macro level change, as too many people of color have had their diversity devalued. This has led ultimately to the internalization of negative self-images on the individual level and harmful national images on a collective level.[19] Indeed, this devaluation of diversity has caused people of color to positively validate those whom they are economically and politically disenfranchised by. As Lykes and Liem[20] report, such views challenge the proscription separating professional practice from political action. This challenge, however, is not new; many North American psychologists involved with community mental health, public service, and ethnocultural populations have been engaged in it for at least the last three decades. Over the years their responses to the challenge have been variously labelled as liberal, radical, cultural, sociopolitical, or activist approaches to therapy.

In the resultant approaches, we see an emerging form of therapeutic praxis similar to what Latin Americans call *una terapia comprometida*. *Terapia comprometida* refers to a therapy where there is a "bond of commitment," a relationship where the political, social, and psychological alliance between therapist and client is explicit.[21] This is an ethically nonneutral attitude toward the clients' problems that has been most highly developed in work with victims of harsh political repression. In the United States, Indian, Asian, and African-American contributions to this evolving practice have been particularly important in fashioning a critical therapeutic understanding of individual, family, and group survival within racist contexts. We feel that this conscious violation of the neutral stance advocated by traditional psychotherapy creates a framework of solidarity between therapist and client that allows the working through of chronic or recurrent stress and traumatization due to their differentness in an intolerant society.[22] Therapeutic solidarity thus advocates for justice, respect of human rights, and the provision of access to quality health care, human services, and psychotherapy.

Clearly, not all therapists are capable of or desire meeting the high levels of commitment that *terapia comprometida* demands. Thus our progressive approach provides these practitioners with recommendations toward making their practices more competent with diverse populations rather than merely sensitive or relevant as was previously encouraged during past decades by proponents of cross-cultural therapy. The difference is beyond semantics, for competence requires a measurable capacity to *function* effectively with varied social groups at all levels: practice, governance, and policy.

Achieving cultural competence is a developmental process that begins with acknowledging that there have been systematic attempts to ignore, incapacitate, or destroy diverse cultures and that one can learn to become culturally proficient by integrating cultural knowledge into practice and theory. Cultural competence requires a participatory process in the therapist-client dyad, not just the ability of the therapist to know and understand culture. Cultural competence thus involves working collaboratively with natural supports in communities and promoting the self-determination of persons of color. It implies providing the least restrictive or invasive interventions, coordinated care, and outreach to the home base of clients if necessary.[23] Culturally competent therapy requires a capacity for cultural self-evaluation and includes the concept of equal and nondiscriminatory service provision that is responsive to the unique needs of each client.[24]

We have decided to balance our presentation of the theoretical and conceptual components of a diversified psychotherapy with a case discussion format to better illustrate our individual practice styles. In doing so, we have taken as a lead Chin's previous work in developing an interactive forum on empathy and transference issues in psychotherapy with Asian-Americans. As such, our self-directive is to describe cases of individual or family psychotherapy with persons of color geared toward mental health students, trainees, and professionals who have had much or little experience in serving such populations. The focus is on illustrating concepts of transference and empathy, as well as therapeutic strategies that are particularly useful with the specific group each of us describes. The chapters summarize sessions and treatment and capture themes, sequence of issues, and dynamic content. Special attention is given to immigration history, ethnic origin, and family views of racial and gender roles. The overall goal of this work is to illustrate how increasing societal and cultural competence on the part of the therapist and client can lead to empowering and comprehensive interventions.

With such general guidelines, it is worth noting that in comparing clinical perspectives we discovered several cross-cutting themes in our individual approaches to working with persons of color in psychotherapy. We hope you will welcome, as we did, these similarities as well as our very important differences.

WHERE DO WE GO FROM HERE?

We have endeavored to make this book positive in tone and progressive in approach: one providing diverse perspectives and challenges rather than harping on the psychotherapeutic field's inattention to cultural variables. Our purpose is to provide therapists of all theoretical backgrounds with a way of conceptualizing their clients' concerns that includes politics, race, ethnicity, and gender and to provide more appropriate and effective therapeutic strategies. We have offered a sampling of issues that we hope readers will pursue further.

Since our readers may be students or accomplished professionals, we suggest a reading process that acknowledges the realities of both groups—the creation of study groups. We believe that this method holds the most promise for integration of cultural competence into practice models as it is not dependent on being institutionally based. We are all too aware of how slowly these concepts enter the curriculum of undergraduate, graduate, and professional schools and advanced therapy training institutes. We are also painfully aware of how some professions are better at such integration than others. We believe that independent, nonaffiliated, multidisciplinary study groups open to students and professionals alike both reflect how new concepts, theories, and practices actually evolve over time, and serve as a peer collaboration model that creates opportunities for nonhierarchical mentoring.

Within these self-organized groups readers can supportively examine their own assumptions, views, theory, and practice as regards diversity and their clients. They can explore how transference and countertransference issues related to ethnicity and gender manifest in their caseloads. Relevant questions might include: What are the specific differences when the therapist's gender and ethnicity differ from the client's? What are the crucial elements of social and personal esteem for their clients? What external supports to psychotherapy can be used to further empower such esteem?

Our experience and available literature[25] point to the importance of mutual support opportunities for providers serving the disenfranchised and culturally diverse. Peer-led study and discussion groups serve the purpose of minimizing the effects of stress and burnout encountered in the often isolating practice of psychotherapy. We hope that as you read and discuss this book you will increase your collaboration with others, transgress disciplinary turf, learn from your differences, and become increasingly flexible and adaptable in practicing therapy. In a manner that replicates the group-oriented or collective definition of self shared by the ethnocultural groups discussed in this book, study group members can process the experience of cooperation rather than competition. They can explore how to better utilize their own experiences with sexism, diversity, and hierarchies in therapeutic, client-focused self-disclosure.

The final step in this process is to create a continuity in the study group by creating a structure in which to share the challenge in diversifying psychotherapy practice. We would hope that you meet on a certain time schedule, whether it be weekly, biweekly, monthly, or quarterly. More important is regular follow-up, case conferencing, and even didactic sessions regarding legal or social issues impacting clients. Our hope is that you would move into the areas of networking, promoting cultural competence, and community advocacy on behalf of increasing diversity in your mental health services, neighborhood clinics, and social agencies.

NOTES

1. M. Moreno Vega (1992). The politics of art. *Under One Sun: News and Events of the Caribbean Cultural Center*, Winter, 1–3.

2. T. L. Cross, B. J. Bazron, K. W. Dennis, & M. R. Issacs (1989). *Towards a culturally competent system of care*. Washington, DC: CASSP Technical Assistance Center, Georgetown University Child Development Center.

3. V. De La Cancela (1991). Salsa and control: An AmeRican response to Latino health care needs. *Journal of Multi-Cultural Community Health*, 1(2), 23–29; E. de la Vega (1990). Considerations for reaching the Latino population with sexuality and HIV/AIDS information and education. *SIECUS Report*, 18(3), 1–8.

4. R. M. Howell (1990). Native Americans, stereotypes and HIV/AIDS: Our continuing struggle for survival. *SIECUS Report*, 18(3), 9–15.

5. J. E. Trimble (1990). Application of psychological knowledge for American Indians and Alaska Natives. *Journal of Training & Practice in Professional Psychology*, 4(1), 45–63.

6. R. La Due (1990). An Indian by any other name or don't "Kemo Sabe" me, Tonto. *Focus: Notes from the Society for the Psychological Study of Ethnic Minority Issues*, 4(2), 10–11.

7. B. R. Tong (1990). "Ornamental Orientals" and others: Ethnic labels in review. *Focus: Notes from the Society for the Psychological Study of Ethnic Minority Issues*, 4(2), 8–9.

8. M. McGoldrick, J. K. Pearce, & J. Giordano (Eds.) (1982). *Ethnicity and family therapy*. New York: Guilford Press.

9. D. W. Sue, E. I. Richardson, R. A. Ruiz, & E. J. Smith (1981). *Counseling the culturally different: Theory and practice*. New York: John Wiley & Sons.

10. L. Fulani (Ed.) (1987). *The politics of race and gender in therapy*. New York: Haworth Press.

11. V. De La Cancela (1991). The endangered black male: Reversing the trend for African-American and Latino males. *Journal of Multi-Cultural Community Health*, 1(1), 16–19.

12. C. Ahuna, G. Cornell, J. Fong, C. A. Tanaka, & J. Yang (1991). Graduate students' perspective on cultural diversity. *Focus: Notes from the Society for the Psychological Study of Ethnic Minority Issues*, 5(2), 9–10; V. De La Cancela (1991). Working affirmatively with Puerto Rican men: Professional and personal reflections. *Journal of Feminist Family Therapy*, 2(3/4), 195–211.

13. V. De La Cancela & G. M. Sotomayor (1992). Rainbow warriors: Reducing institutional racism in mental health. *Journal of Mental Health Counseling*, 15(1), 55–71.

14. S. Oskamp (1990). The editor's page. *Journal of Social Issues*, 46(3), iv–v.

15. T. S. Sloan (1990). Psychology for the Third World? *Journal of Social Issues*, 46(3), 1–20.

16. de la Vega (1990), Considerations for reaching the Latino population; K. Meeks (1992). Congressman Rangel calls for health care for all Americans at forum. *New York Amsterdam News*, February 1, 11.

17. G. Albee (1986). Toward a just society: Lessons from observations on the primary prevention of psychopathology. *American Psychologist*, 41, 891–98.

18. Sloan (1990), Psychology for the Third World?

19. M. Montero (1990). Ideology and psychosocial research in Third World contexts. *Journal of Social Issues*, 46(3), 43–55.

20. M. B. Lykes, & R. Liem (1990). Human rights and mental health in the

United States: Lessons from Latin America. *Journal of Social Issues*, 46(3), 151–65.

21. D. Becker, E. Lira, M. I. Castillo, E. Gome, & J. Kovalskys (1990). Therapy with victims of political repression in Chile: The challenge of social reparation. *Journal of Social Issues*, 46(3), 133–49.

22. V. De La Cancela (1991). Progressive counseling with Latino refugees and families. *Journal of Progressive Human Services*, 2(2), 19–34.

23. Cross et al. (1989), *Towards a culturally competent system*.

24. Commissioner's Task Force (CTF) (1991). *The Commissioner's Task Force report on mental health services for children and adolescents*. New York: Department of Mental Health, Mental Retardation and Alcoholism Services.

25. J. E. Carrillo & V. De La Cancela (1992). The Cambridge Hospital Latino health clinic: A model for interagency integration of health services for Latinos at the provider level. *Journal of the National Medical Association*, 84(6), 178–82; V. L. De La Cancela (1978). On being a minority student in clinical psychology. *Journal of Contemporary Psychotherapy*, 9(2), 178–82.

CHAPTER TWO

HISTORICAL OVERVIEWS: THREE SOCIOPOLITICAL PERSPECTIVES

Yvonne M. Jenkins, Victor De La Cancela, and Jean Lau Chin

THE SIGNIFICANCE OF SOCIAL HISTORY TO PRACTICE

As people of color increasingly take responsibility for their own accounts of history, it becomes clearer that, despite their considerable courage and resilience, those of African, Asian, Latino, and American Indian heritages have persistently experienced "extremes of prejudice, segregation, and discrimination" on the basis of difference.[1] This is consistent with Hopps's view that "oppression has been the most severe, deeply rooted, persistent, and intractable for people-of-color."[2] A culturally competent understanding of this is particularly important to the practice of psychotherapy in that *therapists cannot develop empathy with the world views and daily realities of people of color in the United States without being aware of their historical and sociopolitical struggles*. Furthermore, therapists' self-understanding in these contexts is fundamental to empathizing with the historical and sociopolitical realities of others.

Many of the realities endured by these populations have not been acknowledged in anglocentric accounts of U.S. history. Therefore, an exclusion from history has developed more systematically and extensively for some groups than others. The dynamics and dialectics of domination (i.e., control through devaluation, exploitation, restriction, annihilation), which have characterized the oppression of people of color, have been particularly destructive for groups whose historical experiences have been omitted, poorly recorded, or lost over the course of time. In addition, much of the anxiety about difference, social distance, and related acts of aggression that have plagued this nation for centuries suggests that estrangement from the histories of these populations has also been costly to society at large.

Accurate and inclusive accounts of history that value diversity empower by providing contexts for understanding the past, overcoming present challenges, and defining progressive directions for the future. Such contexts may be gained from awareness of distinguishing factors that have influenced the arrivals of various racial and ethnocultural groups in the United States, the sociopolitical challenges they have encountered (e.g., racism, segregation), and other unique and important determinants of their world views and experiences. Furthermore, analyses of these factors may facilitate development of culturally consistent guidelines for the practice of psychotherapy, higher utilization rates, and improved therapeutic outcomes for these populations.

HISTORICAL OVERVIEWS

With this perspective, we have limited our discussion to U.S. residents of African, Chinese, and Puerto Rican heritages to communicate how the relationship between social history and psychotherapy is perceived and practiced. We confine our reporting to the groups we know best, with whom we feel most competent, and whose world views and sociopolitical realities we can capture most accurately.

African-Americans

For African-Americans, a historical and sociopolitical overview must address the condition of their arrival in the United States, their struggle for justice and equality, as well as their focus on reclaiming and embracing their identity. Among the most significant developments have been: (1) slavery, (2) racist and discriminatory legislation, (3) subsequent legislation to combat racism and discrimination, and (4) progression from a narrow perception of racial and ethnocultural identity based on skin color to one that acknowledges the rich cultural heritage of this group.

Early Presence

African-Americans have endured a history of oppression that dates back to 1619 when the first Africans arrived on a Dutch frigate as indentured servants at Jamestown, Virginia. By 1640, some Africans were required to serve white plantation owners for life, whereas white servants were required to continue for only one additional year. After the period of indentured servitude expired, some Africans were assigned land until 1651. Others worked for many more years before earning enough to purchase freedom. Many free blacks settled in Washington, DC, northern cities, and liberal areas of the south. Yet, the majority of the Africans remained enslaved. Those that eventually secured quasi-free status were permitted to hire themselves out for work. Until 1650, many whites believed that "Blackness is evil in the sight of God."[3]

In 1661, Virginia became the first colony to legalize slavery. Whites viewed Africans as animalistic and in need of control.[4] As the labor interests of plantation owners expanded, they increasingly relied on the Africans to meet their needs. Consequently, the Africans increasingly lost what little control they had over their destiny. Thereafter, slavery spread to most other colonies and territories that eventually became the southern states.

By 1790, the African population of this nation exceeded 750,000. Nearly 700,000 were enslaved. Meanwhile the British, Dutch, and French continued to force West Africans onto slave ships where they endured "Middle Passage," the deadly voyage to the Americas. Disease, caused by inhumane transporting conditions, claimed the lives of thousands while others chose death in the icy waters of the Atlantic over a future in slavery. Survivors were subjected to an extremely inhumane and immoral existence.

Slaves were automatically relegated to subhuman status and legally deprived of basic human rights. For example, no exact records of births and deaths were kept, and marriages were not legally acknowledged. What is presently recognized as sexual, physical, and psychological abuses were commonplace as were countless other traumas and human indignities. Original African names were erased from existence. Kinship bonds were radically disrupted. Some families were temporarily separated while others were permanently disrupted just to meet the needs of plantation owners. Mothers were separated from children. Husbands and wives were separated from one another. Members of tribes were separated from one another, often making it nearly impossible to communicate since different tribes spoke different languages and dialects. Over time the continuity of distinct ethnocultural practices and traditions was modified along some dimensions and lost among others due to the estrangement from these imposed by slavery. This institution endured for nearly 250 years and "set the tone for [peoples of African descent] to be treated as inferior" in the United States.[5]

Skin color became a primary determinant of privilege and social class. Those slaves of darker skin color were more often assigned to the harshest labor while those of medium to light brown hue commonly became house servants. Usually the latter group included mixed-race children conceived as a consequence of rapes committed by white plantation owners and overseers against female slaves. Other mixed-race children were conceived as a result of psychological pressures and the needs of the whites and slaves to feel valued and empowered. Internalization of society's belief in white supremacy impaired the self- and group-concepts of many African slaves and their descendants for generations.

By the 1820s, Africans were driven away from Independence Square in Philadelphia on the Fourth of July since whites believed they had no part in establishing the nation, even though Crispus Attucks, a runaway slave, had been the first person killed during the Boston Massacre in 1770. Between 1820 and 1860, most southern whites believed that slavery was good for the development of the nation and a means to "protect" uncivilized and dependent blacks.[6] However, emancipation was imminent. Initially, President Lincoln proposed payment of $300 per slave to owners to colonize the entire slave population in another part of the world. This proposal was opposed. However, in 1862 the emancipation proclamation became law and slaves in Washington, DC, were freed. Government funds were designated to support the voluntary emigration of this group to Haiti and Liberia. Strikingly, "colonialization . . . seemed almost as important to Lincoln as emancipation."[7]

Slavery was not legally abolished until 1865 with the passage of the Thirteenth Amendment and the end of the Civil War in which 180,000 Africans fought. This was followed by the period of Reconstruction, which was intended to empower former slaves. Instead, this period perpetuated the system of white supremacy and entrapped former slaves in powerlessness. Their powerlessness was subsequently reinforced by *Plessy vs. Ferguson* (1896), the landmark "separate but equal doctrine," which relegated them to second-class citizenship. By 1900, peoples of African ancestry were classified "Negro" and "colored." The Jim Crow laws, a discriminatory system, blocked the access of this group to fair voting practices, equal education, and economic opportunities, particularly in the south. Especially denigrating was the segregation of public accommodations and facilities by signs designating "colored" and "white." Meanwhile, Negro soldiers were used in U.S. efforts to dominate smaller countries inhabited by people of color. One example was Puerto Rico, which had a large Negro population. The island was supervised very cautiously to insure that its Negro citizens would not have liberties that would inspire Negroes in the United States to fight more intensely for human rights on the mainland.

At the turn of the century, many white Americans believed that Negroes had failed to advance because of innate inferiority while the systemic impact of societal disorders (e.g., racism, discrimination, prejudice) was completely denied. Between World War I and World War II, racial segregation was viewed as justifiable on the basis of research that claimed to prove that Negroes were inferior.[8] A particularly exploitative and inhumane study initiated during this period (1932) was the Tuskegee Experiment on syphilis conducted by the U.S. Public Health Service in collaboration with several state and federal agencies. This followup study, which lasted for 40 years, involved the deception of 400 African-American males and their families to gain their participation. They were never told that the experiment was intended to study untreated syphilis nor that they had contracted the contagious and deadly disease. Because they were never treated, most died without ever knowing they had contracted the disease.[9]

The Struggle for Justice and Equality

In 1954, the immorality of racism was acknowledged by the passage of the *Brown vs. Board of Education of Topeka, Kansas* decision by the Supreme Court. This landmark decision "declared that segregated school facilities were inherently unequal and unconstitutional."[10] In 1955, Rosa Parks's refusal to sit at the back of a bus because of her race led to the now historic Montgomery bus boycott and the emergence of Dr. Martin Luther King, Jr. Between 1957 and 1965, Congress passed five civil rights acts that secured and protected voting rights and prohibited discrimination in public accommodations and government-funded programs. Meanwhile hostility between civil rights proponents and white supremacists escalated. Particularly tragic during this period was the assassination of Medgar Evers, leader of the Mississippi National Association for the Advancement of Colored People (NAACP), who was shot in the back outside his home one night in 1963. Evers was committed to equal rights and to restoring positive social identity to his people. In addition, homes of civil rights leaders and black churches were bombed. Civil rights organizations peacefully protested racial discrimination. However, civil rights advocates were continuously subjected to violent lynchings, bombings, attacks by vicious police dogs, high-pressured water hosing, unjust arrests, rapes, beatings, and deadly force. They were also unjustly fired from jobs and denied loans while mortgages were foreclosed on their homes. Nevertheless, Negroes and sympathetic whites persisted in the struggle to pursue justice and equality.

The 1960s was a period of revolution. Descendants of slaves began to define themselves as "black Americans." New group pride surfaced through the Black Power Movement as evidenced in themes like "Black Is Beautiful" and "I'm Black and I'm Proud." The psychological inception of the black revolution was August 28, 1963, when more than 200,000 participated in the March on Washington for Jobs and Freedom where Dr. Martin Luther King, Jr., gave the historic "I Have A Dream" speech. The Voting Rights Act of 1965 subsequently paved the way for black Americans and other people of color to be elected to public offices. By then Malcolm X, eloquent spokesman for the Black Muslims, had begun to challenge society's definition of blacks and to raise the consciousness of whites. The Black Muslims were committed to the basic tenets of the Islamic religion and racial separatism for black Americans. Malcolm X was eventually ousted by the Black Muslims after describing the assassination of President Kennedy as "chickens coming home to roost."[11]

Later during a trip to Mecca, he experienced a spiritual transformation that resulted in modification of his stance from separatism to collaboration. Malcolm X established a separate group in accordance with his views. His rift with the Black Muslims grew larger. In 1965 Malcolm X was assassinated before his family and followers at a mass meeting of his group in New York City. For his followers and many others who did not necessarily agree with his views, the violent nature of his death was another sad commentary on the intolerance of diversity in the United States. Three years later, the assassination of Dr. King angered, disillusioned, and led to the despair of civil rights proponents even though some had previously criticized his philosophy and approach. The realization that Dr. King, an eminent proponent of nonviolence, was murdered influenced some to give up on nonviolence as a viable option for confronting racism, discrimination, and prejudice.

The Postsixties Sociopolitical Climate

The postsixties sociopolitical climate has been mixed. By the early 1970s, increasing numbers of immigrants from the Caribbean and Africa came to the United States for economic and educational purposes. At the same time, the Black Muslims and other groups advocated racial separatism as a solution to the plight of blacks in the United States. Meanwhile, the Black Panther Party for Self-Defense "called for full employment, decent housing, black control of the black community, and an end to every form of repression and brutality."[12] Others advocated for social change through the ballot box. In 1976, the black vote was central to the election of Jimmy Carter who appointed more African-Americans to key positions than any other president had in the past. In addition, African-American mayors, state legislators, and congresspeople were elected in greater numbers. Yet, the Reagan and Bush eras that followed the defeat of President Carter in 1980 posed severe setbacks to previous civil rights gains.

Efforts to capture their identity more accurately continued as blacks redefined themselves "African-Americans." Meanwhile, the candidacy of Rev. Jesse Jackson for president in 1984 and 1988 inspired the hope of many. In addition, the election of the nation's first African-American governor, Douglas Wilder of Virginia, in 1985 was both ironic and progressive since Virginia was the first colony to legalize slavery.

Presently several realities indicate that peoples of African descent are at risk in the United States:

1. the desperate plight of the black underclass and working poor;
2. the high rates of infant mortality, illiteracy, homelessness, substance abuse, HIV infection, and AIDS among this population;
3. the susceptibility of young African-American males to incarceration or early death by violence;

4. increasing recognition that the Clarence Thomas–Anita Hill hearings represented one of the most systematic exercises in race and gender devaluation
   and exploitation that has taken place in the twentieth century; and

5. lack of social-change-oriented responses by the U.S. government to the plight
   of peoples of African descent throughout the world as evidenced by pre-
   mature lifting of economic sanctions against South Africa, the turning away
   of Haitian refugees from U.S. shores while others are readily admitted, and
   the delayed response to the starving people of Somalia.

Despite past and present challenges, increasing numbers of successful
African-Americans are mentoring African-American youth. Their ability
to mobilize hope through expressing concern for youth and modeling
success is extremely valuable. Particularly encouraging is the interest of
African-American celebrities who convey positive images that value diversity and nurture self-esteem. For example, Arsenio Hall, Spike Lee,
Bill Cosby, and others model a nonaggressive, yet assertive way of being
"a brother" through their masculine "cool poses," candor, and creative
approaches to social problems. Also, Oprah Winfrey emphasizes the
importance of self-esteem and constructive approaches to problem solving through her talk show. This is particularly valuable because low self-
esteem and poor conflict resolution skills are among the determinants
of violence and early death in communities of color.

In conclusion, the historical and sociopolitical struggles of African-
Americans have involved: (1) oppression through domination, exploitation, devaluation, annihilation, and restriction facilitated by racism,
discrimination, and prejudice; (2) the fight for equality and justice; and
(3) the process of embracing and reclaiming a rich ethnocultural heritage.
In psychotherapy, these struggles impact on: (1) the worldview of the
client, (2) perceptions of psychotherapy and the therapist as a member
of a particular reference group, (3) what is discussed, and (4) what
approaches prove to be most effective. Even though African-Americans
have become more diverse in thought, ethnicity, and social class over
the years, social justice and equality remain at the forefront of their
agenda.

Chinese-Americans

Early Presence

Economic and political crises in the Canton province of China (i.e.,
starvation due to devastating floods, overpopulation, and pillage by
military uprisings) mobilized the immigration of Chinese to the United
States in the 1850s. Many Chinese viewed immigration as an opportunity
for physical survival and responded to the appeal of the California Gold

Rush. Traders to Canton, a seaport, offered cheap passage and created an indentured servant system. By 1885, approximately 300,000 had migrated to Pacific Coast areas, most of them Toisanese Chinese seeking a temporary sojourn in search of the "Golden Mountain," as San Francisco was called. These early immigrants intended to return to China to their wives and families.

The early Chinese immigrants found employment in factories and were recruited as cheap laborers to build the transcontinental railroad. The low cost of Chinese labor was initially welcomed in the service occupations. However, their movement into the declining gold mining industry triggered anxiety and hostility among whites who believed their economic security to be threatened. Because of this, early Chinese immigrants were subjected to mob violence, discriminatory miner's and fisherman's taxes, strikes, boycotts, and riots, which threatened their employability and safety.[13] This resulted in the restriction of most Chinese-Americans to the laundry business. The depression era of the 1870s escalated anti-Chinese sentiment. Chinese-Americans were viewed as a threat to economic security and were scapegoated for their willingness to work for low wages.

Restrictive Legislation

Hostility toward Chinese immigrants was also expressed through extensive anti-Asian legislation. Multiple acts were passed by Congress and states and cities in the western United States.[14] In 1882, the Federal Exclusion Act suspended Chinese immigration and made those born in China ineligible for U.S. citizenship; this was repealed in 1943. Between 1908 and 1924, many laws were passed severely restricting the rights of Chinese immigrants in virtually all aspects of civil life.

During this period, illegal entry of Chinese into the United States occurred, mostly men. With culture misunderstood and physical safety threatened, Chinese harbored themselves within Chinatowns throughout the United States. Chinese-Americans became suspicious in response to continued harassment by immigration officials and hostility by many white Americans. As few Chinese women had immigrated to the United States, the harsh and stressful existence for many Chinese-Americans promoted gambling and prostitution. Derogatory perceptions of Chinese-Americans by white Americans were common.

During this period, laws were enacted specifically targeted against Chinese. The Gentlemen's Agreement of 1908 enabled the San Francisco School Board to segregate all Asian children by forcing them to attend one inadequate school. Two years later, this order was rescinded after Japan registered a complaint with President Theodore Roosevelt. In 1917, literacy tests became a requirement for immigrants. In 1918, the California Alien Land Law (Webb-Henry Bill) declared that those ineligible literacy tests became a requirement for immigrants. In 1918, the California Alien Land Law (Webb-Henry Bill) declared that those ineligible for citizenship were prevented from owning or leasing land. Although this was enacted in response to the anxiety of whites toward successful Japanese truck farmers, it affected the Chinese. In 1908 and 1921, the Emergency Quota Act of 1924 imposed quotas on the entry of Chinese immigrants to the United States. The Immigration Exclusion Act of 1924 denied admission to all persons ineligible for U.S. citizenship, thereby terminating immigration from China and other Asian countries.

While immigration restrictions against Chinese were repealed in 1943, this was at the height of World War II. Japan was considered a threat to American security while China was considered an ally. This repeal together with the incarceration of Japanese-Americans in detention camps only served to pit Chinese-Americans against Japanese-Americans. Chinese-Americans were given different privileges than Japanese-Americans. For example, they were classified as white while Japanese-Americans were classified as black during segregation in the south. This classification of Chinese-Americans was short-lived.

McCarthyism

As China became ruled by a Communist government, paranoia and suspicion toward Chinese-Americans once again escalated, this time based on their political threat. Chinese-Americans now feared deportation and became "paranoid" as McCarthyism resulted in surveillance and harassment of Chinese-Americans and their businesses. They strove toward academic achievement to ensure physical and social survival within the United States. This adaptation fit with Asian values and resulted in this perception of Chinese as a "model minority." Many Chinese did not want to bring attention to themselves for fear of reprisal and because they would have no recourse in the courts—thus, the root of the saying, "You don't have a Chinaman's chance." This was further escalated by the onset of the Korean and Vietnam Wars. Asians were viewed as "gooks" who placed little or no value on their own lives.

The Postsixties Sociopolitical Climate

It was not until the Immigration and National Act of 1965 that discriminatory provisions of citizenship ended. Immigration of Chinese from Hong Kong, a British colony, began. Reunification of Chinese men with their families occurred through enactment of legislation allowing for "confession" of one's illegal entry into the United States. This coincided with the Civil Rights Movement of the sixties. Immigration of Chinese and other Asians became increasingly diverse.

For Chinese-Americans, a sociohistorical overview must address their ambiguous status since their first arrival in the United States. Most significant has been:

1. the extensive anti-Asian legislation directed at Chinese-Americans;
2. the ambiguity of racial classification;
3. the ramifications of the model minority myth; and
4. the scapegoating of Asian-Americans during periods of economic and political unrest.

In the postsixties climate of the Civil Rights Movement, one must also consider immigration of Chinese from China, Taiwan, Hong Kong, Vietnam, and other Asian countries. This diversity is significant because of their different sociopolitical histories and relationships with the United States. For Chinese-American immigrants, one cannot ignore the political backdrop of communism and the one-child-per-family policy in China; nor can we ignore the history of the United States and Taiwan as political allies. The urban and cosmopolitan nature of Hong Kong, a British colony, is contrasted with the refugee status of Chinese-Vietnamese fleeing from persecution and war trauma. All these differences prevail against a backdrop of the early anti-Asian sentiment toward Toisanese-Chinese who are now second and third generation American-born Chinese. This diversity will influence perceptions of sociopolitical history in relationship to self-identity. The friendly U.S.-Taiwan relationship, the colonization of Hong Kong, the influence of foreign military powers in China, the "rescue" of Vietnamese Chinese through refugee status, and the history of racism toward Chinese in the United States result in differential perceptions of white Americans that will permeate the psychotherapeutic relationship. Different reasons for immigration will influence adjustment to life in the United States. Chinese from Hong Kong generally come to rejoin families separated because of exclusionary legislation as do Toisanese-Chinese from rural China. Others from China come as scholars as do Chinese from Taiwan. Chinese from Vietnam come as refugees often faced with the aftereffects of war trauma. Yet, Chinese-Americans are only one of more than twenty Asian groups in the United States while Asian-Americans make up only 3 percent of the total U.S. population according to the 1990 census.

While the perceived political threat of Chinese-Americans has decreased, and the Civil Rights Movement has diminished overt hostility and discrimination toward Chinese-Americans, many instances of racism and oppression continue. Overt aggression continues as in the case of Vincent Chin, a Chinese-American killed by two white men on his wedding night because he was mistaken for Japanese. The two men were acquitted because it was their first offense. Splitting continues as Vietnamese refugees are eligible for Medicaid upon arrival to the United States whereas Chinese immigrants are denied eligibility for Medicaid and any other public assistance programs during their first two years here. Colleges have denied admission to qualified Chinese-Americans because they are considered an "overrepresented minority group." Affirmative action policies have excluded Asian-Americans as an eligible category.

The myth of the model minority continues to bias white Americans toward viewing Chinese-Americans as without problems, not needing services, and taking care of their own. This myth continues to oppress Chinese-Americans and other Asian-Americans because of significant discrepancies among diverse segments of Asian-American communities. Asian-Americans are believed to: (1) exceed the median income and educational attainment levels in the United States; (2) experience less social distance from whites; and (3) be more acceptable for marriage to whites than other cultural groups. Sue and Sue emphasized that not only does this myth benefit the powerful, but it is a divisive mechanism that engenders conflict between Asian-Americans and other people of color.[15] Thus, the model minority myth is a barrier to cultural diversity.

Conclusion

In conclusion, several themes emerge in the sociopolitical history of Chinese-Americans that resonate with those of other pluralistic populations. First, racism and oppression have impacted their experience in the United States. Second, their ethnic diversity of powerlessness results in a differential experience and perception of similar issues. Third, they share a common bond of culture and identity.

Puerto Ricans

Colonialization by Spain

The native people of Puerto Rico were the Taino indians prior to the colonialization of the island by Spain in 1493, which lasted for more than 400 years. *Borinquen* is the Taino word for Puerto Rico. A total of 95 percent of the original 50,000 Taino were massacred by the Spaniards by 1514, leaving only 600 alive by 1621.[16] Many of these died of hunger, overwork, or suicide. Male survivors became prisoners of the Spaniards while female survivors became their consorts.[17] From the mid-1500s throughout the 1600s African slaves were brought to the island by the Spaniards to work in the production of sugar cane. The Africans brought their "language, food, musical instruments, religion, and medicine men to the cultural mix of the island."[18] The coexistence of surviving Taino indians, Africans, and Spanish Caucasian poor gave birth to the *"jibaro"* and to a new entity—the "Puerto Rican"—which was to symbolize the integration of the African, Indian, and Spanish cultures and the development of a national identity.[19] During the late 1700s and throughout most of the 1800s Puerto Rico witnessed a surge of revolutionary, antislavery, and anticolonialist activity, which was harshly punished by the ruling Spanish governors. Violent uprisings that protested Spain's control led to the establishment of an autonomous Puerto Rican government in 1897 after Spain granted this autonomy. This experience was short-lived due to the invasion of Puerto Rico by the U.S. military.

Colonialization by the United States

On July 25, 1898, as a result of the Spanish-American War, the U.S. Army invaded Puerto Rico's southwest coast, and a military government was established later that year under the supervision of the U.S. War Department. Thereafter, English replaced Spanish as the language of instruction in the schools. The illiteracy rate of Puerto Rico soared.

The passage of the Foraker Act by Congress in 1900 empowered a governor appointed by the president of the United States and an executive council comprised of six U.S. citizens to take charge of the island. Not only was this a colonial relationship, but it was also a blatantly insensitive move because U.S. citizens were not especially knowledgeable about the Puerto Rican people, their culture, or their economic status, which influenced U.S. politicians to make negative assumptions about Puerto Rico.[20] On March 2, 1917, the Jones Act imposed U.S. citizenship on the island, and two months later the draft was extended to Puerto Rico as the United States entered World War I. Meanwhile, the U.S. War Department continued to administer the island until 1934 when the Department of Interior assumed that responsibility. The first governor of the island was not appointed until 1946 by President Harry S. Truman. The first Puerto Rican governor, Luis Munoz Marin, was elected to office in 1948, one year after the U.S. Congress passed a bill making the position an elective one. Administration of the island by the Department of Interior also ended in 1948, and Puerto Ricans have elected their own governing body since then. Nevertheless, those hopes the islanders have held for gaining independence over the years have been fraught with setbacks, disappointment, and repression.

Between 1900 and 1930, a rural working class developed, and industrialization of the island was fostered by the United States for its own economic interests. Migration served the interests of capitalism and colonialism in both the United States and Puerto Rico as Puerto Ricans became increasingly frustrated with their inability to find work in their own country due to industrialization. At the same time U.S. growers sought out cheap laborers. In addition, Puerto Rico rapidly became the primary importer of goods for the United States. These conditions influenced masses of Puerto Ricans to migrate to New York City and other urban centers of the industrial northeast during the 1950s and 1960s to improve their economic situation. The relatively easy movement between New York and Puerto Rico has become so common that the term "air bridge" has been coined to describe the circular migration between the two locations.[21]

A constitution for Puerto Rico was not approved by Congress until 1952. That same year Spanish was reinstated as the primary language of instruction for Puerto Rico while English was downgraded to a secondary position in the aftermath of conflict between pacifists and militant leaders.[22] Nevertheless, the ambivalent biculturality of the island and its often denied colonial status are continually evidenced by its representation by two flags, two national anthems, two cultures, two languages, and two basic philosophies of life. The Spanish language version of commonwealth, *estado libre asociado* (free associated state), clearly imparts the schizophrenic quality of Puerto Rico's colonial relationship to the United States and its division of national identity.

From 1952 until the early 1960s, the United States increasingly influenced Puerto Rican social history and culture. The island was portrayed as a showcase of U.S.-sponsored economic progress and democracy in Latin America. Yet this showcase scenario, which most U.S. citizens have only a vague recollection of, hid the reality that Puerto Rico did not have full representation in Congress, that it had only a resident commissioner without voting rights in the House of Representatives, and the second-class U.S. citizenship of Puerto Ricans on the island who, by U.S. congressional law, were subject to military conscription without voting privileges in U.S. presidential elections. As a commonwealth, Puerto Rico continues to be excluded from numerous federal programs and limited in participation of others. During the implementation of "Operation Bootstrap" from 1947 until 1960, U.S. corporations and investors operating on the island were able to amass federal, state, and local tax-free profits and pay wages below those prevalent in the continental United States. Another well-hidden fact is an earlier history of promotion of Puerto Rican migration to the mainland to meet the demand for low-wage labor in the farm and garment industries. However, the minimum wage for the United States is presently operant in Puerto Rico.

From 1948 to the present, numerous organizations and governments have denounced Puerto Rico's colonial status under the United States. In 1972 Puerto Rico's right to self-determination was declared by the United Nations Decolonization Committee and was fully recognized by that body in 1978. Several political parties advocating status resolutions exist in Puerto Rico. The *Partido Nuevo Progresista* seeks statehood for the island; the *Partido Democratico Popular* is willing to accept the present commonwealth structure under the United States; and the *Partido In-*

dependentista Puertorriqueno seeks independence along with smaller nationalist, communist, and socialist parties that do not participate in U.S. elections or politics.

The Current Status of Puerto Rican Nationals

Puerto Ricans continue to have an ambiguous relationship with the United States influenced by colonialism and racism. They are expected to be model citizens despite the disenfranchisement of their homeland in mainland elections, lack of congressional and presidential voting power, high selective service draft potential, and increasing poverty and exposure to violence. To complicate matters further, the colonial situation has triggered intragroup conflict in that some second- and third-generation residents of the mainland ("Nuyoricans") are not recognized as "real" Puerto Ricans by some of the more traditional first-generation islanders, even though most are fluent in Spanish, and are treated as such by other Latino ethnic groups and U.S. citizens. On January 28, 1993, a bill was signed by Governor Pedro Rossello giving English equal standing with Spanish as Puerto Rico's official language.

Puerto Ricans in the United States

Puerto Ricans began to migrate to the United States in 1900 but arrived in increasing numbers after World War II. At least 70 percent of those who have migrated to New York have been of African ancestry.[23] Initially, high unemployment caused by the rapid economic displacement of Puerto Ricans through industrialization and the universal military service requirement primarily influenced migration. However, the reasons for migration have expanded to include education, political refuge, adventure, and an attempt to resolve family problems.[24] According to the 1990 census, more than 3 million Puerto Ricans reside in the United States, comprising 13 percent of its Latino population and 9 percent of its total population including the population of Puerto Rico.[25]

Migration and culture shock frequently have an adverse impact on the quality of life Puerto Ricans experience in the United States. Culture shock is often experienced immediately upon arrival due to discrimination and prejudice encountered on the basis of language, cultural differences, and race. Often, dreams for improving socioeconomic conditions are never fulfilled. Valdivieso and Davis offer several explanations for this.[26] They report that most Puerto Ricans are segregated in the secondary labor market as unskilled labor, service, clerical, and seasonal workers. In addition, 38 percent of all Puerto Rican families in the United States are below the poverty income index while 65 percent of those headed by females fall below that index. A total of 67 percent graduate from high school while 11 percent become college graduates. Those born on the island experience higher unemployment rates, school dropout rates, communication problems, and deeper levels of poverty. Considerable estrangement, frustration, and disappointment are experienced in relation to these realities. Since some family members are left behind during migration, emotional support is not always immediately accessible to recent migrants, which results in isolation, despair, anxiety, and resentment. However, natural support systems like *bodegas* in Spanish Harlem have been a particularly valuable source of emotional (and physical) support for new migrants.[27] Children often rebel against traditional practices of parents, view them as inferior, and are torn between cultures and loyalties. A poor self-image, involving low self- and social esteem, often results from this conflict. In addition, parent-child relationships are often strained by the language barrier, which necessitates the use of children as interpreters and leads parents to be disempowered in this process.[28] Understandably, ambivalence toward U.S. domination of Puerto Rico is common among Puerto Ricans in the United States.

Conclusion

The historical and sociopolitical struggles of Puerto Ricans have involved oppression through political and economic domination first by Spain and later the United States' exploitation, devaluation, and restriction. In the United States racism, discrimination, and prejudice have perpetuated their powerlessness. Conflict between national solidarity and a divided national identity has been influenced by the colonial relationship between the United States and Puerto Rico.

Perceptions of Race, Ethnicity, Culture, and Gender

The diverse historical backgrounds of African-Americans, Chinese-Americans, and Puerto Ricans influence differential perceptions of race, ethnicity, and culture, which have significant implications for psychotherapy.

The Meaning of Race

In the United States, the anglocentric definition of race is entrenched in perceptions of white superiority and involves a black-white dichotomy. "The white race [is] defined by the absence of any nonwhite blood, and the black race [is] defined by the presence of any black blood. Thus, the offspring of [other races] who intermarr[y] with blacks become black. Race [is] genetically or biologically defined, . . . and [cannot] change over a person's lifetime."[29]

Peoples of African descent in the United States have always been defined by the white majority according to their race rather than their culture. The basis of this has been skin color with little appreciation for the interface between the African heritage and U.S. values, economics,

language, and culture.[30] Race has also acquired sociopolitical and ethnocultural meanings for African-Americans and is viewed as a barrier
to opportunities for acceptance, success, social justice, and the "American dream."[31] Until the mid-1980s, this definition was internalized by
many without critical evaluation. However, since this group has begun
to define its own identity, its perception of race has expanded to include
a more global cultural connection to peoples of African descent throughout the world, embracing ethnic differences.

The meaning of race for Chinese-Americans has included having their
worth and needs defined by white missionaries, pejorative labels, objectification, and gross devaluation. Missionaries traveled to Asia to
"convert the heathen" because they were viewed as having no religion
and in need of being saved. Also, the visibility of race set Asians apart
as "exotic," thereby objectifying their human status. During wars with
Asian countries, the United States also devalued Asian life with statements that conveyed value for the lives of white soldiers over the
"gooks" who could be killed. This was projected to Asian heroism with
pejorative stereotypes of the *samurai* and *kamakazi*, which erroneously
suggested that Asians place a low value on human life. Finally, the
meaning of race for Chinese-Americans has meant being perceived as
physically indistinguishable from many other Asian ethnic groups in
the United States. The perception that "all Asians look alike" was one
factor in the death of Vincent Chin in 1982.[32]

For Puerto Ricans, race is a cultural rather than a physical construct
that varies in meaning from culture to culture.[33] Race also identifies a
group of people who are similar somehow in their "essential nature . . .
[dependent] on . . . physical appearance, class, education, manners and
other 'social' variables."[34] Yet, these are not viewed as bases for discrimination. In addition, race is perceived as a social phenomenon that
is changeable over time, from place to place, and ranges along a continuum of racial categories (e.g., *mestizo*, *triguено*, *indio*, *moreno*). "Consequently, [one] can go from being white in Puerto Rico to mulatto in
Mexico to black in the United States."[35]

The Meaning of Ethnicity

Ethnicity refers to connection based on commonalities (i.e., religion,
nationality, region, political) where cultural patterns are shared and
where their transmission over time creates a common history.[36] The
meaning of ethnicity for most African-American descendants of slaves
is less prominent than for other peoples of color who made the choice
to migrate to the United States. This difference is influenced by estrangement from ethnic origins imposed by slavery, the narrow definition of identity based on color that has subsequently persisted, and
other transgressions endured in the United States. African-Americans

define their ethnicity on the basis of bi- or multiculturality while religious affiliations or regional identification are primary sources of identity for others, even though these sources are not necessarily understood to be components of ethnicity in the formal sense of the word. Many others, inspired by Alex Haley's *Roots*,[37] have begun to trace their backgrounds to African origins in an effort to reclaim and embrace ethnicity as authentically as possible.

The Chinese-American perception of ethnicity includes a strong element of philosophy and culture, which bonds the group. Asians do retain their ethnic identity based on country of origin and make between-group distinctions based on nationality, culture, and physical traits. Furthermore, many Asians define self-identity in terms of nationality while identity as Asians takes on a more sociopolitical connotation.

For Puerto Ricans, ethnicity means nationality of origin, political identity (i.e., immigrant or native), and traditional and ethnospecific religious practices. Nationality is an important variable that distinguishes Puerto Ricans from other Latino populations. Puerto Ricans have maintained a strong ethnic identity in response to circular migrations, restricted opportunities, the "radicalizing environment setting," and other stressors encountered in the United States.[38] Even though the U.S. Caucasian majority persists in defining Puerto Ricans as "minorities," "AmeRican" has become an alternative self-definition that is "personal, collective and multiple" and "reflects a community-empowerment response."[39] The political aspect of ethnic identity tends to be influenced by whether or not one has been raised in the United States or Puerto Rico. Ethnospecific religious beliefs and practices (a blend of African religious rites with folk practices of Catholicism, *espiritismo*, and folk healing) also influence the meaning of ethnicity for Puerto Ricans.[40]

The Meaning of Culture

For African-Americans, culture is a dimension of self- and group identity that includes: (1) a shared experience of oppression in the United States; (2) dual socialization; and (3) reclaiming and embracing African heritage. Despite adversities endured by this population, the oral tradition, reverence for family kinship, spirituality, and other significant cultural patterns have endured. Some attribute this to "soul," "a form of group consciousness . . . identity . . . the essence of blackness . . . a folk conception of the . . . African-American's . . . 'national character.' "[41]

Soul music includes the gospel, jazz, rock and roll, and rhythm and blues forms that so creatively capture the African-American experience. Aretha Franklin and James Brown have been honored with the titles "Queen of Soul" and "Godfather of Soul." Soul food includes some of the low-cost, filling foods, often of low nutritional value, that whites made available to slaves "([chitlins], hog maws, ham hocks, ox tails) and foods with an African flair (e.g., black-eyed peas, red beans and rice, collard greens, cornbread . . .)"[42] that were transported from West Africa or resulted from the efforts of slaves to recreate West African cuisine.

Unique language and communication patterns are also prominent in African-American culture. For example, Negro spirituals preserved the culture through communicating hidden meanings that enabled slaves to escape to freedom. Folk tales, sermons, and rap have also maintained the oral tradition while art, literature, cinema, and the performing arts have creatively captured the African-American experience.

Finally, socialization of African-American children until the 1970s routinely involved teaching them to survive in the black and white worlds. Even though many parents and elders continue this practice, others are not as attentive to this issue because of lifestyle transitions influenced by civil rights legislation over the years, denial that racism and other societal disorders continue to exist, and estrangement from history and traditional ethnocultural values.

The meaning of culture for Asian-Americans is prominent as a dimension of self- and group identity but strongly influenced by the pressure of westerners and U.S. citizens to acculturate to the U.S. culture. Acculturation, the criterion for belongingness and fitting in from social and economic vantage points, has been complicated by race and mainstream definitions. It has created an artificial dichotomy in the evolution of cultural identity for many Asian-Americans. Therefore, some have felt compelled to acculturate to the U.S. culture while others have valued preserving their "Asian" heritage. Many Asian students attribute greater status to being a "foreign student" than to being an immigrant or Asian-American because the latter is associated with low socioeconomic status.

Biculturality for Asian-Americans is associated with strong cultural traditions set against a historical context of the melting pot theory. The "marginal man" concept, promulgated in the sixties to describe the failure to fit into either culture, reinforced an artificial dichotomy in which Asian-Americans felt compelled to choose between cultures. This was complicated by the fear of earlier Toisanese Chinese-Americans of the negative consequences of visible cultural identity, which had legal, immigration, and political ramifications. Now that Asian-Americans have established legal and social status within the United States, they can stress biculturality from a positive position and express their culture visibly. Filial piety and modesty are two cultural concepts significant within Asian cultures that are often misunderstood in western cultures. While they form the basis for folk tales, social discourse, and group consciousness to model behavior, they have been translated into negative traits of submissiveness and self-denigration by Westerners.

The Puerto Rican culture involves a rich blend of heritages (i.e., African, Spanish, Taino), social classes, and island agrarian and urban mainland lifestyles. Rooted in a strong communal orientation, the essence of Puerto Rican culture is expressed through its values for family, spirituality, dignity, respect, mutual assistance, and personalism. The common bond of oppression influenced by centuries of colonialization also has a significant influence on the meaning of culture for Puerto Ricans. Cultural lifestyles are represented by "salsa" and African-American "soul."[43] Salsa, also known as Latin jazz or world beat, is a political voice of the people and "a necessary approach to Latino activism" that "educates, inspires, humourously criticizes, and organizes [their anger]."[44] Salsa also addresses "[Latin] American unity, empowerment, colonial legacies, racism, capitalist materialism, social and economic injustice, U.S.-Latino identity, and oppression."[45] Similar to musical expressions of the African-American experience (e.g., Negro spirituals, gospel, and civil rights anthems), salsa advocates autonomy and provides direction for the survival and prosperity of the culture. *Jibaro* music, the new song movement, and Puerto Rican rap are also expressions of Puerto Rican culture. An expression of the Puerto Rican culture in mental health is *espiritismo*, a traditional healing practice in which practitioners believe in the coexistence of material and spiritual worlds.[46] Cultural expressions are also found in the foods, arts, and literature of Puerto Rico.

The Meaning of Gender

Gender roles of African-Americans are primarily egalitarian in their integration of expressive and instrumental behaviors[47] and extend in function to others outside the family of origin. Gender roles within the African-American family represent adaptations to oppression. In two-parent families power, decision making, and role responsibility are often shared, and there is a balance among communication, conflict resolution, and affection.[48] Of course there are role variations based on differential background variables such as socioeconomic class, personality types, and family structure (e.g., single parent, two parent, extended). Despite the advancement of some women in the workplace, most still devote much of their energy to caretaking and nurturing. Although men in two-parent families often become involved in nurturing and caretaking, much of their attention is still devoted to fulfilling the role of provider. Majors and Bilson highlight the "cool pose" as a prevalent coping strategy among some young African-American males.[49] Consistent with the perception some have of masculinity, this strategy is protective, reveals no vulnerability, and limits opportunities for intimacy and emotional support.

As alternatives to traditional gender roles become more acceptable in society, more African-American men are assuming the responsibilities of single parenting, more men and women are adopting children as part of single- or two-parent families, increasing numbers of men and women are postponing marriage and parenting to pursue career goals, and others more freely pursue alternative lifestyles. Finally, grandparents are increasingly assuming primary roles in parenting as parents spend longer hours in the workplace, are overwhelmed by the pressures of single parenting, or are no longer available to their children due to serious illness, incarceration, or early death.

African-American women in the skilled trades and professions have only begun to confront sexist injustice in an organized manner during the past two decades. Increased awareness of sexism as a reality for African-American women was influenced by the Clarence Thomas–Anita Hill hearings. However, many still fail to be aware of their own victimization or to believe the victimization reported by others. This is linked to psychosocial factors commonly associated with abuse (e.g., denial, low self-esteem, an inability to distinguish appropriate from inappropriate behavior, a delay or failure to report), socialization (e.g., blaming the victim, double standards of behavior for men and women), lack of education, and the fact that historically racism has posed an even more serious threat to their daily survival.

The meaning of gender among Asian-Americans has generally been secondary to culture and racial/ethnic identification. Historically, Asian culture was male-dominated. Women were subservient to men in social, familial, and community roles. Women viewed men as the privileged, and family and social structures were organized accordingly. Ancestral lineage followed male lines. The primary role of women involved bearing children, maintaining the family, and behaving modestly and obediently. As such, they were mothers, wives, daughters-in-law, and daughters first. Men's roles involved being the patriarch or becoming the elder of the family and gaining the respect of the clan.

These roles defined identity and translated into specific guidelines for behaviors in the countries of origin. The warrior and scholar were celebrated in Asian folklore but were reserved as roles for males. Women were accorded secondary status and roles. Women achieved notoriety only when they stepped out of traditional roles and disguised themselves as men, such as the Woman Warrior. Also common in Asian folklore were stories celebrating and exaggerating the roles of unrelenting sacrifice made by women.

U.S. society defined different values that interacted with Asian cultural values. Changing gender roles presented new challenges for Asian women. Despite the wish to preserve basic tenets of their heritage, traditional Asian roles posed conflicts for Asian women as they became more highly educated, entered professional roles, became more involved in the political process, and struggled to achieve economic mobility.

Employment for women and men within garment and restaurant industries, respectively, conflicted with the ability to retain traditional roles. Extended work schedules made it difficult for fathers to adequately maintain the patriarch role. As the work demands of parents increasingly infringed on the time families once spent together, grandparents became more involved in the primary caretaking of children.

For Puerto Ricans there is a clear demarcation of gender roles with distinct cultural meanings. In the most traditional sense, these roles have supported women's subordination to men's power and authority. Two distinct codes of behavior among this group are *marianismo* and *machismo*. In the role of *marianismo* women are defined as spiritually superior to men and capable of enduring all suffering inflicted by men.[50] *Machismo* defines men as providers, responsible for the welfare, honor, and protection of the family,[51] as well as sexually available.[52] *Hembrismo*, a powerful role consistent with social and political goals of the women's movement, represents a cultural revenge to *machismo*.[53] According to traditional codes of behavior, women are expected to be submissive, gentle, dependent, sentimental, and timid. Men are expected to be cold, authoritarian, strong and brave, intellectual, rational, and independent.[54] However, traditional codes are in transition.

Education and exposure to U.S. society seem to have a modifying effect on traditional gender roles to a degree. Yet, acculturation is a source of complexity. In addition, differentials such as ethnicity or nationality of origin, social class, and migration make it particularly difficult to define specific differentials in gender issues.

As treatment paradigms become more responsive to the issues of Puerto Rican and other men of color, it is expected that more men may relax sexist attitudes by becoming open to learning important relationship skills from women, discarding "macho" childrearing and conflict resolution practices, and gaining awareness of how stereotypes, myths, and other misconceptions disempower them in society.[55] Comas-Díaz advocates feminist therapy as a paradigm for aiding Latina women with negotiating traditional gender roles.[56]

PARALLEL THEMES

From "Melting Pot" to "Cultural Mosaic"

The traditional practice of psychotherapy was developed to meet the needs of western Europeans. In the United States, the "melting pot" ethic has influenced perspectives on theory and practice. Based on a belief in white superiority, this ethic fostered cultural blindness and assimilation to white norms rather than cultural awareness and appreciation of diversity. "To belong and to be embraced, people were en-

couraged to change their names, disown old country values, beliefs, and
language; relinquish familiar cultural practices; and become generally
ashamed of any identity that was less than '100 per cent red-blooded
American.' "[57] For decades this often resulted in marginality, identity
confusion, or despair. In psychotherapy as in society, *the "melting pot"*
ethic perpetuated the oppression of people of color by blaming these groups for
their difficulties rather than acknowledging the systemic nature of their oppres-
sion. Psychotherapists have often failed to differentiate between social
and intrapsychic determinants of health and illness. For example, treatment planning has often failed to consider whether some clinical syn-
dromes were influenced or exacerbated by social conditions like
unemployment, poor housing, or violence. Therefore, people of color
and the poor have often been shortchanged by the treatment process.
The "blame the victim" stance continues to exist despite the progression
of the field toward cultural competence. An absence of culturally competent perspectives perpetuates the oppression of people of color in the
United States through: (1) devaluation of their world views; (2) perceptions of difference as deviance, inadequacy, or inferiority; and (3) limited
awareness of how ethnocultural factors and societal disorders influence
identity, psychosocial development, and variations in treatment needs.

Even though consumers of psychotherapy have become increasingly
diverse, theory and practice have just begun to reflect a more progressive
orientation that "values cultural pluralism and acknowledges our nation
as a cultural mosaic."[58] This is influenced by increased awareness that
acknowledgement rather than denial of diversity nurtures psychological
security, capacity for understanding, and appreciation of difference.[59]

"The Browning of America"

The rapid expansion of the population of the United States has been
referred to as "the browning of America." Sue attributes this transition
to rising immigration rates among people of color and declining fertility
and birth rates among an aging white population.[60] People of color and
women are increasingly occupying critical positions in the workforce
that have a powerful impact on the economy and influence the general
well-being of everyone. Therefore, society has much to gain from embracing diversity.

Systematic Oppression and Disempowerment

Each of the groups discussed here has been subjected to systematic
oppression. This has involved domination, exploitation, devaluation,
annihilation, and restriction of liberty reinforced by racism, discrimination, and other injustices. Consequently, they have been systemati-

cally disempowered and forced into marginal positions in society (e.g., indentured servitude, slavery, compromised citizenship, the working poor, the underclass), which have compromised not only their own well-being but that of society-at-large.

IMPLICATIONS OF SOCIAL HISTORY FOR PSYCHOTHERAPY

The social histories of the racial and ethnocultural groups we have discussed have implications for psychotherapy with these groups as well as other pluralistic populations in the United States. Therapists who treat these groups must:

1. examine their own as well as clients' perceptions of race, ethnicity, and gender;
2. examine their own as well as clients' experiences with difference;
3. be aware of how oppression influences perceptions of psychotherapy; and
4. be willing to work within culturally syntonic treatment frameworks that facilitate personal and social change through collaboration.

Effective psychotherapy does not take place in a vacuum. Therefore, significant historical, sociopolitical, and cultural realities must be acknowledged. For the therapist, this must involve coming to terms with feelings about belonging to one's own racial, ethnic, and gender groups. Without acknowledging or embracing social as well as other aspects of one's own identity, it is impossible to completely embrace or nurture the identity of others. In the United States, whites tend to overlook or deny the racial component of their identity while ethnicity[61] and gender are more often acknowledged. In contrast, race and ethnicity/culture are more often bases of identification for people of color. These differences in self-identity are often influenced by how these groups are defined by the larger society and on what bases they have experienced oppression. Pinderhughes offers guidelines for examining personal perceptions of difference that enhance the therapeutic relationship.[62]

People of color often view psychotherapy with mistrust and suspicion. For decades, much of the racism, ethnocentrism, and sexism that has permeated society has reinforced a legacy of mistrust and suspicion in the field of mental health and limited the availability and quality of mental health services to these populations. Therefore, healthy cultural paranoia, a refusal to identify with and trust those who differ in color, lifestyle, and social class values,[63] evolved in response to this legacy. Parallels between society and psychotherapy influence some clients to initially view therapists as extensions of the establishment. This perception is not limited to alliances between white therapists and people of color. A belief in white supremacy influences some clients to automatically view therapists of color as second-rate[64] or incompetent. When these issues are denied or overlooked in psychotherapy, the therapeutic alliance becomes a conditional one that fails to embrace diversity. Consequently, the legacy is perpetuated.

Social histories of the groups we have focused on suggest that adaptive socialization practices and other culture-specific strengths have enabled them to survive societal disorders and even prosper at some levels despite enormous obstacles. Their strengths are certainly worthy of more attention so they can be nurtured more adequately through psychotherapy.

Family, group, and social therapy approaches are particularly effective when tailored to the world views of pluralistic populations. Integrated family therapy orientations based on systems perspectives can enable families to understand the role of social or external stressors in difficulties encountered without denying the role of internal conflicts. In view of sociopolitical realities that have dominated, devalued, exploited, and restricted these populations, practical and flexible approaches that involve direct problem solving, active versus process-oriented management, and external resolution can be assuring at times. Group therapy can provide a supportive forum for expanding personal awareness, psychoeducation, and behavior change while social therapy promotes active participation in social change. Behavior therapy is also a crucial modality since some clients from pluralistic populations are more open to addressing psychophysiological symptoms (e.g., migraine headaches, back pain, gastrointestinal distress) initially. Behavior therapy ameliorates some of the powerlessness these groups experience in society because it is guided by a contractual agreement that enables the client to have a directive role from the outset in determining the outcome. Furthermore, behavior therapy can easily be integrated with other modalities when appropriate to achieve desired therapeutic results. Finally, indigenous practices (e.g., folk healing, confession, prayer) as adjuncts to psychotherapy have potential effectiveness for clients who value these practices. Other approaches to psychotherapy may also be effective with pluralistic populations when modified to fit their world views.

CONCLUSION

Therapists cannot empower people of color through psychotherapy without an appreciation of historical and sociopolitical realities that impact on their experiences. It is also necessary for therapists to come to terms with their own personal truths (e.g., attitudes, feelings, stereotyped perceptions, conflicts) concerning difference in order to intervene with these populations effectively and to facilitate the social change necessary to reinforce and sustain positive therapeutic outcomes.

NOTES

1. J. A. Axelson (1985). *Counseling and development in a multicultural society.* Belmont, CA: Brooks/Cole, 67.

2. J. Hopps (1982). Oppression based on color. *Social Work,* 27(1), 3–5.

3. Axelson (1985), *Counseling,* 69.

4. *Ibid.*

5. N. Boyd-Franklin (Ed.) (1989). *Black families in therapy.* New York: Guilford Press, 10.

6. Axelson (1985), *Counseling,* 69.

7. J. H. Franklin and A. A. Moss, Jr. (1988). *From slavery to freedom.* New York: Alfred A. Knopf, 189.

8. Axelson (1985), *Counseling,* 69.

9. H. Jones (1981). *Bad blood: The Tuskegee syphilis experiment.* New York: Free Press. Quoted in H. Bulhan (1985). *Frantz Fanon and the psychology of oppression.* New York: Plenum Press, 87.

10. Axelson (1985), *Counseling,* 69.

11. Franklin & Moss (1988), *From slavery,* 377.

12. *Ibid.,* 459.

13. M. O. Wong (1988). The Chinese American family. In C. Mindel & R. W. Habenstein (Eds.), *Ethnic families in America: Patterns and variations.* New York: Elsevier, 230–57; W. Peterson (1978). Chinese Americans and Japanese Americans. In T. Sowell (Ed.), *American ethnic groups.* Washington, DC: Urban Institute Press, 65–106.

14. Axelson (1985), *Counseling,* 89–91.

15. D. W. Sue & D. Sue (1990). *Counseling the culturally different.* New York: John Wiley & Sons, 189.

16. Peoples Press Puerto Rico Project (1977). *Puerto Rico: The flame of resistance.* San Juan: Peoples Press, 9.

17. N. Garcia-Preto (1982). Puerto Rican families. In M. McGoldrick, J. K. Pearce, & J. Giordano (Eds.), *Ethnicity and family therapy.* New York: Guilford Press, 164–86.

18. K. Wagenheim & O. J. Wagenheim (Eds.) (1973). *The Puerto Ricans.* New York: Anchor Books.

19. Peoples Press Puerto Rico Project (1977), *Puerto Rico,* 9.

20. L. Comas-Díaz & E.E.H. Griffith (Eds). (1988). *Clinical guidelines in cross-cultural mental health.* New York: John Wiley & Sons, 205.

21. C. Nelson & M. Tienda (1988). The structure of Hispanic ethnicity: Historical and contemporary perspectives. In R. D. Alba (Ed.), *Ethnicity and race in the U.S.A.: Toward the twenty-first century.* New York: Routledge, 49–74.

22. Comas-Díaz & Griffith (1988), *Clinical guidelines,* 205.

23. S. Rodriguez (1992). Multiculturalism: A third generation approach to managing diversity. *EAPA Exchange* (March), 14–19.

24. Garcia-Preto (1982), Puerto Rican families, 166.

25. R. H. Dana (Ed.) (1993). *Multicultural assessment perspectives for professional psychology*. Needham Heights, MA: Allyn & Bacon, 65–67.

26. R. Valvidieso & C. Davis (1988). *Hispanics: Challenging issues for the 1990's*. Washington, DC: Population Reference Bureau.

27. E. De La Cancela & V. De La Cancela (1989). "La Bodega": A natural support system in mainland Puerto Rican communities. *El Boletin: Newsletter of the National Hispanic Psychological Association*, 6(2), 3–6.

28. Garcia-Preto (1982), Puerto Rican families, 165.

29. C. E. Rodriguez (1991). Another way of looking at race. *The Boston Sunday Globe*, May 12, 69–70.

30. B. A. Bass, G. E. Wyatt & G. J. Powell (1982). *The Afro-American family: Assessment, treatment and research issues*. New York: Grune & Stratton.

31. E. B. Pinderhughes (1989). *Understanding race, ethnicity and power*. New York: Free Press.

32. Sue & Sue (1990), *Counseling*, 3.

33. Rodriguez (1991), Another way, 70.

34. *Ibid.*

35. *Ibid.*

36. Pinderhughes (1989), *Understanding race*.

37. A. Haley (1976). *Roots*. New York: Doubleday.

38. Nelson & Tienda (1988), The structure of Hispanic ethnicity, 68.

39. V. De La Cancela (1991). Salsa and control: An AmeRican response to Latino health care needs. *Journal of Multi-Cultural Community Health*, 1(2), 23.

40. V. De La Cancela & I. Závala-Martínez (1983). An analysis of culturalism in Latino mental health: Folk medicine as a case in point. *Hispanic Journal of Behavioral Sciences*, 5(3), 251–74.

41. Bass et al. (1982), *The Afro-American family*, 74.

42. *Ibid.*, 75.

43. V. De La Cancela (1991), Salsa, 23.

44. *Ibid.*

45. *Ibid.*

46. De La Cancela & Závala-Martínez (1983), An analysis of culturalism.

47. M. B. Thomas & P. G. Dansby (1985). Family structures, therapeutic issues, and strengths. *Psychotherapy* 22(2S), 398–407.

48. Boyd-Franklin (1989), *Black families*, 226.

49. R. Majors & J. M. Bilson (1992). *Cool pose: The dilemmas of black manhood in America*. New York: Lexington Books.

50. E. Stevens (1973). Machismo and marianismo. *Transaction-Society*, 10(6), 57–63.

51. C. E. Sluzki (1982). The Latin lover revisited. In M. McGoldrick, J. K. Pearce, & J. Giordano (Eds.), *Ethnicity and family therapy*. New York: Guilford Press, 492–98.

52. E. Habach (1972). *Ni machismo, ni hembrismo (Neither machismo nor hembrismo)*. Coleccion: Protesta. Caracas: Publicaciones EPLA.

53. L. Comas-Díaz (1982). Mental health needs of mainland Puerto Rican women. In R. E. Zambrana (Ed.), *Work, family and health: Latina women in transition*. New York: Hispanic Research Center, Fordham University, 1–10; L. Comas-Díaz (1989). Feminist therapy with Hispanic/Latina women: Myth or

reality? In L. Fulani (Ed.), *The psychopathology of everyday racism and sexism*. New York: Harrington Press, 39–62.

54. Comas-Díaz (1989), *Feminist therapy*.

55. V. De La Cancela (1993). "Coolin' ": The psychosocial communication of African and Latino men. *Urban League Review*, 16(12).

56. Comas-Díaz (1989), *Feminist therapy*.

57. B. Solomon (1976). Social work in multiethnic society. In M. Sotomayer (Ed.), *Cross-cultural perspectives in social work practice and education*. Council on Social Work Education, 176.

58. D. W. Sue (1992). Multiculturalism: The road less traveled. *American Counselor*, 1(1), 8.

59. Pinderhughes (1989), *Understanding race*, 4.

60. Sue (1992), Multiculturalism.

61. Pinderhughes (1989), *Understanding race*.

62. *Ibid*.

63. W. Grier & P. Cobbs (1968). *Black rage*. New York: Bantam Books.

64. Boyd-Franklin (1989), *Black families*.

CHAPTER THREE

DIVERSITY AND SOCIAL ESTEEM
Yvonne M. Jenkins

Many variables impact on the individual's capacity to value the self and to feel valued by others. Among the most salient ones of a sociopolitical nature are race, ethnicity, gender, and social class. Based on the sociohistorical overviews offered in chapter two, it is clear that societal disorders associated with these variables (e.g., racism, ethnocentrism, sexism, and classism) have challenged the capacities of people of color in the United States to value themselves and to feel valued by others since precolonial times. Cultural blindness, a basic tenet of the "melting pot" ethic, has perpetuated the oppression of people of color by systematically devaluing their world views and by denying the impact of societal disorders on their overall well-being.

As the United States becomes a more pluralistic society, the concept of diversity is embraced now more than ever before. This is evidenced by the fact that much attention is now being paid to the impact of diversity on psychosocial development, interpersonal relationships, academic performance, and worker productivity. In addition, identity development models have become more inclusive of racial, ethnocultural, and other sources of sociopolitical diversity.[1] Furthermore, progressive practice models expand our understanding of how embracing cultural diversity,[2] ethnic validity,[3] and social empowerment[4] benefits the treatment process. Moreover, accreditation bodies now require training programs for counselors and psychologists to offer courses on cross-cultural issues. Some educators are also making a more conscientious effort to integrate cross-cultural perspectives into other subject areas. Finally, although the importance of cultural sensitivity is still recognized, it is no longer considered a sufficient indication of readiness to address the mental health needs of people of color. In addition to cultural sensitivity, those in training are required to demonstrate *measurable competence* of readiness to address the needs of pluralistic populations.

Although these developments are long overdue, they suggest that cross-cultural issues are now respected in mental health and have begun to receive the serious attention they deserve. Society at large stands to gain much from these developments. One potential benefit for consumers of color is higher social esteem.

This chapter focuses on diversity and social esteem. Means of nurturing and devaluing diversity are defined. In addition, social esteem is defined conceptually, developmentally, and in terms of implications for psychotherapy. Finally, ways in which race, ethnicity, and gender impact social esteem are described.

HOW IS DIVERSITY NURTURED?

Diversity is nurtured through self-knowledge, multicultural education, and empathy. The absence of these conditions generates anxiety about difference that reinforces racism, ethnocentrism, sexism, and other societal disorders.

Self-Knowledge

Self-knowledge involves awareness of one's own perceptions of difference on the basis of race, ethnicity, gender, and other sources of diversity that may be encountered in the treatment setting. In order to change personal biases and stereotyped images of the culturally different, Pinderhughes contends that therapists and counselors need to explore their own feelings, attitudes, and behavior about difference by responding to questions like the following:

1. What was your first experience with feeling different?
2. What are your earliest images of race or color? What information were you given about how to deal with racial issues?
3. Discuss your experiences as a person having or lacking power in relation to the following: ethnicity; racial identity; class identity; gender identity.[5]

Positive identification with one's own racial or ethnocultural group is essential to developing an appreciation of diversity in others. As a consequence the therapist is enabled "to control or resolve unfavorable reactions [to the client] and . . . [to promote] greater sensitivity to responses that may be triggered by perceptions of difference" as threatening.[6] There is no doubt that the therapist's modeling of behavior that embraces diversity, influenced by his or her own positive social identity, may have a powerful impact on the client's psychosocial development and functioning.

Multicultural Education

During the 1960s, increased awareness of the social, political, and economic inequities encountered by visible racial and ethnocultural groups in the United States resulted in a movement toward multicultural education. Its initial focus was to educate and to provide exposure to ethnocultural intricacies (e.g., celebration of holidays, native foods, dress, and customs). This proved to be interesting and fascinating but superficial and inadequate for altering stereotypes, prejudice, or facilitating social change. In reality, the lives of people of color involved far more than ethnocultural intricacies. Over the years, many had actively protested their marginal positions in society and the circumstances that engendered and perpetuated their plight. Gradually it became clear to educators that *perceptions of difference* (e.g., attitudes, assumptions, misconceptions) rather than *actual sources of difference* (e.g., race, ethnicity, gender, social class) supported the circumstances that sustained the social and economic disenfranchisement of pluralistic populations. Consequently, a more active and integrated approach to multicultural education was developed with the following objectives: (1) fairness and tolerance; (2) critical thinking and prejudice reduction; (3) resolution of conflict associated with difference; and (4) support for actualization of basic human rights.

The current approach to multicultural education is one of several factors that have influenced training programs for counselors and psychotherapists to more actively address cross-cultural issues in mental health. Practitioners have become much clearer and more concerned about the inadequacies of professional training programs for counselors and psychotherapists as well as service delivery to underserved populations. Progressive training programs now include didactic approaches and attention to self-processes (e.g., exploring how stereotypes and prejudice operate in one's own life) through experiential and applied processes (e.g., race relations and diversity workshops, practica with culturally competent supervision). Many of these programs are also committed to improving the quality of research that is so essential to accurate assessment, relevant service delivery, and favorable outcomes in psychotherapy.

Empathy

Empathy, a basic condition of positive therapeutic alliances, is essential to the empowerment of the client. By establishing a vital connection to the basic human condition, the empathy of the therapist enables the client to feel safe, worthwhile, and to envision personal and social change as real possibilities. The standard concept of empathy is expanded by the therapist's capacity to embrace social and psychological aspects of identity, a prerequisite for embracing diversity in others.

WHEN DIVERSITY IS VALUED

As the United States becomes a more pluralistic society, more people of color are becoming consumers of psychotherapy. Therefore, it is important to acknowledge the benefits of valuing diversity to psychotherapy. Valuing diversity influences more authentic definitions of the mental health needs of pluralistic populations than those offered in the past. For instance, prior to the social unrest of the sixties, attempts by people of color to define many of the social realities that compromised or stifled their well-being were overlooked, denied, or distorted in psychotherapy as in society. This impeded opportunities for training culturally competent therapists, designing relevant and cost-effective service-delivery systems, and conducting vital clinical research for direction on how to address the needs of these populations more effectively.

WHEN DIVERSITY IS DEVALUED

> When people are clear and mainly positive about their own identity and its meaning, difference then becomes less of a threat.[7]

In the past, the devaluation of diversity in the United States has led to cultural isolation, marginalization, and restriction of pluralistic populations to certain segments of society. The underlying mindset for these conditions has been prejudice, anxiety about difference, and perceived threats to personal and economic power. Without adequate support systems, targets of devalued societal perceptions have suffered serious assaults to the self-concept (e.g., low self-esteem, lack of confidence, poor body image), impaired psychological integration, and persistent levels of emotional distress. Some have become so conditioned to being devalued that they fail to recognize its impact on daily functioning and psychosocial development. Those who hold perceptions that devalue also pay a price in not developing the positive social identity that is vital to their own psychosocial development.

Diversity can be devalued along several dimensions that impact negatively on social esteem.

Devaluation of Cultural Values

Cultural pluralism promotes "unity in diversity." As the United States grapples with realizing this concept, the contrast between western values and those of pluralistic populations becomes increasingly apparent. Rooted in the "melting pot" ethic, western values emphasize individuality, freedom of choice, self-determinism, competition, and winning. Yet, nonwestern values emphasize affiliation and collaterality, interdependence, family bonds, and self-restraint.[8] Because these values simply differ from those rooted in the "melting pot" ethic, conditions valued by pluralistic populations have been viewed as "pathological," "deviant," and "inferior." In chapter four, Chin elaborates on how comparative frameworks for normality have shortchanged pluralistic populations. As a point of clarification, it is important not to confuse western values with Eurocentric values. Even though both have origins on the European continent, considerable diversity exists between these value orientations.

Exoticism

Exoticism, the objectification of a group on the basis of its foreign origin, uniqueness, or rare nature, exploits and dehumanizes by relegating its members to commodity status. This is perpetuated through stereotyping, myths, and labeling. A familiar example is the sexual exploitation of Asian women via the mail order bride business. Chan emphasizes that this practice "demonstrates the objectification and fascination of white America with Asian women as submissive sexual servants."[9] Another common example is the labeling of Latinos as "hot," passionate, and sexual. The stereotype of the "Latin lover" reduces Latinos to mindless commodities whose only priority in life is sexual conquest. African-Americans have been stereotyped similarly.

Devaluation of Indigent Standards of Beauty

Indigent standards of beauty have traditionally been devalued in the United States and are often automatic components of the early socialization process, which can be especially harmful to children and adolescents in the absence of adequate support systems to protect them from assaults to social esteem. While this process has primarily involved prejudice and discrimination on the basis of skin color and hair texture, other physical characteristics associated with race (e.g., eye contour, body stature, and nose structure) have also been targets of humiliation and rejection.

Conformity to Eurocentric standards of beauty can win social approval and access to power. For instance, as mentioned in chapter two, early Chinese immigrants cut their braids or *queues* to gain the social acceptance necessary for success in business.[10] Furthermore, some people of color whose physical traits have resembled those of whites have had more access to privilege than those who have not. This was true for African slaves. Those slaves of darkest skin color and native hair texture were assigned to the harshest work tasks and living conditions, whereas those of lighter skin color and straighter hair texture more often became house servants and were permitted a more humane existence.

In some instances, people of color have embraced these devaluations. For example, some Asian-Americans have rejected the contour of their eyes on this basis. Similarly, some African-Americans and Latinos have perceived darker skin color as "unattractive" or "undesirable," whereas lighter skin tones have been viewed as "attractive," "desirable," or even "prestigious." Along the same lines, the natural or kinky hair texture of African-Americans and Latinos of African descent has often been referred to as "bad hair" while straighter hair textures have been embraced as "good," "pretty," or "nice." Additionally, "the brown paper bag test," as described by some African-American coeds, has been a means of admission for some men and women to social clubs and parties. This test has also represented an index of desirability to the opposite sex. With the color of the brown paper bag as the reference point, those with darker skin tones are believed to be more often rejected in some circles, whereas those with lighter skin tones are believed to be more often accepted. A counterpart of "the brown paper bag test" is "the hair comb test": "the more easily a comb [flows] through the hair, the higher one's chances of gaining . . . admission [or acceptance]."[11] Sadly, the perpetuation of these devaluations by the media, clothing and beauty industries, and other persuasive mechanisms poses a serious challenge to social esteem.

Although the Black Power Movement and Puerto Rican Studies Movement enhanced appreciation of indigent standards of beauty, these devaluations still exist. Some people of color are painfully aware of these standards and struggle constantly to resolve related conflicts. Others, however, are naively unaware that Eurocentric standards of beauty influence their perceptions. In fact, many unconsciously internalize these perceptions, which, in turn, impact their choices of friends, spouses, and associates. The fact that this mindset continues to influence perceptions and behaviors more than a century after the abolition of slavery attests to the power of its influence on standards of beauty and perceptions of difference in this society.

Rejection of One's Own Reference Group

Low social esteem can be expressed as rejection of one's own reference group. This can take the form of: "badmouthing" or verbal bashing of the group; avoiding members of the group due to embarrassment or shame associated with group identity; intragroup violence, hostility, and defacement of neighborhood or community property; and the tendency to emphasize that aspect of one's biracial heritage that is valued more highly by the white middle class and to deny the other, even if the latter is more visible.

Stereotypes and the Double Competency Standard

Stereotypes devalue diversity by applying rigid preconceptions to all members of a particular reference group without regard for individual variations.[12] Stereotypes also rationalize patterns of domination and subordination in society.[13] The danger of stereotypes is that they are impervious to logic or experience.[14] Stereotypes are a tremendous source of pressure for people of color who are often subjected to more rigid standards of performance than their white counterparts due to these distortions. In order to survive racism, discrimination, and prejudice, people of color are often socialized early in life to be twice as competent as their white counterparts to receive equal recognition. This has been particularly true among those from poor and working-class backgrounds. For some, this standard has also resulted in fear that what has been achieved can be easily taken away, "the impostor syndrome," perfectionism, and low self-esteem. These outcomes are also associated with low social esteem.

Invisibility

Some devalue diversity by failing to acknowledge or to take people of color seriously. This is evidenced by an array of subtle and overt behaviors. Commonly cited examples are the white educator's persistent tendency to ignore requests by students of color to recite in the classroom; the uses of minimization and silence as responses in a predominantly white forum to a person of color who confronts racist perceptions or practices; the absence of culturally competent practitioners at some treatment facilities; denial of problems in the workplace associated with discrimination or prejudice; perpetuation of standard approaches to education and psychotherapy rather than culturally inclusive ones; the automatic assumption that persons of color in the board room, college lecture hall, or other esteemed domains need not be taken seriously because they are unqualified, intellectually dull, or are merely present because of affirmative action policy. When such attitudes are internalized by people of color, feelings of inadequacy, unworthiness, and insignificance are often experienced.

Comparisons of Suffering

Unfortunately there are times when suffering is rated comparatively to devalue the experience of people of color. The question becomes who or which group has suffered most or least as a result of oppression. For example, some white ethnics compare the experiences of their immigrant ancestors, who overcame tremendous economic odds, with those of early American Indians, African slaves, and other culturally different groups. Such comparisons often suggest that the culturally different have had equal access to social and economic opportunities but failed to take advantage of them. This "blame-the-victim" stance fails to appreciate the systematic nature of racism in the United States and politics associated with skin color and other unique physical traits.

With the exception of the Irish who fled to escape English domination and the Jews who fled religious and political persecution by the Nazi Party, history indicates that most white ethnics immigrated to the United States by choice rather than by force or influence of white domination or manipulation. Unlike African slaves and some early American Indians, the cultural roots and languages of many white ethnics have remained intact. Of course, there are some who have become estranged from their ethnocultural roots and homelands due to the pressures inherent to the "melting pot" ethic. However, these groups seem to be in the minority.

Although some white ethnics have been targets of racism, discrimination, and prejudice, the majority have not been affected as systematically as visible racial and ethnocultural groups of color. A case in point has been the plight of Haitian refugees who were forcibly returned to persecution in their homeland under the Executive Order of President Bush on May 24, 1992, despite a 1980 law that prohibits "the return of aliens to their persecutors."[15] Congressman Charles Rangel of the state of New York challenged the Bush administration to consider whether this group would have been welcomed if it was not black and poor. African-American civil rights leaders took this further by asserting that "it is no . . . coincidence that Haitian refugees [were] turned back while those seeking asylum from other countries . . . have been welcomed. . . . [T]he Administration's decision to wash its hand of Haitians is tainted with racism."[16] Even though the president's order was overruled by the U.S. Court of Appeals on July 29, 1992, the order served as a reminder that people of African ancestry are not yet valued by some of the most powerful structures of society.

Differentials in human suffering need to be acknowledged if there is to be movement beyond the conditions that cause and perpetuate them. Furthermore, differentials of one group's experience do not invalidate those of others. Comparisons of suffering perpetuate oppression and are detrimental to social esteem.

Minimization, Isolation, and Mockery

The complexities associated with race in the United States have always been a source of anxiety and controversy that some have preferred to avoid or deny because of the discomfort they create. Minimization, isolation, and mockery are common defenses against the harsh realities associated with racism that perpetuate the cycle of oppression. The following passage from Steele's *The Content of Our Character* exemplifies this form of devaluation:

In the literature classes I teach I often see how the presence of whites all but seduces some black students into provocation. When we come to a novel by a black writer, . . . the white students can easily discuss the human motivations of the black characters. But, inevitably, a black student, . . . will begin to set in relief the various racial problems that are the background of these characters' lives. This student's tone will carry a reprimand: the class is afraid to confront the reality of racism. . . . My latest strategy is to thank that student for his or her moral vigilance and then appoint the young man or woman as the class['] official racism monitor. But even if I get a laugh . . . the strategy never quite works. Our racial division is suddenly drawn in neon.

I think those who provoke this sort of awkwardness are operating out of a black identity that obliges them to badger white people about race almost on principle. . . . [T]hese provocations . . . are power moves, that try to freeze the "enemy" in self-consciousness. They gratify and inflate the provocateur.[17]

Steele's appointment of the black student as "racism monitor" and his perception of the student's response as a "reprimand," provocation of awkwardness, and "power play" demonstrate how minimization, isolation, and mockery are employed to protect one from the discomfort associated with racism. This stance invariably perpetuates devaluation of diversity. Steele overlooks his own provocative moves and inaccurate assumption that somehow racism is secondary to or separate from human dilemmas. This distorts the reality that racism underlies many of the difficulties that people of color experience in daily living. Steele's stance also impedes the possibility for open dialogue necessary to broaden understanding and to facilitate social change.

"Hate Crimes" and "Fighting Words"

Racism, prejudice, and discrimination are the bases of "hate crimes" and "fighting words." Hate crimes are hostile macroaggressions toward an individual or group on the basis of difference. Among those sources of difference most frequently targeted are race, ethnicity, gender, sexual preference, and social class.

In the United States, hate crimes have included: murder; rape; assault;

bombings; the defacement of public and private property with racist, vulgar, and derogatory symbols (e.g., swastikas, burning crosses); and other forms of political terror. One hate crime that received considerable attention by the media was the vicious assault of Rodney King, an un-armed African-American, by four white Los Angeles police officers. Even though the officers did capture King for speeding, prior to his arrest they proceeded to brutally assault him by beating him with batons, stomping on him, and kicking him. Eighty-four seconds of this crime were videotaped for the world to see by an amateur cameraman. Despite this evidence a jury initially acquitted the officers involved. Against a backdrop of social frustration associated with economic disparity, polit-ical disenfranchisement, and the government's lack of commitment to ideals that would create a fair and equitable multicultural society, the initial acquittal is believed to have provided the spark that ignited the revolt in south central Los Angeles in 1992.[18]

"Fighting words" are threats, slogans, and racial epithets that injure and provoke anger and rage. Some citizens believe that fighting words are encompassed under the right to free speech stated in the Bill of Rights. However, this stance seems to distort the meaning of this basic human right.

Hate crimes and fighting words devalue diversity and, therefore, min-imize social esteem.

Historical Exclusion

Fulfillment of the need to belong is vital to self-esteem development.[19] Although racial and ethnocultural identification are integral aspects of this process, meaningful connections to time and history[20] are also nec-essary to satisfy the "deep psychological need[s] for . . . continuity, se-curity and identity"[21] associated with social esteem development. The historical exclusion of African-Americans, as described in chapter two, has been particularly costly to social esteem. Much of their present ex-perience in the United States involves retrieving, reclaiming, and em-bracing as much of their history, culture, and social identity as possible.

SELF-ESTEEM OR SOCIAL ESTEEM? IS THERE REALLY A DIFFERENCE?

According to Bednar, Wells, and Peterson, self-esteem is a psycho-logical attribute, a central component of personality, and a subjective and enduring aspect of realistic self-approval.[22] In Maslow's hierarchy of needs, self-esteem is only second to the highest of all human needs, self-actualization.[23] The need for self-esteem encompasses a self-image of worthiness, approval, respect, competence, prestige, and other valued conditions. The more congruent this value orientation is with the self-concept, the more likely the need for self-esteem is fulfilled. The fact that the need for self-esteem is immediately preceded in Maslow's hierarchy by needs for belongingness and love suggests that satisfaction with racial and ethnocultural identity is essential to self-esteem development. It seems then that the therapeutic process must genuinely embrace critical sources of diversity like race, ethnicity, and gender in order to facilitate and promote healing and growth.

Maslow's hierarchy is based on anglocentric values. Therefore, its relevance to people of color in the United States is limited because it fails to be guided by those values most consistent with their world views. U.S. culture "define[s] the psychosocial unit of operation as the individual."[24] According to this framework, identity is defined autonomously to the group. In contrast, the psychosocial unit of operation for most pluralistic populations in the United States is "the family, group, or collective society."[25] Identity then is a group-centered concept. Among the values that support this are interdependence, affiliation, and collaterality.

Maslow's hierarchy, like other anglocentric concepts of ideal mental health, fails to recognize that *for collective societies, group esteem is practically synonymous with the anglocentric conceptualization of self-esteem.* Therefore, the concept of social esteem is preferred here as an alternative to self-esteem to reflect the interdependence between value of self and reference group identity that are central to the world views of most pluralistic populations in the United States. Social esteem, like self-esteem, is essential to healthy psychosocial development and lends a necessary context to perceptions of the self, others, and personal power. Social esteem also enhances the capacity to cope with adversity.

Low social esteem develops when there is dissonance between one's image of self and culture-specific definitions of worthiness, approval, respect, and competence. Consequently, the person feels unworthy and insecure, may find it difficult to trust, and may exercise insatiable needs for dependence or dominance in an effort to find acceptance, assurance, or love. These characteristics have been observed in women with dissonant expectations as described in chapter six.

SOCIAL ESTEEM DEVELOPMENT AND PSYCHOTHERAPY

Social esteem development is a continuous psychosocial maturational process influenced by personal factors and societal conditions that impact on social identity development. Social esteem, a critical component of social identity development, may range anywhere from an overly positive identification with the white majority accompanied by disdain for one's own reference group, to valuing and appreciating one's own reference group as well as others. Therefore, the task of psychotherapy may involve anything from helping the client to develop a positive image of his or her own reference group to educating him or her about the systemic nature of oppression.

A framework for promoting social esteem development in psychotherapy follows based on the Racial and Cultural Identity Development Model.[26] However, this model is limited in its applicability to all pluralistic populations and does not recognize some of the unique developmental experiences that occur in different ethnocultural groups.[27]

Stage 1: *Conformity*. Little or no social esteem is displayed at this stage. The client expresses negative perceptions of his or her reference group or may overidentify with whites (e.g., avoids members of the reference group, mimics white patterns of speech and appearance) to feel valued and powerful. Therefore, the person of color at this stage of social esteem development is likely to prefer a white therapist. If the therapist is, indeed, white, he or she can help the client to work through the need to overidentify with whites. If the therapist is a person of color, he or she can facilitate a working through of negative feelings toward the reference group. The therapist's use of self is critical for intervening with the person at this stage of racial and cultural identity development.

Stage 2: *Dissonance*. Social esteem surfaces at the dissonance stage as the client expresses interest and pride in his or her own reference group. Yet, the negative perceptions of the previous stage occasionally intrude and create a state of dissonance. Resolution is initiated through self-exploration.

Stage 3: *Resistance and immersion*. Social esteem is more prominent at this stage as the client finds the group a source of pride and personal enhancement and actively seeks information and artifacts to establish a deeper connection. Racism is a primary concern at this stage accompanied by healthy "cultural paranoia" and resentment. The therapist may enhance social esteem at this stage simply by listening, displaying openness, acknowledging suspicions of psychotherapy as an extension of the establishment, and by tolerating the intense affect that might accompany this perception. A nondefensive posture, unconditional acceptance, and emotional support are essential to promoting social esteem at this stage.

Stage 4: *Introspection*. Even though the client at the introspection stage exhibits social esteem, he or she experiences conflict in the need for a meaningful connection to the reference group within a dominant cultural framework that values a differentiated sense of self. At times this conflict is misperceived as group devaluation. In order to preserve social esteem, the task of psychotherapy here is to support the client's efforts to establish an interdependent relationship between the reference group and the self.

Stage 5: *Integrative awareness*. The client at the integrative awareness stage is committed to social change. He or she may complain about lacking the support of others for facilitating change or may feel overly responsible for inequities in society. This client is more likely to choose a therapist on the basis of a mutual world view rather than on the basis of race. Active listening, emotional support, reality testing regarding the role of the social system in the scheme of socio-political realities, and the building of limit-setting skills are helpful for reinforcing social esteem at this stage.

OTHER IMPLICATIONS FOR PSYCHOTHERAPY ASSOCIATED WITH SOCIAL ESTEEM

Social esteem is influenced by the client's ethnocultural world view. Therefore, every aspect of the treatment process must be influenced by that world view in order to meet the need for belongingness that promotes social esteem. Although diverse world views are represented among people of color in the United States, their value orientations consistently emphasize affiliation and collaterality, interdependence, collective responsibility, family bonds, and self-restraint.

The therapeutic setting may nurture social esteem by being located in the community of clients served or easily accessible to them by transportation. Culturally inspired decor and culturally consistent seating capacities also convey respect for the culture. For example, culturally inspired pictures, crafts, or sculptured objects might be displayed. Bright tropical flowers, plants, and aquariums often enable clients of Latin, Central American, and Caribbean origins to feel more connected because these serve as reminders of familiar settings. The possibility that the family or extended family may accompany a patient to sessions is consistent with the collective orientation of people of color. Informal settings like family homes, churches, and outdoor spaces where confidentiality can be protected can also occasionally be appropriate for treatment.

The time-orientations of culturally different populations often vary from that of the white middle class. Therefore, it is practical for the therapist to have a flexible approach to time.

The tone of the therapeutic relationship is set by how the therapist greets the client. In view of the significance of collaterality and affiliation among people of color, it is important for the therapist to be pleasant, open, and relaxed. A verbal greeting accompanied by a nod of the head may convey warmth to some Asian-American clients. It can be more appropriate to greet those whose value orientation is more traditional with "How is your family today?" than "How are you today?" since strong family bonds are of value.[28] Greetings may be accompanied by a handshake with African-American, Latino, and American Indian clients. For centuries, no formal titles were used to address African-Americans because of their low social status in society. Instead, they were addressed, with unwarranted familiarity, by their first names, racial epithets, and other titles of disrespect (e.g., "boy," "wench"). Therefore, as a gesture of respect it is now especially important for therapists to initially address adult clients as "Mrs.," "Ms.," or "Mr." followed by the surname until the client gives permission or expresses a preference for being addressed otherwise. The therapist's use of appropriate self-disclosure (e.g., discrete but relevant background that conveys sensitivity to the client's needs, description of professional experience, interests) can be more appropriate than immediately exploring the problem during early stages of treatment. Instead, developing a positive relationship with the client is extremely important.

If the clientele served is primarily bilingual, the therapist and support staff need to be bilingual to establish rapport and communication and to enhance progress in psychotherapy. The emotions of the patient are often captured most accurately by the language of origin. For Asian-American clients, "saving face" is preferred to western perceptions of honesty, openness, and confrontation. Therefore, to push for conformity to western standards is disrespectful and counterproductive to the treatment process. This may also jeopardize social esteem.

The capacity to appropriately manage power, reflected by mutuality or reciprocity, is essential in view of the oppression that people of color have endured in the United States. For example, *personalismo*, the personal aspect of interaction, is valued by some Latino clients. *Personalismo* is associated with expectations that the therapist is a good person, capable of intimacy, personally invested in progress, and open to mutual generosity.[29] For example, a Puerto Rican woman who was offered free treatment by her college counseling center expressed appreciation for the therapist's interest and help by making her small holiday gifts. Mutuality and reciprocity are also valued by clients from other cultures. An unemployed African-American male with skills in graphics designed an impressive "certificate" for his therapist and offered it to her during their final session. The certificate expressed his gratitude for services rendered that enabled him to realize a career goal. The reciprocity conveyed through the therapist's acceptance of the gifts was a source of empowerment that reinforced the self-esteem as well as social esteem of both clients.

Negative assumptions about men of color often prevent their inclusion in therapy. Not only do such assumptions devalue their diversity but they compromise the therapeutic process. For instance, therapists need to make a conscientious effort to develop an alliance with mothers *and* fathers of youth in treatment. Since some fathers hold more than one job simultaneously, a flexible approach is often necessary to permit their participation. Fathers' participation in treatment may be enhanced by finding out their perception of the problem and how they would like for treatment to be helpful, the availability of evening or weekend sessions, and phone contacts or letters when they are unable to be present. Men of color have important roles in collective societies. Their lack of participation in the treatment process does little to enhance social esteem.

Respect for other culture-specific variables like definitions of normal versus abnormal behavior, help-seeking patterns, and alternative healing modalities also values diversity and enhances social esteem. People of color are more likely to seek treatment for physical complaints than for emotional distress. Therefore, it is important for physicians and other health care providers to be aware of help-seeking patterns and to be careful to determine when referral to a mental health provider is appropriate. *Espiritismo*, a traditional healing sect among Puerto Ricans; *santeria*, an alternative healing cult for Cuban-Americans; *curanderismo*, a Mexican folk healing practice;[30] and evening prayer and revival meetings at churches in African-American communities are examples of belief systems and spiritual practices that provide natural collective support systems. However, some authors have cautioned against the use of folk healing practices that reinforce powerlessness through the denial of personal responsibility, "delay . . . referrals to establishment practitioners," or pay minimal attention to medical implications of organic involvement in some disorders.[31] It is also critical for culturally competent mental health professionals to consult health care facilities and social service agencies that serve people of color.

Finally, the social esteem of people of color is also nurtured by acknowledging their strengths and relabeling those behaviors that have enabled them to survive oppression:

[This] credits their struggle to survive . . . and acknowledges an appreciation for . . . how hard they have struggled to be loyal to their culture. . . . Relabeling survival behaviors such as opposition, stubbornness, reaction formation, passive aggression, manipulation, domination, striking back, . . . dependency and passivity can help clients learn that these manuevers . . . are based on the natural wish of all people to have a sense of power. . . . [Particular] [c]redit is given to adaptability, creativity, and [the] resilience . . . these mechanisms represent.[32]

When appropriate, this can also offer insight into how critical strategies for managing oppression "have become exaggerated and inflexible."[33] "Under stress, adaptability can slip into inconsistency, toughness and strength into abuse and power behavior, persistence into stubbornness, caution into immobility, and hard work into driven education."[34]

RACE, ETHNICITY, GENDER, AND SOCIAL ESTEEM

While there are many sources of diversity, we have chosen to highlight race, ethnicity, and gender. The broad meaning of race in the United

States encompasses several aspects of diversity including "differences between peoples based on color"[35] and other distinct physical traits shared by a group. At times the meaning of race is confused with that of ethnicity and social class. Given the actual and assumed meanings of this variable, perceptions of race often impact negatively on social esteem. Like other key sources of diversity, racial differences are commonly devalued. This practice is sustained by racism.

Ethnicity encompasses the unique social and cultural heritage of a group according to nationality, religion, region, or tribe. Because ethnicity influences the development of values, perceptions, needs, modes of expression, behavior, and identity, it is a critical determinant of social esteem.

Gender roles also influence social esteem. Some roles are real and ascribed, influenced by ethnocultural and family traditions and social class. Others, however, are projections of the dominant culture motivated by fantasy, self-aggrandizement, and anxiety about difference. Dependent upon the circumstances, actualization of ascribed gender roles may enhance or decrease social esteem.

For women of color, lower levels of social esteem can be associated with occupying gender roles that promote self-denial and "help others to adapt to, rather than to change, social oppression in order to survive" (e.g., "martyr," "superwoman," "systems balancer," and "tension reliever").[36] To the contrary, higher levels of social esteem can be associated with actualizing roles that promote social change through positive ethnocultural and historical identity development,[37] sociopolitical awareness, involvement with organizations that address the psychosocial growth and development of youth of color, collaboration with men of color on relationship issues,[38] and continuous self-development.

Because men of color have been perceived as threatening, they have endured a history of coercion,[39] severe character emasculation, and disempowerment in their roles as husbands/partners, providers, and fathers. Terms like "cool pose,"[40] "coolin',"[41] and "masking"[42] have been used to describe the facade of being in control or power some men display in response to disempowerment. While these strategies are adaptive, they can also be self-defeating in that they distance some men of color from necessary sources of emotional support despite justifiable frustration, anger, and despair. Tragically, these feelings are often turned against the self, loved ones, or other men of color. Yet some men defy the indignities of oppression in constructive ways by making valuable contributions to their families, communities, and society. For example, leaders from several urban communities of color promote self-esteem and social esteem among youth through varied activities that build and strengthen character, provide exposure to positive role models, and provide alternatives to accepting disempowerment. Their involvement also conveys that men of color are competent and valuable. De La Cancela describes other interventions that seem to have value for building social esteem among men of color.[43] Among these are manhood training, psychoeducation about alternatives to sexual and family violence, and "brotherhood" training workshops for African-American and Latino youth.

CONCLUSION

Valuing diversity promotes the social esteem of people of color. When centered in the world view of the client, psychotherapy can empower underserved populations through nurturing this critical component of social identity.

NOTES

1. D. W. Sue & D. Sue (1990). *Counseling the culturally different.* New York: John Wiley & Sons; C. Oler (1989). Psychotherapy with black clients' racial identity and locus of control. *Psychotherapy*, 26(2), 233–41; W. E. Cross, Jr. (1971). The negro-to-black conversion experience: Towards a psychology of black liberation. *Black World*, 20, 13–27.

2. Sue & Sue (1990), *Counseling*.

3. F. B. Tyler, D. Brome, & J. Williams (1991). *Ethnic validity, ecology and psychotherapy.* New York: Plenum Press.

4. L. Fulani (1988). Poor women of color do great therapy. In L. Fulani (Ed.), *The psychopathology of everyday racism and sexism.* New York: Harrington Press, 111–120.

5. E. B. Pinderhughes (1989). *Understanding race, ethnicity, and power.* New York: Free Press, 217.

6. *Ibid.*, 21.

7. *Ibid.*, 37.

8. D. Lum (1986). *Social work practice and people of color.* Monterey, CA: Brooks/Cole.

9. C. S. Chan (1988). Asian-American women: Psychological responses to sexual exploitation and cultural stereotypes. In L. Fulani (Ed.), *The psychopathology of everyday racism and sexism.* New York: Harrington Press, 35.

10. Sue & Sue (1990), *Counseling*.

11. M. Okazawa-Rey, T. Robinson, & J. V. Ward (1988). Black women and the politics of skin color and hair. In M. Braude (Ed.), *Women, power, and therapy.* New York: Harrington Press, 89–102.

12. Sue & Sue (1990), *Counseling*.

13. Pinderhughes (1989), *Understanding race.*

14. Sue & Sue (1990), *Counseling*.

15. National Association for the Advancement of Colored People (NAACP) & TransAfrica (1992). Letter recruiting participants for demonstration of civil disobedience to protest treatment of Haitian refugees, July 10; S. La Franiere (1992). U.S. court overrules return of Haitians. *The Boston Globe*, July 30, 1, 5.

16. NAACP & TransAfrica (1992), Letter.

17. S. Steele (1990). *The content of our character*. New York: St. Martin's Press, 3–4.

18. J. L. Sacks (1992). After the riots: Counselors essential in the healing process. *Guidepost*, 34(14), 1.

19. Pinderhughes (1989), *Understanding race*.

20. A. Arce (1982). Cultural aspects of mental health care for Hispanic Americans. In A. Gaw (Ed.), *Cross cultural psychiatry*. Littleton, MA: Wright-PSG, 137–48.

21. Pinderhughes (1989), *Understanding race*, 10.

22. R. L. Bednar, M. G. Wells, & S. R. Peterson (1989). *Self-esteem: Paradoxes and innovations in clinical theory and practice*. Washington, DC: American Psychological Association.

23. A. Maslow (1954). *Motivation and personality*. New York: Harper & Row.

24. Sue & Sue (1990), *Counseling*, 35.

25. Maslow (1954), *Motivation*, 35.

26. D. R. Atkinson, G. Morten, & D. W. Sue (1989). A minority identity development model. In D. R. Atkinson, G. Morten, & D. W. Sue (Eds.), *Counseling American minorities: A cross-cultural perspective*. Dubuque, IA: W. C. Brown, 35–52.

27. G. Morten & D. R. Atkinson (1983). Minority identity development and preference for counselor race. *Journal of Negro Education*, 52, 156–61; J. T. Gibbs (1987). Identity and marginality: Issues in the treatment of biracial adolescents. *American Journal of Orthopsychiatry*, 57, 265–78.

28. Sue & Sue (1990), *Counseling*.

29. Pinderhughes (1989), *Understanding race*.

30. H. Lefley (1986). Why cross-cultural training? Applied issues in culture and mental health service delivery. In H. Lefley & P. Pedersen (Eds.), *Cross-cultural training for mental health professionals*. Springfield, IL: Charles C. Thomas, 11–37; V. De La Cancela & I. Závala-Martínez (1983). An analysis of culturalism in Latino mental health: Folk medicine as a case in point. *Hispanic Journal of Behavioral Sciences*, 5(3), 251–74.

31. S. Arenas, H. Cross, & W. Willard (1980). Curanderos and mental health professionals: A comparative study on perception of psychopathology. *Hispanic Journal of Behavioral Sciences*, 2, 345–64; De La Cancela & Závala-Martínez (1983), An analysis of culturalism.

32. Pinderhughes (1989), *Understanding race*, 172.

33. *Ibid.*

34. *Ibid.*, 173.

35. *Ibid.*, 89.

36. Fulani (1988), 115; E. B. Pinderhughes (1982). Minority women: A nodal point in the functioning of the social system. In M. Ault-Riche (Ed.), *Women and Family Therapy*.

37. L. Fulani (1988). All power to the people! But how? In L. Fulani (Ed.), *The psychopathology of everyday racism and sexism*. New York: Harrington Press, xi–xix.

38. V. De La Cancela (1993). "Coolin' ": The psychosocial communication of African and Latino men. *Urban League Review*, 16(12).

39. *Ibid.*

40. R. G. Majors & J. M. Billson (1992). *Cool pose: The dilemmas of black manhood in America.* New York: Lexington Books.

41. De La Cancela (1993), "Coolin'."

42. P. Thomas (1987). *Down these mean streets.* New York: Alfred A. Knopf.

43. De La Cancela (1993), "Coolin'."

PART TWO

Deborah Ridley Brome

In part one Chin, De La Cancela, and Jenkins planted the seeds from which culturally competent frameworks sprout and eventually blossom. The seeds were the redefined concepts of race, ethnicity, culture, and empathy. In addition, social esteem was introduced and the saliency of gender was emphasized. In part two the authors present three frameworks for developing an overall, culturally competent framework. Each perspective is grounded in enhancing empathy by maximally recognizing and understanding how history and culture interface in shaping how we perceive ourselves and others and how we ultimately change. Also, each perspective empowers the client by extending his or her range of knowledge about those things that impact feelings and behavior from cultural, systemic, and interpersonal bases. Pathology is not viewed as endemic to the person but is conceptualized as a manifestation of the individual's response to his or her environment and personal circumstances.

In chapter four, Chin critiques traditional models of psychotherapy on the basis of their assumptions. She argues that the assumptions upon which the standard practice of psychotherapy rests articulate a particular world view, possess cultural values, and are biased. She goes on to further identify and describe ten concepts that negate the development of culturally competent therapy yet are implicit in the assumptions of traditional psychotherapy paradigms. These concepts include the notion of "more or less," universality, mainstreaming, acculturation, modern versus traditional, the mythical ideal, objectivity, labelling, resistance, and standard practice. In addition she provides the reader with an alternative set of concepts that are inclusive and respectful of diversity.

Chin provides examples of how these "troublesome" concepts are intricately woven into our approaches to healing and impede our ability to empathize with clients and to give accurate diagnostic assessments. Further, she utilizes her inclusive concepts to analyze the difference between western and Asian world views along a number of dimensions.

In chapter five, De La Cancela emphasizes a different perspective in conducting culturally competent psychotherapy. Although his ideas are different, De La Cancela's and Chin's perspectives are compatible. De La Cancela purports that the psychotherapist who works with pluralistic populations must guard against mistaking the social features related to poverty and poor education for culture. He discusses how this type of mistake is the result of psychotherapists ignoring the cultural and social ecology of these populations and their inattention to historical legacies of oppression. He articulates four basic stances that therapists can take in addressing and embracing diversity and in empowering people of color. These stances are: (1) a progressive approach that explores and challenges the status quo as part of the psychotherapy process; (2) political activism that challenges therapists to reexamine their role and function as agents of change; (3) an interdisciplinary perspective that requires that we adopt the approaches and ways of knowing of other disciplines in our work as healers; and (4) an expansive world view, which challenges therapists to utilize other than Eurocentric perspectives in working with pluralistic populations.

De La Cancela challenges therapists to examine the ways in which they contribute to myth perpetuation, maintain the status quo, and limit their range of effectiveness in the community. He views therapy as a vehicle through which we can achieve social change and empower people of color.

In order to maximize its use as a vehicle for change, however, we must take action within our professions in pushing for a redefinition of accepted practice. De La Cancela discusses the concerns of men of color as an example of how a more political approach can be utilized to empower a group historically oppressed in the United States.

Whereas Chin provides a world view–based perspective and De La Cancela a sociopolitical-based perspective, in chapter six Jenkins provides a gender-based perspective of culturally competent psychotherapy. She focuses her discussion on African-American women. Yet, the ethnocultural dimensions that she examines with respect to this group are applicable to other groups of women of color. These dimensions include self-esteem and dissonant expectations, historical legacy as an oppressed gender, and sexism. Jenkins's application of these dimensions to the African-American woman illustrates how a particular race or ethnic group's history of oppression and culture interact with gender role expectations to create a set of complex clinical issues and themes in psychotherapy. For example, Jenkins identifies the themes of being unlovable and the imbalance of achievement/work and family as common among a particular set of African-American women. These themes arise from these women's personal life circumstances and hold cultural and historical significance in tracing the sexism, racism, and gender role expectations of women of African ancestry living in the United States.

In the chapters that follow, Chin, De La Cancela, and Jenkins present three perspectives and approaches that further elaborate those concepts and ideas needed in order for psychotherapists to make necessary shifts to culturally inclusive and compatible paradigms. Collectively their approaches encompass a shift toward alternative world views, a definition of therapists as political change agents, and ethnic- and gender-specific perspectives.

CHAPTER FOUR

TOWARD A PSYCHOLOGY OF DIFFERENCE: PSYCHOTHERAPY FOR A CULTURALLY DIVERSE POPULATION

Jean Lau Chin

Why the need for a psychology of difference? The population of the United States is increasingly characterized by racial/cultural diversity. No longer can we ignore racial/ethnic differences as extraneous variables in the provision of psychotherapy. The rapid growth of visible racial/ethnic groups in the last two decades, particularly of Latino and Asian populations, requires a reexamination of existing theory and practice in psychotherapy. Whereas uniformity of psychotherapeutic practice has been the norm for a society that promoted homogeneity through the "melting pot" theory, there has been increased recognition that this often has been not only irrelevant but also discriminatory toward communities of color.[1]

The purpose of this chapter is to examine issues of difference and how an ethnocultural group perspective can contribute to working with diversity in psychotherapy. This chapter questions not the theoretical models but rather the underlying assumptions used by therapists and the assumptive frameworks used to evaluate psychopathology and guide therapeutic practice.

Work with racial/ethnic groups[2] and low income populations[3] has resulted in a knowledge base of special issues critical to people of color and culturally competent psychotherapy. Race, culture, and social class are now deemed to be significant contextual variables for effective psychotherapy with a racially/culturally diverse population. These issues can contribute immensely to the "standard" practice of psychotherapy. While claims that psychotherapy is value free have been criticized and largely rejected,[4] models that integrate issues of culture into the practice of psychotherapy are few.

Some racial/ethnic psychologists have questioned the applicability of "mainstream" theories of psychotherapy to diverse ethnic populations. Others have spoken of the need for modification. Yet others have argued for the relevance of particular theoretical approaches—such as humanistic,[5] self-psychology,[6] and structural family therapy[7]—for racial/ethnic groups. Some have emphasized the importance of a framework, such as value orientation[8] and world views,[9] in psychotherapy with racial/ethnic groups. Tyler et al. developed an alternative model—the Ethnic Validity Model—as more appropriate.[10]

From these criticisms, the training of therapists to work with culturally different clients often takes the form of educating therapists on cultural content. These efforts start with the premise that we need to first learn about a client's culture. McGoldrick et al. take this approach of providing basic content on a culture as a prerequisite for working with clients from that culture.[11] While this is important, it is often not sufficient in enabling therapists to establish an empathic alliance. Moreover, this approach often presumes that effective psychotherapy with culturally different clients represents deviations from "traditional" practice.

ASSUMPTIVE FRAMEWORK

More critical than knowledge of ethnic content are the underlying assumptions used by therapists to define psychopathology and psychotherapy. Both clients and therapists bring these "assumptive frameworks" to the therapeutic relationship. These can be called world views, cultural values, or biases. More importantly, these assumptive frameworks define the ways in which therapists and clients understand one another. To achieve a therapeutic alliance, therefore, therapists must examine how their assumptive frameworks differ from that of the culturally different client. They must examine how their theoretical frameworks and therapeutic practice are dictated by these assumptive frameworks. Several principles are important in evaluating these assumptive frameworks.

First, it is necessary that a framework values differences. Gardner[12] argues that because therapists tend to be ethnocentric, one must actively advocate for: (1) the positive presentation of the values, potentials, and lifestyle of the culturally different client; and (2) shift from a deficit hypothesis to a difference hypothesis to provide culturally competent psychotherapy. We need to assume an ethnocentric bias as consistent with a therapist's sense of self-worth and look to its potential pitfalls in the countertransference. Therapists who value themselves will value people like themselves and may devalue those who are different.

Second, it is necessary that a framework integrates cultural variables as the context of psychotherapy. To do this, we must acknowledge that cultural differences exist and examine theoretical frameworks for their inherent bias against these differences. We need to presume that cultural behaviors that have survived the test of time have served an adaptive value for that cultural group and need to be examined for their inherent strengths.

Third, it is important to view cultural variables not as good or bad but as whether they facilitate achieving psychotherapeutic outcomes. Too often, cultural behaviors are categorically viewed as reflecting lesser degrees of acculturation, as hindrances to be overcome in the practice of psychotherapy, or as resistances by the client to psychotherapy.

Common concepts underlying frameworks in psychotherapy often emphasize sameness and commonality, resulting in troublesome concepts that preclude the recognition of difference. Ten concepts that bias thinking toward "mainstream" thinking are listed in Table 4.1. Culturally competent concepts are proposed as alternatives to promote a perspective that values differences. Specific examples drawn from psychotherapeutic practice with Asian-American clients are given in the table to illustrate how world views different from western perspectives will influence the psychotherapeutic process commonly thought to be standard. In sum, this chapter argues for a psychology of difference, that is, a valuing differences framework needed to practice culturally competent psychotherapy for a racially and culturally diverse population.

TROUBLESOME CONCEPTS

In recent years, there have been great strides made in acknowledging the need for racial/cultural competency in the delivery of psychotherapy services. Yet, the "mainstream" literature, when discussing racial/ethnic differences, often emphasizes concepts that continue to bias service delivery systems toward a "mainstream" culture. These concepts are troublesome for several reasons. The assumptive frameworks underlying these concepts reflect a Eurocentric view presumed to be universal and dominant. Differences in cultural experiences are defined from a Eurocentric view, and differences in world views are interpreted as resistances. These concepts continue to dictate psychotherapy models such that psychotherapy practice is less effective for the racially/culturally different client because it stresses outcomes and processes not valued by the client. These impasses in psychotherapy often result in "blaming the victim"; in other words, the client is defined as resistant, or cultural value is deemed a hindrance to psychotherapy. These concepts become popular ways to characterize work with racial/ethnic clients. These concepts are troublesome because they do not value the different assumptive framework brought to psychotherapy by the client.

Table 4.1
Diversity in Psychotherapy

Troublesome Concept	Culturally Competent Concept
More or less	Different
Universality	Cultural context
Mainstreaming	Ethnic specific
Acculturation	Bicultural
Modern vs. traditional	Empowerment
Mythical ideal	Diversity
Objectivity	Valuing differences
Labelling	Seeking alternatives
Resistance	Reframing in the client's world view
Standard practice	Cultural competence

More or Less: The Deficit Hypothesis

Much of psychology and psychotherapeutic practice is premised on the deficit hypothesis. In psychology, this is the underlying assumption of trait theories. Tests are designed to measure quantitatively how much an individual has of some trait or behavior. An individual is deemed deficient when he or she has more or less of this trait. In psychotherapy, this concept guides the diagnosis of psychopathology.

This concept is troublesome because people of color will generally be compared as to whether they have more or less of these traits than whites. This will generally result in people of color being judged less favorably or as deficient because it is often compelling to be ethnocentric in evaluating normality. For example, African-Americans have been described as "more angry," Asians as "more passive," and Latinos as "more hysterical" than whites. The use of this comparative framework results in prescribing therapeutic outcomes and interventions that are biased against racially/culturally different populations.

Universality: The Normative Framework

There is often an emphasis on sameness and commonality in describing human experience because the notion of difference is often anxiety provoking. Difference often connotes tension and disagreement in human relationships. Consequently, people frequently refer to the universality of human experience to establish a common bond. Unfortunately, this often results in ignoring subtle but important differences. This was the essence of the melting pot ideal. All immigrants to this country were expected to achieve this universal ideal of blending in with everyone else. We are still realizing the absurdity of this myth for people of color.

The concept of universality is troublesome because it prevents therapists from grappling with their anxiety about differences. It mitigates against therapists establishing specific and relevant norms for racially/culturally different clients. It lulls therapists into a false sense of security about having established a therapeutic alliance with racially/culturally different clients—"We are one; we are all people." It results in therapeutic interventions that may in fact have antitherapeutic outcomes.

Mainstreaming as a Goal

As there is increased sensitivity to the differences among racial/ethnic groups, there is increased recognition of the barriers they face in access to and utilization of services. Unfortunately, this often translates into mainstreaming as a goal. Culturally specific services designed to address racial/ethnic and language differences are often viewed as alternative systems or, worse yet, as inferior systems of care. They are viewed as needed only until clients can be "mainstreamed," that is, use the services designed for mainstream populations and speak the language of the mainstream culture.

This concept is troublesome because it fails to recognize the importance of diversity in the delivery of services. In psychotherapy, it defines the predominant model as mainstream and intended for all. It takes an ethnocentric view and presumes that the client must adapt to fit the service. It sets up an ideal that may not be accepted by different racial/cultural groups.

Acculturation as an Outcome

Acculturation is often defined as an outcome for immigrants and refugees. Newcomers to this country are often expected to adapt to the existing culture by changing their "old" behaviors and habits and adopting new ones. This process of "westernization" or "becoming American" often implies changing one's essence and values. Moreover, acculturation is often reduced to mean learning to speak English.

This concept is problematic because it presumes the adjustment of immigrants and refugees to be a one-way process. Failure to adopt these changes is viewed as an adjustment failure, whereas the adoption of "mainstream" norms is viewed as a measure of successful acculturation. It is also problematic because it places the responsibility for acculturation upon the newcomer and says nothing of the host culture's rejection of the newcomer's culture of origin. It absolves the host culture of the responsibility for validating differences.

When used in psychotherapy, this view fails to take into consideration the interactive process occurring in adapting to a new environment or in establishing a therapeutic relationship, that is, to change and be changed. It also fails to recognize the importance of maintaining one's cultural roots as a core to self-identity and cultural values.

Modern versus Traditional Equals Good versus Bad

Ethnic practices are often viewed as traditional while white middle-class practices are often viewed as modern. Traditional often has connotations of being bad because it is viewed as outdated, conservative, and maladaptive. On the other hand, modern has connotations of being good because it is viewed as adaptive and in tune with the times.

This dichotomy is troublesome because it polarizes and negatively judges cultural behaviors; it suggests that racially/ethnically different groups must give up their cultures to adapt. It fails to value cultural practices that have survived the test of time and have served a functional value in solving human problems. When used in psychotherapy to evaluate adaptive behavior, it fails to recognize the importance of cultural or "traditional" practices for the development of self-identity and maintaining a sense of affiliation. Indeed, it leads to labelling the racially/ethnically different client as primitive, undifferentiated, deprived, disadvantaged, and deficient.

The Mythical Ideal: Deviations from Standard Practice

There is often a belief in the "mythical ideal," that is, there is a single best and right way. In psychotherapy, this translates into how psychotherapy should be practiced, or standard practice. Racially/culturally different groups have often been found to reject the assumptions underlying these methods, to "underutilize" services, and use "alternative healing practices." Sometimes, these practices are romanticized as going back to basics. More often, these are viewed as deviant from "standard practice" and therefore inferior.

This concept is troublesome because it creates a false expectation that there is only one way in which psychotherapy should be practiced. Inexperienced therapists might search in vain for "how it should be done." They might worship a mythical ideal and become harsh critics of those who do not measure up. The use of this ideal is likely to result in psychotherapy becoming irrelevant for the racially/culturally different client. It is also likely to result in rigid adherence to "standard practice" and an intolerance for difference. As a result, treatment failures might be judged as client resistance.

Objectivity

Objectivity is a goal of scientific inquiry. The null hypothesis, statistical significance, and normative data—concepts of scientific inquiry—all rely on facts and figures to establish "objective" standards. In psychology, this emphasis on empirical data often serves to validate as objective those concepts that are, in fact, culture bound. In psychotherapy practice, diagnostic categories are often viewed as objective criteria for assessing psychopathology. Often, pressing concerns about human existence central in present-day society manifest themselves in the problems presented by clients in psychotherapy and our diagnosis of them. During Victorian times when sex roles were more rigid and sexuality more repressed, women were more likely to be diagnosed as hysterical. Within the more recent emphasis on the "self" (i.e., "me" generation), borderline diagnoses have been more commonly reflecting of struggles with self-identity and ego boundaries. Preoccupations with the possibility of nuclear war have resulted in a prevalence of post-trauma stress disorders.

While this may oversimplify the fluidity of our diagnostic categories, it highlights the worship of objectivity in therapists' assumptive frameworks. The concept is troublesome because it lulls therapists into a false belief that objective standards exist to measure human behavior and normality. It prevents therapists from evaluating their assumptive frameworks when working with culturally diverse populations.

Labelling: Problem of Overgeneralization

People often need to create labels to bring order to their environment. They generalize from their own experiences to categorize people and events using descriptive labels. In evaluating human behavior, limited experiences under specific contexts with different racial/cultural groups are often overgeneralized, resulting in racial and cultural stereotypes. The limited display of affection in public by Asians, for example, is often generalized to imply a lack of emotion. The media is often criticized for creating stereotypic views through its negative portrayal of racial/cultural groups.

This concept is troublesome because it reflects categorical thinking in evaluating human behavior and experience. The tendency to overgeneralize precludes recognition of diversity within a group. In psychotherapy, this biases therapists toward fitting clients to a syndrome in their choice of diagnoses. Therapists become biased toward finding the clients to fit the therapy rather than designing therapy to meet the needs of clients.

Resistance and Noncompliance: The Easy Answer

People who do not behave according to expected social codes are often described as resistant or noncompliant. There is extensive discussion in the literature about resistance in psychotherapy. Resistance is often interpreted in the context of a client's dynamics. When clients do not do well in psychotherapy, they are often deemed resistant and considered poor psychotherapy candidates.

This concept is troublesome because it has been overused with culturally different groups. It is the easy answer to explain differences and therapeutic failures. It blames the victim rather than the appropriateness of the method. It shifts the focus toward defining faults of the client instead of evaluating the shortcomings of the therapeutic interventions.

Standard Practice: The Way to Do Therapy

Too often, good therapists are believed to adhere to a "standard practice." This is based on the assumption that there are rules governing good clinical practice. Training presumably teaches these rules to the neophyte therapist. Unfortunately, psychotherapy practice was developed for specific ethnocultural groups and influenced by a specific set of sociocultural contexts. For example, Freudian theory and psychoanalysis was developed during the Victorian era when the prevailing social context was characterized by a more homogeneous society and rigidity about sexual mores. Present-day society in the United States is increasingly diverse. Different racial/ethnic groups make up significant numbers in actual and potential clientele. These differences in world views, rules for social conduct, and expectations of therapy significantly influence how therapy must be practiced.

Standard practice is a troublesome concept because it presumes that the practice of psychotherapy is a static process and that the potential client pool is homogeneous. It also presumes the psychotherapy practice involves a set of principles in which race and culture are viewed as influencing the content of psychotherapy but not the process.

CULTURALLY COMPETENT CONCEPTS

The troublesome concepts described above are popular in use. They often provide assumptive frameworks for therapists that are inappropriate for working with racial/ethnic populations. They result in biases that prevent therapists from practicing in culturally competent ways.

They often serve to dictate funding and service-delivery priorities that are insensitive to racially/ethnically diverse groups. It is important to introduce a different set of concepts to change these assumptive frameworks, such as those described below, for therapy to become more relevant to a culturally diverse population.

Different versus More or Less

We need to look at qualitative rather than quantitative differences when comparing racial/ethnic groups. Individuals or groups can be different in their linguistic skills rather than more or less verbal than some given norm. For example, a particular racial/ethnic group may show a tendency to use metaphors or to emphasize brevity in its use of language. This shift will enable us to view the strengths rather than deficits of a particular group. In psychotherapy, it shifts the focus away from repairing and toward building.

Cultural Context versus Universality

Rather than searching for universal norms as criteria for evaluating behavior, we need to look at norms as culturally specific. Behaviors are set in a cultural context. What is common and expectable will change if the cultural context changes. This shift enables us to use different evaluative criteria with different groups. For example, the definition of independence may rely on different criteria or be less valued within a particular culture. Therefore, we cannot use the same measure (e.g., leaving home) as a criteria for all racial/ethnic groups in achieving independence. In psychotherapy, it should force us to define the context first before we interpret a particular behavior as pathological or adaptive.

Ethnic-Specific versus Mainstreaming

Rather than trying to mainstream people, we need to emphasize ethnic-specific services. Different solutions are needed for different populations; one size does not fit all. Ethnic-specific services include services that integrate the fabric of cultural values and beliefs into diagnosis and treatment. This is a challenge to the service-delivery system, which tends to emphasizes a "mainstream" model.

While "ethnic-specific" has been used by the mainstream system to define "transitional" services for "newcomers" to the United States, the challenge is to define ethnic-specific psychotherapy as a form of cultural competence. This means it must be viewed as the treatment of choice, not as a precursor to mainstreaming. It means that therapeutic outcomes will emphasize not how a client learns to fit into the mainstream culture, but rather those skills needed to adapt to specific tasks the client wants to accomplish.

Bicultural versus Acculturation

Whereas models of psychopathology emphasize an integrated identity as an indicator of adaptive psychological functioning, it is often more adaptive for bicultural individuals to maintain more fluid and discrete identities. It is not uncommon for the bicultural individual to develop different behavior patterns and identities to fit the cultural context. A bicultural individual will often switch cultural behavior patterns as he or she moves from a cross-cultural to a cultural-specific context. This form of splitting might be characterized as a developmentally primitive defense mechanism within a western model of human behavior. With racial/ethnic groups, splitting within this context is, in fact, an important adaptive mechanism. In contexts where cross-cultural values conflict, it is often more adaptive to ignore inconsistencies than to reconcile them.

Bicultural individuals heighten or minimize different cultural behavior patterns depending on the cultural context, such as to avoid being discriminated against or to enhance a sense of affiliation as they participate in different contexts. Rather than emphasizing acculturation as the outcome, we should stress the bicultural experience of racial/ethnic groups. In doing so, we show a recognition and respect for the duality of adjustment in achieving a sense of self, that is, the development of a bicultural identity.

The shift to bicultural identity, however, complicates the interpretation of self-identity. Cultural identity is generally more prominent in self-definition for people of color and immigrants than for whites and nonimmigrants. Visible racial/ethnic group members typically include race as an adjective of self-definition in response to the question, "Who am I?" whereas race is less prominent as an adjective of self-definition for whites. In adjusting to a bicultural environment, identity problems may arise that are reactive to this transition. These identity problems can reflect shared group phenomena or transitional phenomena rather than failures in individual identity formation.

In psychotherapy, this shift forces therapists to ask how a client defines himself or herself vis-à-vis culture. Failure to do so can result in defining these problems as pathological as opposed to developmental. The client's choice and development of bicultural identity influence the nature of the psychotherapeutic relationship. In same-race dyads, it can facilitate a positive identification with the therapist, or it can affirm a sense of inferiority. In cross-race dyads, it can heighten racial self-hatred or dilute a sense of ethnic identity.

Empowerment versus Traditional/Modern

Rather than emphasizing a traditional versus modern paradigm, we should shift to empowerment of diverse groups. In psychotherapy, this reflects a shift away from categorizing client behaviors and toward emphasizing client skills and behavior outcomes. Instead of judging an individual behavior as normal versus pathological or adaptive versus maladaptive, this shift emphasizes the therapeutic process of enhancing client strengths. Instead of looking at hindrances in psychotherapy, it encourages therapists to look at those factors which facilitate behavior and therapeutic change.

Diversity versus Mythical Ideal

When we subscribe to the mythical ideal, we falsely define as deviant those behaviors that do not fit the ideal criteria. Clients who behave differently are deemed a poor fit for psychotherapy. Specific forms of practice are deemed the treatment of choice. In shifting toward diversity as a defining principle, we acknowledge multiple alternatives for behavior and multicultural groups in our society. Instead of searching for the perfect society, we seek to grapple with the complexities of difference. We shift from narrow and criticizing definitions of ideal client and therapeutic fit to fluid and progressive definitions of who the client is and the context in which psychotherapy is practiced.

Valuing Differences versus Objectivity

The worship of objectivity, based on the scientific method of inquiry, lulls us into a false sense of security that concrete, tangible variables are able to define the complex process of human experience. The search for an objective standard presumes a simplicity that is often not possible. In contrast to using objectivity as a standard, Howard uses the concept of "cultural tales" to characterize a narrative approach to thinking, cross-cultural psychology, and psychotherapy.[13] This is analogous to an oral history approach to capture the richness and nuances of cultural experience not often possible through the scientific method and logical deduction. Using this approach, the development of identity can be viewed as "an issue of life-story construction; psychopathology as instances of life stories gone awry; and psychotherapy as exercises in story repair." With such an approach, the client comes to psychotherapy with a story to tell. Some aspects of this story may be missing (i.e., denial and repression), poorly written (i.e., adjustment problems, trauma), or deficient (i.e., character problems). The role of the therapist is to understand this story and help the client rewrite it.

This shift emphasizes the importance of differences in human experience, and the need to capture these differences, in the practice of psychotherapy. The concept of valuing differences originates from work at Digital Equipment Corporation in building sensitivity and respect for gender, ethnic, racial, and other differences in the corporate world through support groups. It has been used as a model for change in organizational cultures and for communication across different and diverse populations. It is currently applied to psychotherapy.

In shifting from objectivity as a standard, a difference framework suggests that cultural differences are to be valued and used in the practice of psychotherapy. Manifestations of cultural phenomena in psychotherapy are viewed as contextual. Clinical interventions would seek to utilize cultural values and world views in the therapeutic process rather than to eliminate them. Positive reframing would be used to resolve discrepancies between patient and therapist world views. Psychotherapy models would be viewed as culture bound and reflective of therapist ethnocentric bias and present-day social concerns. Psychotherapy interventions would consist of examining the positive potential of the values and practices of a culture for adaptation.

Seeking Alternatives versus Labelling

In evaluating human behavior, we need to recognize the importance of process over content. A labelling approach is more static and emphasizes content to be studied for "goodness of fit." An approach that seeks alternatives recognizes and accepts that there are multiple options to solving human problems. It recognizes cultural differences and differences in experience that influence the choice of different alternatives. When encountering a behavior, instead of asking, "What do we call it?" we would ask "What does it accomplish?" Instead of searching for the right label (i.e., diagnosis), we would search for the right alternative (i.e., solution).

Reframing in the World View of the Client versus Resistance/Noncompliance

People form views of the world they live in, and they share these views with others from their culture. These world views are used to organize day-to-day functioning; they are used to guide social and interpersonal behaviors. Kluckhohn and Strodbeck describe these views as involving four value orientations:

1. person-nature: the relationship of a person to the environment;
2. activity: the behaviors by which a person is judged or judges himself or herself;

3. time: the relative emphasis on past, present, and future time; and
4. relational: the nature of a person's interpersonal relationships.[14]

This sociological perspective has been applied to psychotherapy.

Ibrahim described the importance of these world views in cross-cultural psychotherapy,[15] and Inclan in psychotherapy with Puerto Ricans.[16] World views are often subtle, not verbalized, but strong governing forces of human behavior. Consequently, they influence therapist-client behavior and the choice of psychotherapeutic goals. When therapists confront world views different from their own, they may find clients unwillingly to follow therapeutic directives. They may find themselves unable to see eye to eye with positions taken by the client. Therapists must recognize how these differences in world views can promote miscommunication and misalliances; therapists must avoid inappropriately imposing their world views on clients. Therapists must avoid labelling these behaviors as resistance or noncompliance. Because world views are often immutable, they should be valued.

In shifting toward a paradigm of reframing in the world view of the client, therapists must grapple with whether they are merely educating the client to the ways of western psychotherapy or molding psychotherapy to match the ethos of the client's culture. Therapists are inherently biased from the vantage point of their own world views and professional training; thus it is often difficult, if not impossible, to step out of these perspectives. Reframing in the world view of the client requires taking the client's perspective. Several principles help to dictate therapist behavior and to promote this approach.

Client behaviors must be viewed as functional attempts to adapt to the client's environment.

Failures in psychotherapy are to be viewed as the therapist's inability to empathize with the client's world view and assumptive frameworks.

Key questions to be asked by the therapist include: How does the client see it? What does he or she gain from this? What values are being supported?

Cultural Competence versus Deviation from Standard Practice

The emphasis on "standard practice" creates a mind set that defines a single way to practice and classifies anything different as deviant. It fails in being responsive to diverse populations. Once again, we need to shift to a different paradigm; we need to define different practices for different populations. This shift emphasizes the importance of psychotherapy practice becoming culturally competent.

The concept of cultural competence was originated by Cross et al. and is defined as a system of care that is sensitive to culture at all levels—policy, governance, practice, and consumer.[17] Using a continuum of competence, Cross ranks behaviors and attitudes in a system reflecting increasing levels of competence for different cultural groups. This model, however, has been applied primarily to service-delivery systems rather than psychotherapy practice.

In psychotherapy practice, the emphasis on culture has generally been limited to cultural sensitivity, often defined to mean knowledge of a client's culture. This often results in an emphasis on cultural content. Using Cross's model, cultural competence in psychotherapy suggests an examination of all aspects of psychotherapy. Regarding policy, who defines the practice of psychotherapy? Who licenses, credentials, and trains? Are these bodies culturally competent? Regarding governance, what is the administrative structure of our service-delivery systems? Do they promote culturally different clients to utilize the system? Are there barriers that prevent or discourage their entry? Are there different options responsive to different needs of culturally different groups? Regarding practice, how do therapists practice? Do they use assumptive frameworks inconsistent with and devaluing client values? Regarding consumers, who are the clients? How are they different? Are client preferences and world views respected and heard? The shift toward cultural competence promotes a systemic approach to psychotherapy that challenges therapists to examine their perspectives of practice when working with a culturally diverse population.

CONTRIBUTIONS FROM AN ASIAN-AMERICAN PERSPECTIVE

The contrast in world views often noted between Asian and western perspectives can illustrate how differences must be understood to achieve cultural competence in psychotherapy. It can illustrate how a shift in assumptive frameworks can facilitate achieving psychotherapeutic outcomes with culturally diverse populations.

Several differences in assumptive frameworks serve to illustrate these points. Some contrasts between western and Asian perspectives as they might influence psychotherapy are listed in Table 4.2. They are not meant to imply uniformity within cultures or among individuals, but rather to illustrate relative degrees of emphasis or alternative perspectives common in Asian and western cultures. They are also not meant to be followed blindly, although inattention to these dimensions could adversely influence the nature of the psychotherapeutic process. The Asian perspectives[18] are likely to be stronger among Asian immigrants and refugees than those who have been in the United States for more generations. This tendency is not because Asian-Americans have become more acculturated but because they are more able to use behavior switch-

Table 4.2
Diversity in Psychotherapy: Contrasts Between Western and Asian Perspectives

Help-seeking behaviors:	Generalist vs. specialist
Psychotherapy:	Healing vs. self-actualization
Interpersonal relationships:	Hierarchical vs. equal
Emotions:	Catharsis vs. regulation
Communication styles:	Direct vs. indirect
Use of language:	Fluency vs. meaning
Maturity:	Independence vs. interdependence
Belongingness:	Individual vs. social
Identity:	Self-denigration vs. modesty
Parent-child relationships:	Ajase complex vs. Oedipal complex
Time:	Fluid vs. precise

ing as a coping mechanism and because they have become bicultural in their identity and world views.

Also, the differences between western and Asian perspectives are also found in other communities of color. Increasingly, we find other communities of color—Latino cultures, for example—who also share world views not considered to be part of the "dominant" order.

Help-Seeking Behaviors: Generalist versus Specialist

Differences in help-seeking behaviors exist between Asian and western cultures. Asian clients tend to emphasize a holistic approach to the environment. When seeking help for a "social problem," Asian clients are more apt to expect a generalist over a specialist. In establishing a therapeutic alliance, a directive approach is more likely to be facilitative because it confirms the role of the therapist as helper or advice giver. The provision of concrete social services, therefore, is more likely to be perceived as helpful than a "talking cure." Whereas western psychotherapy often emphasizes introspection, Asians are more likely to value this in a personal rather than interpersonal context.

Psychotherapy: Healing versus Self-Actualization

Asians tend to have a holistic view of health in which boundaries between mind, body, and soul are often indistinguishable. Mental health problems are inextricably related to physiological problems. Consequently, Asians with mental health problems will often present with somatic concerns. Dizziness and headaches are often symptoms of depression while heart palpitations are often a symptom of anxiety.

Herbal medicines, commonly used in Asian cultures, follow the principle that health results from a balance among the different systems of the body. The approach to healing is the stimulation of natural systems in the body and the restoration of balance. Western health care takes a more aggressive approach. Medication and surgery focus on elimination of disease and illness. Technological advances and diagnostic procedures in western medicine are often invasive procedures.

When Asian clients come for psychotherapy, they often view their problem as a health problem. The use of somatization reflects a world view in which emotional issues are viewed in the context of mind, body, and soul—that is, a holistic approach. Approaching healing as the restoration of balance reflects a "doing" orientation. Consequently, Asians frequently expect immediate symptom relief, they expect cure through medication to restore an imbalance among the bodily systems.

In psychotherapy, an emphasis on talking is discordant with this expectation. An emphasis on insight reflects a "becoming" orientation, which is also inconsistent with this expectation of healing. An emphasis on restoring an imbalance in the body or family system is more likely to be effective with Asian clients. For insight psychotherapy to be effective with Asian clients, therapists must recognize this initial perception of healing and reframe the emphasis of therapy as educative. "Becoming" in the Asian culture is associated with academic achievement as a self-actualization process, not with physical illness.

Interpersonal Relationships: Hierarchical versus Equal

Each culture has its own behavior code for interpersonal relationships. Many Asian cultures subscribe to the Confucian view of filial piety, which values unquestioning obedience to one's parents, as well as concern for and ministering to their needs and wishes. This translates into deference to authority figures and a hierarchy of interpersonal relationships, concepts which differ from the western emphasis on assertiveness and equality.

In psychotherapy, these discrepancies could be problematic to the therapeutic alliance if the therapist expects the client to take responsibility for his or her problems while the client expects the therapist to be an authority figure and to give advice. Silence cannot be interpreted as agreement if the client believes the therapist, perceived as an authority figure, should not be openly contradicted. While most therapists are sensitive in "educating" clients to the rules prescribed for psychotherapy (e.g., the fifty-minute hour, confidentiality), most take for granted their assumptive frameworks of interpersonal conduct.

When client and therapist come from the same culture, these miscommunications are less common since the culture provides a common context in which to facilitate communication and define acceptable interpersonal behavior. Therapists coming from communities of color are usually more able to bridge these cross-cultural differences because of their biculturality. Therapists from "mainstream" cultures more often expect the client to behave as "everyone else does."

Understanding these interpersonal dimensions in the therapeutic relationship becomes crucial to therapeutic effectiveness. Educating the client on the "rules" of psychotherapy will be insufficient if the relationship is perceived differently between client and therapist. The therapist may need to redefine the relationship and reframe the therapeutic process to fit the world view of the client.

Emotions: Catharsis versus Regulation

Psychotherapy and western values often prescribe catharsis—the release of emotions—to achieve optimal ego functioning. Within Asian cultures, the regulation of emotions is deemed more important to ego development than its release. As a corollary, there are negative sanctions against public displays of emotion. When westerners encounter Asians only in public settings, they are exposed to only one aspect of emotional behavior. When this is overgeneralized, they are likely to perceive Asians as unemotional. When westerners advocate for "expressing oneself," they may fail to understand the positive importance attached to "controlling oneself"; consequently, they are likely to view Asians as constricted. It is important to recognize these differences in emphasis between Asian and western cultures in psychotherapy. An emphasis on the regulation of emotions and private displays of emotion as therapeutic goals is more likely to facilitate better therapeutic outcomes with Asian clients.

Communication Styles: Direct versus Indirect

Asian cultures emphasize harmony with one's environment while western (especially U.S.) culture emphasizes mastery over and antagonism with one's environment. To preserve this harmony in interpersonal relationships, the use of indirect communication is often valued. Interrupting others is considered impolite; consequently, silence is often used by Asians to communicate disagreement. This contrasts with western emphasis on mastery over nature and on actively changing one's circumstances. Disagreement is considered healthy, and silence constitutes agreement.

In psychotherapy, confrontative techniques, viewed as direct and open by westerners, may be viewed as aggressive and inappropriate by Asian clients since it escalates conflict over cooperation. Resolution of conflict as a therapeutic goal can be viewed as disruptive since it violates the basic value of maintaining harmony. Use of these techniques could inhibit rather than facilitate psychotherapy with Asian clients.

Use of Language: Fluency versus Meaning

Language, as a medium of communication, provides words for expressing affect and meaning. Various forms of nonverbal communication—body language, spatial boundaries, facial expressions, eye contact, touching, and so on—have differing connotations and degrees of freedom in different cultures.

Asian cultures have been defined as high-context cultures where more information comes from the context than from the content of verbal information.[19] In the Chinese language, for example, emphasis is on brevity and the use of metaphor as the mark of scholarliness. Implicit meaning is stressed, and often considered more significant than the actual words used. This contrast with western uses of language, which emphasize clarity in getting one's point across and verbal fluency.

This contrast in use of language between western and Asian perspectives is likely to influence how Asian clients are perceived in psychotherapy. If western criteria are used to evaluate the language skills and communication styles of Asian clients, the clients are likely to be viewed as verbally deficient in psychotherapy. This contrast also suggests that the push for verbal expressiveness in psychotherapy is likely to be discordant with assumptive frameworks of many Asian clients. Psychotherapy models that promote the use of metaphor, symbolism, and nonverbal nuances are more likely to be sensitive to these subtle phenomena among Asian clients.

Maturity: Independence versus Interdependence

Maturity is often defined by western cultures as the achievement of independence from the family. Family enmeshment is considered pathological and self-differentiation healthy within family therapy frameworks. Cultures, however, differ in the degree to which "enmeshment," as defined by western cultures, is considered pathological.

Asian cultures emphasize mutual interdependence as the criteria of maturity, that is, caring for one's family. In the Asian culture, the extended family is viewed as mutually interdependent and as a supportive network. Maturity is defined not as separation from the family but rather as integration into the extended family network. This contrasts with the goal of achieving independence, defined in western cultures as the ability to leave the family.

Therapists need to recognize these differing definitions of maturity. A therapist may erroneously view a client as "enmeshed" when the diagnosed behaviors may be part of appropriate cultural protocol. In fostering independence as defined by western cultures, a therapist may inappropriately foster greater cultural dissonance and misunderstanding with family and other support systems rather than helping the client achieve maturity.

Belongingness: Individual versus Social

A sense of belonging is often important to psychological well-being. How this is defined often differs from culture to culture. Within the Asian culture, emphasis is on "we" rather than "I," that is, a social rather than individual orientation. For example, significant life events of an individual are shared with the family and community. An event that has brought shame to an individual is experienced and shared by an entire family or community. This concept of shame as a shared phenomenon contrasts with western cultures, in which shame is viewed as an individual experience.

This contrast in world views helps us to understand differences in suicidality among Asian clients. Suicidal attempts for poor grades are more common among Asian clients. Academic achievements, on the other hand, are often considered successes for the family as well as the individual. The burden and obligation, therefore, can be enormous for the student whose poor academic grades are viewed as bringing shame upon the family. A suicidal attempt may be viewed as an attempt at restitution, less as the obliteration of oneself.

Identity: Self-Denigration versus Modesty

Modesty is an important value in defining cultural identity within the Asian culture. However, this can only be understood along with the coexisting value of reciprocity. It is not uncommon for Asians to mutually elicit praise from one another by putting down oneself. Since the principle of reciprocity requires the listener to challenge this put-down, it enables one to remain modest while obtaining recognition from others. Westerners who do not understand this phenomenon often view this behavior as reflecting poor self-worth and self-denigration. In psychotherapy, these subtle nuances to cultural behaviors are important in defining therapeutic interventions. An Asian client may be helped to see that these behaviors are less adaptive in cross-cultural contexts rather than confronted for his or her lack of self-worth. An Asian client may be supported for his or her modesty rather than "helped" to change his or her self-definition.

Parent-Child Relationships: Ajase Complex versus Oedipal Complex

The Oedipus complex, based on Greek mythology, has been a pivotal concept in defining parent-child relationships within western cultures. Yet, its universality has been challenged by Japanese psychoanalysts who have focused upon the Ajase complex based on an Indian myth.

Prince Ajase not only kills his father, as does Oedipus, but he has a very special, intense, and culturally syntonic relationship with his mother. Prince Ajase, who was destined to kill his father, becomes king. He later tries to kill his mother because she is loyal to his father, the dead king. However, Ajase is not able to accomplish this because of his guilt feelings. Apparently, as punishment for his transgressions, sores develop on his body, and an odor emanates from them so offensive that no one will come near. His mother is the only person willing to care for him. King Ajase's heart responds to his mother's display of affection and forgiveness, thus he and his mother are reunited.[20]

Unlike Oedipus from the Greek traditions, Ajase, from the Buddhist tradition, places emphasis on the mother-son dyad rather than the father-son dyad. Ajase's guilt feelings are raised because of the mother's love for her son, while in Oedipus, the guilt feelings are due to the fear of retaliation by the father.[21] In the Ajase myth, we see an emphasis on maternal sacrifice, somatic symptoms, and family reunion. In Oedipus, the emphasis is on paternal aggression and retribution and gratification of incestuous wishes.

The contrasts between the two myths have significant implications as the universality of European mythology is applied to communities of color. The perceived universality of the Oedipus complex has resulted in the definition of mother-son conflicts as more primitive. It has influenced views of aggressive phenomena as adaptive and self-sacrifice as aggression turned inward. We need to rethink these phenomena that influence therapeutic practice from other, nonwestern perspectives.

Time: Fluid versus Precise

Asian cultures tend to believe that every system has its own sense of time whereas the western culture tends to emphasize integration of systems together and the urgency of time. This is reflected in linguistic structures, for example, where a clock "walks" in the Spanish and Chinese languages while it "runs" in English. The precision of time in western cultures translates into practice in an emphasis on appointments and promptness, that is, when events start and end. Within Asian cultures, perception of time is more fluid; events are more accommodating to individual schedules.

Time is an important issue in psychotherapy practice. Patients are expected to be prompt, to call to cancel, to come for fifty minutes, to terminate appropriately, and so on. It is clear, however, that this definition of time may not fit with prevailing views for clients from nonwestern cultures. While "standard rules" of practice may be considered sacrosanct (such as the fifty-minute hour), they may be misunderstood by Asian clients. Asian clients who come late or announce themselves unexpectedly should not automatically be judged as resistant or noncompliant.

CONCLUSION

In conclusion, our assumptive frameworks influence the ways in which we view human behavior and practice psychotherapy. As our society becomes increasingly diverse, we need to recognize how culture bound our existing theories and practice are. We need to develop a framework that values differences to practice psychotherapy in the context of culture. To achieve this, we need to eliminate the use of troublesome concepts that reflect bias in our assumptive frameworks and replace them with culturally competent concepts that value differences. We need to empower clients, not therapists, and seek alternatives that reframe psychotherapy from the clients' world views.

NOTES

1. G. Albee (1977). Does including psychotherapy in health insurance represent a subsidy to the rich from the poor? *American Psychologist,* 32, 719–21; J. L. Chin (1981). Institutional racism and mental health: An Asian American perspective. In O. A. Barbarin, P. R. Good, O. M. Pharr, & J. A. Siskind (Eds.), *Institutional racism and community competence.* Washington, DC: U.S. Government Printing Office, 44–55; L. Gardner (1980). Racial, ethnic and social class considerations in psychotherapy supervision. In A. Hess (Ed.), *Psychotherapy supervision: Theory, research and practice.* New York: John Wiley, 474–508; S. Sue & J. K. Morishima (1982). *The mental health of Asian Americans.* San Francisco: Jossey-Bass; E. Toupin (1980). Counseling Asians: Psychotherapy in the context of racism and Asian-American history. *American Journal of Orthopsychiatry,* 50(1), 76–86.

2. G. R. Dudley and M. R. Rawlins (1985). Special issue: Psychotherapy with ethnic minorities. *Psychotherapy,* 22(2S); E. E. Jones & S. Korchin (1982). *Minority mental health.* New York: Praeger; A. C. Jones (1985). Psychological functioning

in black Americans: A conceptual guide for use in psychotherapy. *Psychotherapy*, 22(2), 363–69; D. W. Sue, E. I. Richardson, R. A. Ruiz & E. J. Smith (1981). *Counseling the culturally different: Theory and practice*. New York: John Wiley & Sons; A. Thomas & S. Sillen (1972). *Racism and psychiatry*. New York: Brunner/ Mazel; S. Sue (1982). Ethnic minority issues in psychology. *American Psychologist*, 38, 583–92.

3. H. Aponte (1976). Under-organization in the poor family. *Family therapy: Theory and practice*. New York: Gardner Press, 432–48; F. X. Acosta, J. Yamamoto, & L. Evans (1982). *Effective psychotherapy with low income and minority patients*. New York: Plenum.

4. A. E. Bergin & S. S. Garfield (1971). *Psychotherapy and behavior change: An empirical analysis*. New York: John Wiley & Sons; C. Buhler (1962). *Values in psychotherapy*. New York: The Free Press; P. London (1986). *The modes and morals of psychotherapy*, 2nd ed. Washington, DC: Hemisphere; C. M. Lowe (1976). *Value orientations in counseling and psychotherapy: The meanings of mental health*, 2nd ed. Cranston, RI: Carroll Press; M. Rosenbaum (Ed.) (1982). *Ethics and values in psychotherapy: A guidebook*. Riverside, NJ: The Free Press; H. H. Strupp (1980). Humanism and psychotherapy: A personal statement of the therapist's essential values. *Psychotherapy: Theory, Research, and Practice*, 17 396–400; A. C. Tjeltveit (1989). The ubiquity of models of human beings in psychotherapy: The need for rigorous reflection. *Psychotherapy*, 26(1), 1–10.

5. A. H. Jenkins (1985). Attending to self-activity in the Afro-American client. *Psychotherapy*, 22(2S), 335–41.

6. L. Comas-Díaz & M. Minrath (1985). Psychotherapy with ethnic minority borderline clients. *Psychotherapy*, 22(2S), 416–418.

7. S. Minuchin (1974). *Families and family therapy*. Cambridge, MA: Harvard University Press.

8. F. R. Kluckhohn & F. L. Strodbeck (1961). *Variations in value orientations*. Evanston, IL: Row, Peterson; J. Inclan (1985). Variations in value orientations in mental health work with Puerto Ricans. *Psychotherapy*, 22(2S), 324–34.

9. F. A. Ibrahim (1985). Effectiveness in cross-cultural counseling and psychotherapy: A framework. *Psychotherapy*, 22(2S), 321–23; D. W. Sue (1978). World views and counseling. *Personnel and Guidance Journal*, 56, 458–62.

10. F. B. Tyler, D. R. Sussewell & S. J. Williams-McCoy (1985). Ethnic validity in psychotherapy. *Psychotherapy*, 22(2S), 311–20.

11. M. McGoldrick, J. K. Pearce & J. Giordano (Eds.) (1982). *Ethnicity and family therapy*. New York: Guilford Press.

12. Gardner (1980).

13. G. S. Howard (1991). A narrative approach to thinking, cross-cultural psychology, and psychotherapy. *American Psychologist*, 46(3), 187–97.

14. Kluckhohn & Strodbeck (1961).

15. Ibrahim (1985).

16. Inclan (1985).

17. T. L. Cross, B. J. Bazron, K. W. Dennis & M. R. Isaacs (1989). *Towards a culturally competent system of care*. Washington, DC: CASSP Technical Assistance Center, Georgetown University Child Development Center.

18. W. Tseng (1973). The concept of personality in Confucian thought. *Psychiatry*, 36, 191–202.

19. E. T. Hall (1976). How cultures collide. *Psychology Today*, July, 66–97.

20. Okonogi as quoted by Tatara (1980) as cited by J. Yamamoto (1982). *Beyond Buddhism*. Downers Grove, IL: Intervarsity Press.

21. T. Iwasaki (1971). Discussion, cultural aspects of transference and countertransference by G. Ticho. *Bulletin of the Menninger Clinic*, 35(5), 330–34.

CHAPTER FIVE

A PROGRESSIVE CHALLENGE: POLITICAL PERSPECTIVES OF PSYCHOTHERAPY THEORY AND PRACTICE

Victor De La Cancela

In this chapter, some strategies for proactive psychotherapy and perspectives are offered that focus not simply on the patient but on therapists and on the larger, socioeconomic and political macrosystems that frame all of psychotherapy.

Since people of color often have difficulty in dealing with these social systems, therapeutic approaches must attend to and promote social change and empowerment of clients within these systems. The progressive "ecostructural" approach recognizes the importance of families, external support,[1] and community support groups or self-help organizations. Participation in such proactive therapy can empower the individual and family member as well as the wider community.

FOUR BASIC ISSUES

Some readers may be surprised to find that the following discussion of affirming psychotherapy with people of color is one that they easily resonate to. This in part may be due to the awe or aversion that psychotherapists and others in our society have been socialized to experience toward anything that smacks of being "political." However, most therapists and especially psychologists trained in progressive clinical, counseling, and community programs will recognize that much of what is offered here as political activism or empowering concepts are tenets of practice in which they already engage. The difference here is that the "political" aspects are clearly articulated, made conscious, and not obfuscated within claims of "value-free" practice.

The chapter is organized along five major areas. It begins with discussion of four basic issues that are potentially helpful in conceptualizing an empowering therapy and actual practice:

1. Developing a *progressive approach* to psychotherapy services delivery, such that we explore and challenge the sociopolitical status quo. Integration of social reality with psychotherapy must occur in the theoretical conceptualization and psychological praxis of the practitioner. This approach to therapy differs from traditional psychotherapy in the value it attaches to clients interpreting their social struggles.[2]
2. Integrating *political activism* and lobbying into the role definition of service providers.
3. Training interdisciplinary psychotherapists as *agents of multicultural and socioeconomic change* who are responsive to community needs.
4. *Overcoming Eurocentricity* in therapy educational efforts as well as the repressive aspects of psychotherapy supervision models that are nonpluralistic.

By way of illustration, the aforementioned four issues are combined in a brief review of specific mental health concerns regarding African-American, Latino, and Asian men of color. The chapter thus concludes with a report on developing class-based interventions that recognize the need for a "sociocentric" approach, wherein definition of masculine selves is within the context of family and community rather than an exclusively individual context.

Developing a Progressive Approach

Upon introducing the first basic issue—developing a progressive approach—a brief discussion of the historical context for clinical practice and theory is needed because a thorough understanding of psychotherapy requires exploration of its political aspects. Some argue that psychotherapy is and should be politically neutral and value free. This view, however, is itself a political statement because it requires that clinicians avoid challenging the sociopolitical status quo and thereby accept it. In contemporary society, psychotherapy and organized psychiatry, social work, psychology, and mental health nursing often function in the interest of the dominant social order, which in the United States is capitalist. For example, corporations set up employee assistance programs and staff them with therapists in order to treat the employees' mental health problems that interfere with business, such as authority conflicts, alcoholism, and absenteeism.[3]

Similarly, dominant social science views and psychological literature have ethnocentrically depicted low-income, ethnic clients and people of color as pathological, genetically and culturally deficient, deprived, or disadvantaged. These labels have served the ideological interest of a social order that requires economic and social handicaps to exist for some groups so that others might profit.[4]

Although these examples exhibit mechanisms for social *control*, psychotherapy is a synthesizing educative and social process that also contains elements for *liberation*. There are therapists who engage in education, advocacy, brokerage, mediation, and even bureaucratic rule-breaking in order to better serve their clients. Another component of this dialectical interchange has recently been pressed by cross-cultural, radical, feminist, and gay/lesbian psychotherapists, and it is apropos for examination of the therapist's attitudes toward racism, sexism, sexual orientation, and social action.

Critical appraisals of psychotherapy date back to Sigmund Freud's own lifetime when some psychoanalysts attempted to synthesize radical theory and/or Marxism and psychoanalysis. From the 1960s onward, others such as Frantz Fanon, Herbert Marcuse, and R. D. Laing have attempted a sociopolitical, psychotherapeutic perspective which aims to analyze the social structure and political ideology of capitalism. Their aim is to help clients gain insight into attitudes and behaviors that are related to competitiveness, prestige, conformity, elitism, and class divisions. Here, the therapist is encouraged to progressively practice by stepping outside the "authoritarian role" and being supportive of client participation in the analysis-treatment process. Progressive practitioners must also be able to state the limits of therapy clearly and to suggest social action when this may be a more appropriate alternative.

The progressive therapist seeks to integrate into what Závala-Martínez calls a clinical community-oriented praxis.[5] This does not require therapists to possess the time, knowledge, or inclination to provide political education. Rather, Závala-Martínez states that meaningful praxis with clients implies an integration of community education, the development of participatory projects, and the equal distribution of mental health knowledge and skills.[6] She suggests that the progressive approach must reflect the struggle for growth and survival that characterizes diverse communities.

Integrating Political Activism/Lobbying

The delivery of psychotherapy services is shaped by the capitalist economy in which we live and by the policies of those who control the economy. Regardless of our individual, subjective beliefs regarding psychotherapy and its relationship to the sociopolitical environment, we cannot escape the objective effects of capitalism. Reductions in expenditures for human services, tightening of productivity controls, cost-benefit analyses, increased caseloads, and corporate-like hierarchical division of labor are all aspects of psychotherapeutic practice in the public and private nonprofit sphere that therapists confront as workers.

Most therapists are part of the "new" working class. Whereas psychotherapists once held a certain privileged professional status, we have become part of the labor force in the vast social enterprise—and business enterprise—of therapy. Without the mystique and ideology of professionalism, therapists are seen as what they are: laborers who are dependent on wages, just like other workers.

The sooner we begin to understand and accept this "new" working class status, the sooner we can appreciate the need to develop political strategies that link us with the real-world community of workers, empowering them and ourselves—to lobby for better funding and delivery of mental health services. Many who identify themselves as professionals think that political activity and noise-making is "unprofessional," that we can use more sedate, "professional" means to challenge the status quo. But consider the chilling professional silence that has allowed legislators and administrators to "dump" the mentally ill out of hospitals and onto the streets, under the guise of providing community-based services for them. Think also of how the ill-planned deinstitutionalization of severely disturbed persons has cost society dearly in terms of victimization of people with psychiatric labels by criminals, their own entrance into the justice system as perpetrators in some cases, and the resulting stigmatizing public perception of the persistently ill and the whole mental health field.

Look at the economic policies spurred on during the Reagan and Bush years, and still continuing today, which have forced thousands of families and homeless individuals onto the streets—people without jobs, without homes, and, often, without hope. How can we ignore the mental devastation that is wrought by powerful political and economic forces, particularly for low-income ethnics and people of color? How can we develop meaningful therapeutic interventions without addressing the socioeconomic environment in which they take place? How can we practice competently if we do not address the diversity engendered by the patient's political status, such as immigrant, native, refugee, asylum seeker, exile, alien, undocumented, citizen?[7] How can we as mental health professionals genuinely acknowledge that many therapists have been no more competent, liberal, or urgent in addressing these issues than society in general; and that doing so will be of value to all of us even as it may make us question our comfortable theories and practice?

Therapists who wish to serve clients as agents of change must consciously question the political results of their clinical practices. We must ask ourselves, for example, if by treating prison inmates, we are participating in and legitimizing the existing punishment process. We must consider whether or not by evaluating applicants for welfare we are helping to maintain a supply of workers for the hardest and lowest paying jobs; whether our participation in Head Start programs helps adjust children to the poor education they will receive; and whether intake systems operate to screen out clients and artificially create a scarcity of services.

When therapists consciously examine the sociopolitical effects of their clinical practices, many hidden issues will begin to surface. Here are just a few to consider:[8]

- Referral mechanisms deal with clients in need by not really addressing their needs; rather they refer them to others who ostensibly are better able to deal with their "category" of problems (e.g., drug users are referred to chemical dependency services instead of the therapist seeing their drug use problem more holistically).

- Short-term therapy aims to move service recipients out of the agency as quickly as possible regardless of their need for services.

- Insistence on clients keeping appointments is meant to encourage behavioral conformity and steady cash flow.

- Mandates of professional objectivity and emotional neutrality are akin to other capital-oriented work practices that encourage emotional disengagement from work in order to ensure a uniform product. For example, visible racial ethnic group therapists have been counseled to avoid countertransferences in which they overidentify with their clients of color. It is believed that this may lead them to do more for these clients than they might otherwise do for others who are not of their ethnic racial background.

The psychotherapist who seeks to work with multiethnic clients should be prepared for the potentially highly politicized nature of this work: politics that include the referral of low-income clients without the benefit of any discussion, exploration, or explanation to account for their referral; and policies that guide some therapists to select medication as the "treatment of choice" for ethnics and low-income clients, which has been criticized as serving custodial functions.[9] For example, LeVine and Padilla question practices that potentially impose directive therapies on Latinos out of fears that their behavior must be controlled or because it frees the therapist to spend more time with preferred middle-class clients.[10]

We need a conscious political approach to mental health that recognizes that *therapy is not and can never be "neutral."* If we are truly concerned about the betterment of human welfare, we must challenge society at large for not being able to provide jobs at a living wage for all who want them. We must uncover why and how the receipt of medical, mental health, and social services is made unpleasant and/or stigmatizing particularly for the poor. We must try to teach our colleagues that a tra-

ditional clinical practice is not and can never be an adequate response
to the fundamental problems of exploitation, denial, and dehumanization in capitalist society.

This reaching and teaching process also means empowering clients
by facilitating their awareness of how social forces impact on their lives.
In carrying out this work, many of the specific skills that traditional
training has given therapists can still be used, but with very different
notions of direction, purpose, values, and roles. Hence, supporting
clients includes keeping them informed of political/legislative developments that go against their best interests and helping them to channel
their energies toward community action and other advocacy strategies.[11]
It means providing them a "therapy aimed at social action and the
alleviation of discrimination and poverty."[12] Empowerment also suggests determining in concert with the client how much separation or
conformity to the dominant social order will facilitate personal growth.[13]
Ultimately, empowering therapy requires the cultivation of the client's
critical thinking capacities toward more conscious decision making.

Despite the humanistic values inherent in a progressive practice, it is
highly likely that the therapist who aspires to such practice will be
plagued by difficulties. These will stem from the fact that adhering to
these values is itself a political move, one that will be viewed suspiciously
because of its underlying premises: a concern with ideology and an
employment of radical or nontraditional concepts. Because of these
premises such therapists must be prepared to confront the realities of a
capitalist structure, that is, that traditional "neutral" psychotherapy
practitioners occupy the editorial boards, grant review committees, graduate programs, and employment settings that most professional therapists come in contact with. Hence manuscript or research proposal
rejections, as well as placement, tenure, and advancement denial, are
more apt to occur than not.[14] Similarly, charges of unethical and unprofessional concerns with politics may surface,[15] leading to dismay,
frustration, resignation, and little job security.

Even when such direct impact on the "challenging" therapist's livelihood is not experienced, and even if the therapist eschews a radical
practice, the effects of capitalist society will be felt. For example, the
simple act of writing a letter to a medical journal shows how deeply
capitalism, competitiveness, and guild issues can invade the therapist's
profession.

In attempting to understand why there were but three cross-cultural
index entries in an American Psychiatric Association publication *Treatments of Psychiatric Disorders*,[16] two authors agreed to write a letter to the
editor of the *American Journal of Psychiatry*. This letter basically explored
the possible reasons for such a paucity of cross-cultural issues. Selected
segments from the draft letter follow:

Why is that? Could it be reflective of the alleged remedicalization of psychiatry in which social factors are ignored and prominence is given to biological etiologies in understanding mental illness? An analysis of the book's chapter headings reveals that the majority of articles indeed do not emphasize social factors, though a few reflect trends in the delivery of mental health services, i.e., employee assistance programs.

Why is that? Is it that one of the more primitive psychological defense mechanisms—denial, is being utilized on a grand scale by some of the most prominent United States psychiatrists and esteemed mental health professionals who served as editorial advisory board members, consultants and contributors to this massive five volume set that has been hailed as the treatment bible of U.S. psychiatry? Denial that each person's ethnic, racial and social cultural background provides a contextual definition of normality and pathology. Denial that prominent African-American psychiatrists like Drs. Pouissant and Pinderhughes have devoted a significant portion of their careers to examination of effective therapies for the socioculturally and racially diverse. Populations that United States psychiatrists encounter in community mental health centers, psychiatric wards, general hospitals and one would hope in their private practices.

Why is that? Is it that U.S. psychiatry reflects the biases and prejudices of a mainstreaming society wishing to ignore the multi-class, multi-racial and multilingual reality of its masses? The fact that the only chapter that includes references to African-Americans, Latinos and Asians is on sexuality and that the terms used to identify them are the less politically preferred ones of Orientals, Hispanics and Blacks does little to reassure the reader that psychiatrists do not share the same myths and stereotypes held by a generally ethnocentric society.

Have we forgotten the message that concerned clinicians, therapists and mental health researchers over the past three decades have endeavored to bring to their psychiatric and psychological colleagues? In the 70's, students in training complained of institutional racism in graduate program curriculum while "established" psychiatrists suggested that traditional psychotherapeutic techniques might alienate linguistic minority clients such as the Spanish-speaking. During the 80's, therapists were warned against ignoring intragroup differences and critically advised to attend to the legacy of rampant discrimination, prejudices and stereotypes expressed in a psychological literature that spoke of the socioculturally different as pathological and culturally deprived.

Practitioners must continue to examine the connections between the psychosocial distress of stigmatized, scapegoated and socially devalued ethnic individuals and people of color and the sociopolitical realities of their reference groups. In this manner hopefully we will not blame the victim nor ascribe to culture what may be socioeconomically related. Through the integration of social analysis, biological models and psychological approaches, we can move towards further modification of our treatment models and enhanced examination of the hidden, unconscious, or denied ideology, politics, values and class biases of traditional treatment perspectives.

"Educar es poder. Poder es educar." To educate is power. Power is to educate. It appears then that our psychiatric colleagues at the APA publication office have exerted their power in publishing a book that denies a prominent tendency in the U.S. mental health field's movement towards a pluralistic therapy model.

As such, it has done a disservice to its ethnic minority constituents specifically and to psychiatric education in general. It has engaged in an exercise of monocultural dominance and turned a deaf ear to the mandate to continually question and learn which it allegedly adheres to. It has chosen to neither learn or empower practitioners via educating them so that "each one can teach one." Why is that?[17]

This draft letter was shared with several self-described "ethnoculturally active" psychiatrists with the intent of gathering cosignatures to enhance the impact of the critique. Similarly, the input of the presidents of the four major national ethnic minority psychological associations and other psychologists was solicited. Then guild issues began to surface as follows: Several psychiatrists dropped out after agreeing to sign the letter because they felt it was an attack on psychiatry by psychologists, which was part of the continuing battles between the two APAs and professions regarding lay versus medical psychotherapy. The original two authors suggested inclusion of nursing and social work colleagues as well as modification of the letter toward allaying competitive or conflictive interpretations and refocusing on our joint responsibilities to patients, constituents, and ethnocultural mental health education and research.

After said modification, some of the more prominent psychiatrists reconsidered and now were only in agreement with having one nonpsychiatry cosigner—the original psychologist coauthor. He refused, reminding his psychiatric colleague that not only was he the primary author of this letter but that other psychologists were solicited to be cosigners in a stance of unity. The psychiatrist, however, agreed to pursue writing the letter on his own, and a modified but recognizable form of the letter was published and cosigned by twenty psychiatrists.[18] The irony in this story is that the editor's response to this letter suggested that its cosigners should bear "the burden of self-criticism," as the development of the publication was discussed at many of the American Psychiatric Association's meetings and in print (*Psychiatric News, New York Times*). He questioned how these transcultural activists made no previous moves to see the material or meet with the task force as other interest groups did.[19] Although this response might appear to be defensive, it does suggest that health professionals must be better organized, ever vigilant, and ready to intervene if they are to have greater impact in the area of fostering sociocultural competence.

Therapists, as professionals committed to alleviating suffering and promoting freedom and well-being for individuals and society, appear to have a professional responsibility to protect the human rights of the racially and ethoculturally diverse client. Thus, the profession should explore the clients' situation and its civic, legal, and psychosocial aspects.

We need to oppose the bias and persecution that the culturally different experience in this country and insist that their legal rights under the U.S. Constitution, domestic laws, and International Human Rights Law be protected. We can go on record as endorsing their right to free speech, the maintenance of their language and culture of origin, and an end to the threats and harassments from those racist individuals and organizations who are threatened by diversity.

At the local level activist-practitioners can extend their services to ethnic organizations helping them to assess their needs, providing direct services, and creating a resource and referral network. Psychotherapists can provide technical assistance with research; proposal writing; recruitment, selection, and placement of trainees; and identification of potential funding sources. We can supervise and train agency workers to identify serious disturbances, document the effects of repression, and report the results of using different treatment modalities. We can also educate others through our access to local news media, agency conferences, and national conventions.[20]

Our most important lobbying and psychoeducational efforts, however, must target U.S. government agencies. They, in particular, need to understand the psychosocial significance of the treatment accorded by our country to visible racial ethnic groups. They need to know that by denying them socioculturally competent health care (including mental health and social services) our federal, state, county, and municipal agencies consign thousands of people to increased morbidity and mortality needlessly. In addition, attending properly to treatment not only saves lives and suffering, it provides economic gains, savings, and productivity benefits to a society increasingly overwhelmed by escalating social and health costs.

Interdisciplinary Agents of Multicultural and Socioeconomic Change

The third point, which goes hand-in-hand with political activism, is the need for multicultural and interdisciplinary approaches to delivery of health and psychotherapy services.

In efforts to distinguish ourselves from our medical colleagues and as a reaction to their medicocentricity, psychotherapists as a group previously have not fully acknowledged the importance of medical and health concerns in therapy with their clients. Except for the specialized work of psychotherapists and medical social workers working in health and hospital settings, the vast majority of psychotherapists give cursory attention to biological or biomedical factors in their service delivery. Given the biopsychosocial and cultural diversity of the U.S. populace and the fact that the diseases that the people of the United States are increasingly being stricken with and dying from are related to risk behaviors that can be changed, it appears to be a moral, ethical, and professional obligation to include health promotion, education, and disease prevention in our therapeutic repertoire.

Consider, for example, excessive alcohol intake, cigarette smoking, and AIDS as three areas that are amenable to the combined efforts of behavioral therapists, clinical-community psychologists, and public health social workers. Consider also that teenage pregnancy, IV drug use, medically underserved areas, lack of medical insurance, and illnesses related to poor sanitation or overcrowded living conditions can be "societal cofactors" leading to psychological stress, emotional conflicts, fatalism, and even compromising of the individual's immune system.[21] Given the history of heterosexism, racism, ethnocentrism, and classism in medical practice, many people of color and in alternative lifestyles are distrustful of western health services and seek more holistic healing. In this regard, it is important to acknowledge the existence of conspiracy theories and genocidal fears that exist among some in communities of color, feminist groups, and the gay and lesbian community—AIDS as biological warfare and homophobic extermination, or radical mastectomies and hysterectomies as overutilized phallocentric medical procedures.[22]

Racial, ethnic, and culturally diverse psychotherapists serving similarly distinct patients have generally been much more competent, or have had to become so, in the arena of health and mental health interactions for a number of reasons, including: the large number of unresolved health problems of refugees and migrants, be these Asian, Haitian, or Latino; the extent of alcohol abuse, alcoholism, and drug use/abuse, including cigarette smoking, among people of color, especially American Indians/Native Americans, African-Americans, Asians, and Latinos, which leads to heightened morbidity and mortality rates;[23] the reduced access to health care among people of color due to financial, linguistic, cultural, educational, and institutional barriers;[24] varying degrees of the dual utilization of folk beliefs and biomedical systems among people of color, as well as a reported nondifferentiation between physical and emotional concerns among certain groups such as Asians and Latinos;[25] psychotherapy services often being offered as a last resort upon referral from medical and other health service providers;[26] and the existence of a socioeconomically related pattern of seeking health/mental health care for acute, crisis, or emergency conditions rather than preventive or maintenance-oriented primary care.[27]

Drawing from such experiences and from the medical psychotherapy and anthropology literature, cross-cultural psychiatrists and psychologists, among others, have identified the "medical model" health culture that most clinicians practice in and subscribe to. This includes psychotherapists, who would otherwise go to great lengths to distinguish themselves from "biomedical types," referring to their clients as patients whom they are caretakers of or caregivers to rather than cohealers or partners with.[28] Indeed, the prevalent illness model is one that often ascribes individual responsibility, blame, and stigma to the sufferer whose illness is considered to reflect character weakness. Yet in the long run, many of the health problems faced by poor people of color are related to their lack of societal power in changing their possibilities of developing disease, such as malnutrition and asthma.

It has been suggested that both health psychology and community psychology have much to offer to meet the special needs of multicultural and socioeconomically diverse populations, such as control of hypertension among African-Americans and Latinos.[29] By way of illustration, the following is an application of this suggestion in the context of HIV counseling within psychotherapy, a crucial and critical area in which a great deal of stereotyping has flourished.

Some professional circles have offered pseudocultural explanations regarding people of color that create an image of static, exotic, racial, or ethnic features that serve as barriers to accepting messages of AIDS prevention. For example, one author[30] implies that Latinos *routinely* use anal sex as a birth control method while others claim that Latinos invariably reject same-sex liaisons. In opposition to this barrier theory is the stark reality of how problematic it is to counsel any group of people on health-related issues when intervention methodologies are applied indiscriminately and without cognizance of the group's varied social, economic, educational, and political experiences. Hence, in the world of HIV counseling, attempting to change intimate and specific behaviors that are carried out on a personal basis and in interpersonal settings leads to talking about changing behaviors that reflect "established cultural patterns" and lifestyles.

For example, the issue of family life and gender roles in African-American, Asian-American, and Latino communities is not only one of cultural influences but also one of how family members provide reminders of or cue each other into functional behavioral repertoires. It is not simply that African-American, Asian Pacific, or Latino women are unable to ask their partners to use condoms for fear of being rejected or transgressing their culturally defined roles. Rather, it is a fact that in *most* cultural groups women historically have been "kept in their place" by male patriarchs, not just in African-American, Chinese, Puerto Rican, or Chicano cultures. Similarly, it is not only cultural practices but a lack of adequate education and the high cost of health care in the United States that make it difficult to prevent infection by limiting the home-based administration of medicine and vitamins with unsterile needles by friends and neighbors in some Latin American communities.

Therapists should be wary of noncritical cultural perspectives that are limited by overstating traditional stereotypes and paying too little attention to diverse, conflicting, and transitional values and roles in many families of color. All too often, narrow cultural perspectives end up confusing social features related to poverty and poor education, such that socioeconomic and political influences are misconstrued as part of the cultural "heritage" of people of color. For example, access to real jobs, educational services, and training opportunities for men of color depends heavily on the political party affiliation of elected leaders on the federal, state, and municipal level. Yet many men of color are viewed as not sufficiently motivated to lift themselves up by their bootstraps.[31] This type of aberrant logic is apparent in misguided theories of a "culture of poverty" or "welfare culture," which are applied to African-Americans and Latinos. This type of logic leads to *victim-blaming* and creates barriers of suspicion among people of color toward the very people who allegedly are trying to help them.

When seeking to develop HIV counseling models that empower the community, for example, it is important to undertake demographic analysis and consideration of behavioral, economic and sociopolitical realities. A prosocial model must link combating AIDS with the fight for improved access to health care for people of color and the fight against drugs, illiteracy, violence, and crime in their communities. This model involves grass roots organizations and local services in proactive programming by *professionals in partnership with community residents.*

This is a liberating model that says "Yes, we can!" (*Si! Podemos!*) to those who would believe that people of color cannot raise consciousness, take care of their own, educate themselves, and survive. This perspective is empowering because it is characterized by promoting the health and well-being of communities of color and their families, rather than focusing primarily on the well-being of the individual. This model is ultimately geared toward community control over education and prevention efforts that will address AIDS reduction and other medical and mental health needs facing the community.

Expanding Horizons in Psychotherapy Teaching and Supervision

If diversity is to be accepted in psychotherapy theory and practice within the United States, then the field must open itself up to scrutiny and allow exploration of how institutionally ethnocentric, racist, sexist, and classist it has been. One suggested area where initial inquiry might prove fruitful is in researching how therapy is practiced in nonwestern, noncapitalist, non-European, and racially diverse settings. For example in several so-called nonwestern, communist, or socialist countries, psychotherapy places great emphasis on work and community responsibility as integral to the treatment, rehabilitative, and recovery processes. In the former Soviet Union, People's Republic of China, and Cuba, therapy is mostly reality oriented, includes occupational therapy, emphasizes the individual's role as a responsible member of society, and involves family members and the workplace in recuperative efforts.[32] This is also true of psychotherapy in Ghana and several other West African countries where community responsibility is emphasized.

The Chinese psychotherapist focuses on the here and now and development of an analytical creative cognition style; hence emotion and past experience are not emphasized. "Heart-to-heart" talks correspond more clearly to western psychotherapy sessions, yet they are usually only half an hour in length. The Cuban approach includes a public health model of preventive mental health care that includes psychoeducation—informing the client and family of the warning signs of relapse as well as community education and home visits. Though some of these approaches are gaining some prominence in U.S. efforts at rehabilitation of persons with psychiatric labels, these are still not commonplace in general psychotherapy practice, and thus, their application in culturally diverse settings offers us new learning opportunities. Such opportunities include overcoming the elitism of mainstream psychotherapists who view community mental health workers and psychologists who work in community-based organizations as somehow deviant rather than different.

As psychotherapy educators, we have significant power to meaningfully impact on those institutional forces that contribute to the oppressed status of communities of color and other groups in this society. We can all engage in a serious and careful self-evaluation of how our androgyny can empower students, faculty, and staff from diverse ethnic, racial, cultural, and sexual lifestyles.

Key to this examination is a commitment to developing mentoring and "womentoring" possibilities for all members of the psychotherapy field. Such academic/clinical role modeling is necessary given the longstanding influence of race, heterosexist power, and gender politics on tenure decisions in academia and institutional employment, and their contribution to the establishment of mainly Caucasian "male to male" mentor-protégé relationships. In fact, most successful academicians-clinicians admit to having in part achieved their current status because of the backing of influential patrons, guides, or sponsors. A sponsor's importance lies in socializing newcomers into role and organizational requirements, and expectations that lead to surviving.[33] For example, socialization through invitations to coauthor papers for presentations or reviewing for journals provides leads into the publication track.[34]

Recent research indicates that same-race role models and sponsors appear to be better facilitators of the career development and retention of students of color than nonsimilar models. Apparently, these relationships serve as concrete demonstrations to students of color that despite racism they too can become competent professionals.[35] However, faculty members who are not from such backgrounds can also be effective sponsors to persons of color if they support the student's ethnic or racial research or psychotherapy service interests by seeing how these may fit into the senior faculty member's own research or psychotherapy interests. This has the added benefit of enriching faculty research by adding culturally diverse perspectives.

Similarly, given the prevalence of visible ethnic racial group faculty members in junior level and nontenured temporary positions, senior faculty can contribute to their juniors' professional development, promotion, and retention by initiating sponsor-protégé relationships that include them in the networking process that is so critical to advancement. A particular challenge will be creating cooperative and collectivist models of sponsorship that do not recreate the traditional hierarchal and patriarchal relationships of the "old boys' network."

Both feminist-informed and ethnocultural communal perspectives have much to offer in this regard.[36] For example, it has been suggested that network sponsorship models in which two or more people play the roles of sponsor and protégé to each other at different times are more appropriate for female graduate students and faculty, since these are more egalitarian in operation.[37] Another empowering suggestion is the establishment of faculty growth contracts that are developed in consultation with department or program heads to aid junior female faculty to clarify goals, strengths, weaknesses, and resources needed for growth, within the framework of departmental and institutional needs and goals.[38] Native American psychologists suggest that the sponsor is a familiar concept among American Indian cultures and, by extension, other non-European heritages, given the traditional value attached to elders, *griots*, and other wise folk teachers and leaders.[39]

It should be emphasized that sponsorship, mentoring, and womentoring initiatives must also include opportunities for development of public service orientations and expertise. Psychotherapy educational facilities would be remiss if they did not examine how faculty, students, and staff can contribute to both public and professional arenas via business, legislative, political, social, and community organizational activities at the national, state, and municipal levels. Public policy activity must not only be encouraged but given added weight in the promotion and tenure review process.

Finally, multicultural psychotherapy education must truly be inclusive. Caucasians are ethnic as well; their subgroup histories and identities need to be examined and encouraged toward movement from "white cultural unawareness to a multi-cultural and non-racist identity."[40]

Psychotherapy supervision similarly offers us new areas of growth, if we apply the progressive's examination of its political implications. Several critics have asserted that the traditional supervisor-supervisee relationship is one wherein disagreement or a difference in perceptions with the supervisor's authority may be treated as the trainee's psychopathology.[41] Since traditional supervisory relationships are allegedly constructed to teach and enforce the profession's rules and regulations,[42] those concerned with diversity worry that the standards offered are ones that nonmainstream group members have not had a hand in developing.[43] The professional identification through modeling aspects of supervision may also encourage a guild mentality that closes off other viewpoints.[44] In actual experience, changing the supervisory model to reflect the client diversity service model that one wishes to foster will ameliorate some of the aforementioned difficulties. Hence, progressive supervisors will strive to make supervision nonhumiliating, noninfantilizing, democratic, and open.[45]

This approach reveals that supervisor and supervisee are different at times because of class or political, ethnic, racial, and gender memberships that generate conflicting views of the psychotherapist's role and goals. Given differential power relationships in the supervisory enterprise and diversity as defined above, both trainees and supervisors need to examine their "countertransferential oppression"—those beliefs and practices that are discriminatory.[46] Given that the supervisor is already a member of the profession, she or he is the one primarily responsible for advocacy on behalf of the trainee and for actively questioning his or her own and the trainee's beliefs in regards to political ideology, ethnocentrism, racism, elitism, sexism, and classism as these affect the trainee's practice.

Finally, the supportive supervisor must model for the trainee, as the progressive therapist does with a client-appropriate disclosure, by making explicit his or her values, assumptions, and schools of thought. Supervisors should be explicit about their own credentials, the limits of their role as therapist, and the general limitations of psychotherapy.[47]

Treating Men of Color

In this final section an attempt is made to highlight the fact that the previously identified four issues are not purely theoretical or untested concepts. They have been applied specifically in the context of a gender-, ethnic-, and racial-sensitive practice. For example, the author has worked as a psychotherapist to enrich African-American, Asian, and Latino males with regard to their survival. What follows then is a sharing of that experience in a general way to close this chapter.

Much ado has been made about the endangered status of African-

American, Latino, and Asian males, yet the psychotherapeutic profession as a whole has not been at the forefront of addressing these concerns. Instead, there is a legacy of acknowledging men of color only in terms of their alleged absenteeism from the family and a resulting negative impact on children, especially their sons. Asian males, for example, have been alternately viewed as passive, passive aggressive, emasculated, or authoritarian as heads of households. Family therapists have made some efforts to address men-of-color issues in therapy, yet they do not generally deal with the daily losses faced by such men and the concerns women of color have regarding the emotional and physical toll on their families caused by a racist society that exterminates men of color. For some women of color "there are few good men around" as too many are lost to drugs and the streets, crime and jails, or alternative life choices such as homosexuality or interracial affairs. Given a world view that men of color are either dead, victimized, embattled, or embittered, it could be argued that therapists need to provide much bereavement support to families of color.

Even feminist therapists have contributed negatively by not being more critical in their analysis of power relationships, sexual politics, and the conflict of relating as it pertains to men who are often marginalized by both their ethnic/racial and low socioeconomic status (SES) backgrounds. The mainly Caucasian middle-class men's movement in psychotherapy similarly has been nonrigorous in analysis of its theory and practice as it pertains to the real-world diversity of men who are from different classes and ethnic/racial backgrounds or who have serious psychiatric disturbances, substance use problems, and life traumas. As partial remedy to these gaps, this section offers a synopsis of some of the guiding principles used to develop male-affirmative, social-class-based therapeutic interventions for men of color.[48]

To set a cautionary tone for acceptance of these guidelines, the following introduction to a lecture at a public forum over a decade ago on the topic of *machismo* and its psychotherapeutic implications is shared.

Psychotherapists Desk Reference Product Information Report on Machismo

Caution:

— Ethical standards prohibit use of this information for wide generalizations to any person other than members of the population which it describes.

— Ethical standards prohibit dispensing this information without stating its limitations.

— If signs of irritation or sensitivity develop as a result of listening to this material, please note your thoughts, feelings and reaction and formulate questions and criticisms.

— Sift through all your reactions and integrate the material well before use of this data.

Indications:

— These ideas are for use in psychotherapy and mental health/social service delivery to certain Latino males undergoing sex role changes in this country.

Contains:

— Definitions and origins of Puerto Rican *Machismo*; current perspectives in social sciences on *machismo*; method and results of the study; discussion and conclusions.

Expiration Date:

— The day, month, year and moment when it no longer is useful to the individual or group it describes or intends to aid.[49]

This "warning label" approach is admittedly a dramatic manner of highlighting that generic prescriptions for psychotherapy with men of color really do not exist. Rather we must approach individual clients within the specifics of their personal life histories as well as the unique sociopolitical, economic, and cultural factors that shape their gender role, family role, and community behavior.

The primary guideline in work with men of color is treating them *"con respeto"*—respectfully—which means recognizing that more often than not they are treated as less than men. African-American males have historically been considered "boys" or "studs," while Latinos have been portrayed as "machos" with inferiority complexes. These labels connote that the bearers are deprived of intellect and a sense of responsibility but endowed with brawn and immature sexuality. Asian men are viewed either as small, frail, effeminate "wimps," fit only to be restaurant servants and laundrymen, or mysterious, inscrutable, violence-prone martial artists. In fact, their cultural ideals of heroism, like *samurais* or *kamikaze* soldiers, are devalued and understood as reflecting the low value placed by Asians on life.

In the United States, men of color have a history of coercion in which they are told what to do, discouraged from participating, labelled as deviants or delinquents, or denied economic success. In therapy, they are accustomed to being seen as maladaptive, manipulative, violent—in short, pathological—and, more often than not, bad therapy candidates. Asians, for example, are viewed as nonverbal and passive. This all amounts to therapists traditionally making less aggressive outreach and engagement efforts with these men. Therapeutic work, hence, must begin from the standpoint of acknowledging that men of color develop their manhood within a society that denies them full equality. Hence, their male socialization is restricted, is stunted, and includes internalization of both their oppression and idealized, caricatured socioeconomic, cultural images of masculinity (i.e., good economic provider, protectors of the family, heterosexual).

A corollary of respectful therapy is that the interventions made with men of color be empowering and socially contextual—in other words, responsive to their cultural, political, and individual historical life realities in the past, present, and foreseeable future. This approach necessitates ecosystems analysis with much attention placed on the ever-changing family-community-society relationships that allow the emergence of certain adaptive and maladaptive behavior. For example, an area where such analysis is helpful is understanding how men of color respond to the impact of feminism, the increased participation of women in the labor force, and the objective aspects of their largely un- and underemployed status as a group.[50]

The called-for analysis and therapy must be dialectical—that is to say, developmental in perspective and cognizant of contradictory tension in the attitudinal, behavioral, and intra- and interpersonal life of men of color. On a daily basis such men experience these contradictions as ambivalence, confusion, and self- and social alienation. They, therefore, require goal-oriented time-limited, and values-clarifying therapy in which both their positive and their negative male gender behaviors are explored.[51] The called-for therapeutic contract must discuss their progressive and reactionary views of women's roles. It includes a critical analysis of their self-expectations and their perceptions of the expectations of other men as it relates to their behavior. The dialectical model offers a fluid understanding for both the therapist and client in confronting their individual subscription to masculinized ideology. It offers a male-affirmative, empathic, comprehensive, yet critical examination of the gender, ethnic, racial, and political baggage that we all carry around in contemporary society. (Chapter 7 provides a more specific example of this approach applied to clinical work.)

From such dialectical therapy, therapists have developed the belief that men of color can bond with each other when their assets and strong sense of responsibility and accountability to their family and community are engaged. This requires therapists and counselors to be conscious multicultural agents of change committed to inclusionary, collaborative, and progressive educational interventions. For example, such socially competent therapists can help boys and young men of color question the miseducation they might have heretofore received with regard to Martin Luther King, Jr., Malcolm X, the Black Panthers, the Brown Berets, the Young Lords Party, and the Black Power and civil rights movements. In their own time, these individuals, groups of individuals, and movements offered critical models of African-American and Puerto

Rican/Chicano/Latino men attempting to integrate cultural, spiritual, psychological, sociopolitical, and socioeconomic concerns into an empowering agenda for persons of color.[52]

We also need psychotherapy initiatives for men of color that include knowledge of contemporary American Indian, Asian-American, African-American, and Puerto Rican/Latino history. The historical perspective can be especially valuable in the correctional facilities where large numbers of men of color reside. In this way, they might truly have a "corrective emotional experience" that instills pride and responsibility.

Indeed, it can be asserted that one of the most important therapeutic discussions to be had with Asian-American, African-American, and Puerto Rican/Latino males is the relationship of their class or socioeconomic reality to their health/mental health status. Being a poor male of color translates into inadequate health care facilities, shorter average life expectancies, and higher overall homicide, suicide, drug use, and accident rates. Hence, youth of color need psychoeducation regarding what the African-American leader Rev. Dr. Calvin Butts, Latino health care activists Drs. Emilio Carrillo and Carlos Molina, and prominent Asian-American Dr. Jean Chin have espoused: that the alcohol and tobacco industries specifically target the marketing of alcohol and cigarettes to communities of color in racist, sexist, and ethnocentric ways.

As psychotherapists, we too have a particular responsibility to work with our legislators to legislate, lobby, and educate others about drug and alcohol abuse being a leading mental health problem in communities of color. We need more legislative initiatives creating bilingual alcohol treatment centers and job training programs for men in recovery.

These are but a few of the ways in which we can all work together toward increasing political and economic therapeutic competence for Asian, African-American, and Puerto Rican/Latino males. These are shared with the hope that we will achieve this competence as we move steadfastly toward social justice for all people of color and underserved groups—be they the differently abled, women, gay or lesbian, or the poor and working-class members of our society.

CONCLUSION

The four points addressed in this chapter are vital to the creation of an empowering psychotherapy for communities of color. These communities exist within the framework of socioeconomic and sociopolitical macroforces that control their livelihood, health, and, ultimately, their survival. Contextualizing the experience of individual group members requires both differentiating their unique subgroup realities within the United States (e.g., citizen versus undocumented status), and their collective histories in their countries of origin (e.g., African-American slavery in the United States, state-sponsored violence and terrorism in Central America). It is therefore insufficient to focus only on cultural and language diversity in psychotherapy. Examination of patriarchy, classism, and professional elitism and complicity in the disenfranchisement of people of color must occur.

Calls for this level of analysis will certainly heighten the already present anxiety and fears of the dominant group about the growing numbers and power of visible racial/ethnic groups in the United States and the world. The macrocontext challenges to domination will significantly impact the nature of the authoritative relationship in psychotherapy and the professional's role as expert. People of color can no longer be viewed as "pagans" that must be converted to the religions of the west or acculturated and assimilated because they have no culture. People of color are exercising their strong cultural identity and flexing their sociopolitical muscle. They will certainly do so in psychotherapy and in fact may expect psychotherapists to aid them to self-actualize in this direction.

For precisely these reasons, we should anticipate a great deal of resistance within and outside of our professional/academic circles to the true practice of diversity in psychotherapy. Challenges to the established way of doing therapy will be difficult to implement and gradual in impact, therefore therapists will find themselves unaccompanied in these endeavors—all the more reason for us to build strong partnerships with the community and with other health and human service workers.

NOTES

1. H. Aponte (1971). The family school interview: An ecostructural approach. *Family Process*, 15(3), 303–11.

2. J. Reyes (1989). A study of the mental health treatment of Puerto Rican migrants. Ph.D. dissertation, Department of Educational Foundation, University of Cincinnati.

3. V. De La Cancela (1985). Psychotherapy: A political act. *Practice: The Journal of Politics, Economics, Psychology, Sociology and Culture*, 3(3), 48–52.

4. *Ibid*.

5. I. Závala-Martínez (1986). Praxis in psychology: Integrating clinical and community orientation with Latinos. *The Community Psychologist*, 19(2), 11.

6. *Ibid*.

7. L. Comas-Díaz (1990). Hispanic/Latino communities: Psychological implications. *Journal of Training & Practice in Professional Psychology*, 4(1), 14–35; V. De La Cancela (1989). Salud, dinero, y amor: Beyond wishing Latinos good health. *Practice: The Journal of Politics, Economics, Psychology, Sociology and Culture*, 6(3) & 7(1), 81–94; V. De La Cancela & L. P. Guzman (1991). Latino mental health service needs: Implications for training psychologists. In H. F. Myers, P. Wohlford, L. P. Guzman, & R. J. Echemendia (Eds.), *Ethnic minority perspectives on*

clinical training and services in psychology. Washington, DC: American Psychological Association.

8. De La Cancela (1985), Psychotherapy.

9. V. De La Cancela (1985). Towards a sociocultural psychotherapy for low-income ethnic minorities. *Psychotherapy*, 22(2S), 427–35.

10. E. S. LeVine & A. M. Padilla (1980). *Crossing cultures in therapy: Pluralistic counseling for the Hispanic*. Monterey, CA: Brooks/Cole.

11. M. Delgado (1983). Hispanic and psychotherapeutic groups. *International Journal of Group Psychotherapy*, 33, 507–20.

12. LeVine & Padilla (1980), *Crossing cultures*, 256.

13. *Ibid*.

14. De La Cancela (1985), Psychotherapy.

15. D. Gil (1978). Clinical practice and the politics of human liberation. *Catalyst: A Socialist Journal of the Social Services*, 2, 61–69.

16. American Psychiatric Association (APA) (1989). *Treatments of psychiatric disorders: A task force report of the American Psychiatric Association*. Washington, DC: APA.

17. V. De La Cancela (1990). Letter to the editor. Unpublished manuscript.

18. I. Canino, et al. (1991). Letter to the editor. *American Journal of Psychiatry*, 148(4), 543–44.

19. T. B. Karsau (1991). Letter to the editor. *American Journal of Psychiatry*, 148(4), 544.

20. V. De La Cancela (1991). Progressive counseling with Latino refugees and families. *Journal of Progressive Human Services*, 2(2), 19–34.

21. J. E. Carrillo (1988). AIDS and the Latino community. *Centro de Estudios Puertorriquenos Bulletin*, 2(4), 7–14; V. De La Cancela (1989). Minority AIDS prevention: Moving beyond cultural perspectives towards sociopolitical empowerment. *AIDS Education and Prevention*, 1(2), 89–95; J. Pares-Avile (1987). AIDS in the Latino community: A call for action. *El Boletin: Newsletter of the National Hispanic Psychological Association*, 4(2), 8–9.

22. De La Cancela (1989), Minority AIDS prevention.

23. Comas-Díaz (1990), Hispanic/Latino communities; De La Cancela (1989), Salud, dinero, y amor; J. E. Trimble (1990). Application of psychological knowledge for American Indians and Alaska Natives. *Journal of Training & Practice in Professional Psychology*, 4(1), 45–63.

24. Comas-Díaz (1990), Hispanic/Latino communities; De La Cancela (1989), Minority AIDS prevention.

25. V. De La Cancela & I. Závala-Martínez (1983). An analysis of culturalism in Latino mental health: Folk medicine as a case in point. *Hispanic Journal of Behavioral Sciences*, 5(3), 251–74; De La Cancela & Guzman (1991), Latino mental health service; A. M. Padilla & R. Ruiz (1973). *Latino mental health: A review of literature*. Rockville, MD: National Institute of Mental Health.

26. S. W. Keefe, A. M. Padilla & M. L. Carlos (1978). *Emotional support systems in two cultures: A comparison of Mexican Americans and Anglo Americans*, Occasional Paper no. 7. Los Angeles: University of California, Spanish Speaking Mental Health Research Center.

27. Comas-Díaz (1990), Hispanic/Latino communities.

28. De La Cancela (1989), Salud, dinero, y amor.

29. Comas-Díaz (1990), Hispanic/Latino communities; De La Cancela (1989), Salud, dinero, y amor.

30. D. Ward (1991). Disputing the myth: The AIDS problem in the gay community has not been solved. *Journal of Multi-Cultural Community Health*, 1(2), 30–33.

31. V. De La Cancela (1992). Keeping African-American & Latino males alive: Policy and program initiatives in health. *Journal of Multi-Cultural Community Health*, 2(1), 31–39.

32. V. J. Bieliauskas (1977). Mental health care in the USSR. *American Psychologist*, 32(5), 374–79; Y. Camayd-Freixas & M. Uriarte (1980). The organization of mental health services in Cuba. *Hispanic Journal of Behavioral Sciences*, 2, 337–54; C. Ratner (1978). Mental illness in the People's Republic of China. *Far East Reporter*, February, 80–84.

33. M. Miville (1991). Personal and professional perspectives on mentoring and the VREG graduate student. *Focus: Notes from the Society for the Psychological Study of Ethnic Minority Issues*, 5(1), 14.

34. S. Sue (1991). Changing needs for mentoring over the life span. *Focus: Notes from the Society for the Psychological Study of Ethnic Minority Issues*, 5(1), 6.

35. D. C. DeFour (1991). Issues in mentoring ethnic minority students. *Focus: Notes from the Society for the Psychological Study of Ethnic Minority Issues*, 5(1), 1–2.

36. J. Carabajal (1991). Mentoring and the collective experience: A case in point. *Focus: Notes from the Society for the Psychological Study of Ethnic Minority Issues*, 5(1), 3–5.

37. M. A. Paludi, D. C. DeFour, J. Braithwaite, B. Chan, C. Garvey, N. Kramer, D. Lawrence, & M. Haring-Hidore (1991). Academic mentoring for women: Issues of sex, power and politics. *Focus: Notes from the Society for the Psychological Study of Ethnic Minority Issues*, 5(1), 7–8.

38. R. Hall & B. Sandler (1983). *Academic mentoring for women students and faculty: A new look at an old way to get ahead.* Washington, DC: Project on the Status and Education of Women.

39. R. LaDue (1991). Coyote returns: Lessons from the trickster. *Focus: Notes from the Society for the Psychological Study of Ethnic Minority Issues*, 5(1), 10–11.

40. J. Derbort (1992). Racism, bias, and barriers in psychotherapy: The white therapist-client of color experience. *Journal of Multi-Cultural Community Health*, 2(1), 22–25.

41. V. L. De La Cancela (1978). On being a minority student in clinical psychology. *Journal of Contemporary Psychotherapy*, 9(2), 178–82; D. Tennov (1976). *Psychotherapy: The hazardous cure.* New York: Anchor Books.

42. N. Matlin (1976). *Modelos conceptuales para supervision de consejeros.* San Juan: Psicologos de Puerto Rico Asociados.

43. F. Jones (1980). The black psychologist as consultant and therapist. In R. L. Jones (Ed.), *Black psychology.* New York: Harper and Row.

44. Tennov (1976), *Psychotherapy.*

45. M. H. Sacks (1981). Book review, Psychotherapy supervision: Theory, research and practice. *American Journal of Psychiatry*, 138(2), 267–68.

46. I. Závala-Martínez (1981). Personal communication.

47. R. Alvarado (1976). *Racism, elitism, professionalism: Barriers to community mental health.* New York: Aronson, Inc.

48. V. De La Cancela (1991). Working affirmatively with Puerto Rican men: Professional and personal reflections. *Journal of Feminist Family Therapy,* 2(3/4), 195–211; V. De La Cancela (1991). The endangered black male: Reversing the trend for African-American and Latino males. *Journal of Multi-Cultural Community Health,* 1(1), 16–19.

49. V. De La Cancela (1982). Psychosocial Implications of Machismo. Presentation at California Hispanic Psychological Association Public Forum, May. Los Angeles, University of Southern California.

50. V. De La Cancela (1988). Labor pains: Puerto Rican males in transition. *Centro de Estudios Puertorriquenos Bulletin,* 2(4), 40–55.

51. V. De La Cancela (1986). A critical analysis of Puerto Rican machismo: Implications for clinical practice. *Psychotherapy,* 23(2), 291–96.

52. De La Cancela (1991), Endangered black male.

CHAPTER SIX

AFRICAN-AMERICAN WOMEN: ETHNOCULTURAL VARIABLES AND DISSONANT EXPECTATIONS

Yvonne M. Jenkins

Studies of African-American female heads of households and normal female adolescents reveal that these groups display relatively high self-esteem.[1] In fact, the latter display higher self-esteem than their white counterparts.[2] Despite these findings, clinical observations suggest that low self-esteem continues to be a problem for some African-American women who seek psychotherapy.

Even though the majority of African-Americans are able to keep doubts about self-esteem in check,[3] during childhood and adolescence some are deprived of social and psychological conditions that nurture and protect self-esteem. Furthermore, powerfully complex societal disorders (e.g., racism, prejudice, and discrimination) and reality problems (e.g., poverty, violence, substandard housing, inadequate health care, miseducation) impact some African-Americans more traumatically than others. In the absence of adequate social and emotional support systems self-esteem may fail to develop adequately or may gradually deteriorate in response to persistent pressures or assaults to the psyche.

As defined in chapter two, social esteem for visible racial and ethnocultural groups is practically synonymous with the anglocentric meaning of self-esteem. The interdependence among self-esteem, social esteem, and reference group identity is central to the world views and value orientations of people of color in the United States.

Visible racial and ethnocultural groups are commonly assumed to be homogeneous due to their visibility, collectivity, and marginality. This assumption is often a barrier to possibilities for open dialogue between these groups and more powerful segments of society. Societal disorders, anxiety about difference, and the misconceptions that perpetuate these conditions sustain their marginality. In contrast to this assumption, considerable heterogeneity does indeed exist within visible racial and ethnocultural groups. This chapter examines dissonant expectations, a dimension of heterogeneity among African-American women. This chapter also illustrates how understanding the interaction among culture, history, and distinct sociopolitical variables (e.g., race, gender, ethnicity, social class) is central to the process of establishing an authentic empathic connection in psychotherapy. Finally, this chapter applies to other women in that it illustrates how a social history of oppression interacts with gender role expectations to create a set of complex issues and themes.

A WORD OF CAUTION

To assume that low self-esteem and dissonant expectations are unique to or experienced by all African-American women would be inaccurate, misleading, and counterproductive. Instead, this syndrome is more characteristic of a subset of African-American women. Therefore, this discussion is not intended to furnish stereotypes, myths, or misconceptions. Instead it is intended to advance the embracement of diversity. To generalize the content of this chapter to the entire population of African-American women who enter psychotherapy with complaints of unrequited love would be irresponsible and unethical.

LOW SELF-ESTEEM AND DISSONANT EXPECTATIONS

Low self-esteem develops when there is dissonance between a person's self-image and whatever is considered worthwhile, respectable, and competent by the person as well as the reference group. Inherent to low self-esteem is the belief that one is unlovable. When it comes to romance, the woman with low self-esteem is more likely to question whether or not she is worthy of her partner's love than whether her partner is worthy of her love. The belief that she is undeserving triggers endless self-defeating perceptions and maneuvers. It also results in frustration due to unfulfilled needs for love and connection.

Unrequited love, a common complaint among women who enter psychotherapy, is often expressed within the context of dissonant expectations: anticipation of academic and career-related success markedly contrasted by anticipation of failure to realize satisfying love relationships with men. For this subset of African-American women, the latter is believed to be the only alternative with African-American men in particular. This mindset is embraced with tenacity. Dissonant expectations are a manifestation of low self-esteem.

THE WOMAN WITH DISSONANT EXPECTATIONS

The woman with dissonant expectations is single. Her age usually falls between the early twenties and late forties. She is heterosexual, may or may not have children, and is usually a successful college student or professional. She identifies with the middle class; this may be based on actual socioeconomic status or personal value orientation. In the latter, it is common for African-American parents of modest means to value upward mobility. This value is instilled in children to insure their access to a better way of life filled with opportunities that have not been available to the parents. Additionally, the woman with dissonant expectations is more consistent with Schofield's description of the YAVIS (i.e., young, attractive, verbal, intelligent, successful) client despite her possible indigence and cultural dissimilarity, traits he attributes to the less attractive QUOID (i.e., quiet, ugly, old, indigent, culturally dissimilar) client.[4] Furthermore, she tends to be dependent, possessive, controlling, and critical of herself and others. She tends to have limited experience with platonic and love relationships. From her perspective, the meaning of relationship is synonymous with romance. In fact, the only type of relationship she believes is possible with a man involves romance. Therefore, interactions with men are idealized while those with women are often taken for granted or devalued. Her expectations of romance are clouded more than those of most by magical thinking, poor judgment, impulsivity, or intractable pessimism. She may deny herself of companionship for long periods by holding out for the "perfect" partner. Meanwhile she is critical of or sabotages those possibilities available to her. The feelings of powerlessness, entrapment, and hopelessness associated with dissonant expectations may be well defended. For instance, the belief that she is unlovable and related fears of intimacy and failure may influence her to be resistant to introspection and accepting any personal responsibility for change.

ETHNOCULTURAL FOUNDATIONS OF THE AFRICAN-AMERICAN WOMAN'S EXPERIENCE

Slavery

Pejorative myths, stereotypes, and other misconceptions have defined the African-American woman for nearly four centuries and have persistently challenged her capacity to develop and maintain self-esteem. The worth of the slave woman was solely defined according to the economic goals of slavery.[5] Her survival was dependent on this oppressive institution, which exploited her biological reproductive capacity, required her to work, care for, and live *through* others despite her own needs and constant subjection to social malevolence resulting in trauma. Her existence, marital union, and children were not acknowledged by the power structures (i.e., legal, social, political) of society. While the slave woman's capacity for work was valued highly, her social and emotional well-being were grossly disregarded.

In view of these realities, it seems that the underlying ambiance for dissonant expectations was engendered as early as slavery via the gradual but insidious internalization of stereotypes, myths, and other misconceptions that reinforced this exploitative duality and perpetuated "a distorted, [and] devalued image of black womanhood"[6] that has endured for generations. Vestiges of the phenomenon remain engrained into the psyche of *some* African-American women today and deprive them of self-esteem.

Racism and Sexism

As mentioned in chapter three the societal role of women of color embodies a fundamental contradiction: to help others to adapt to, rather than to change, social oppression in order to survive.[7] This role is influenced by racism and sexism. Smith suggests it is a disservice to African-American women to overemphasize racism and sexism as parallel processes. Instead, these processes may be parallel, cumulative, or contextual. "Sometimes her experiences will be rooted in sexism as for all women and/or in racism as in the lives of all African-Americans."[8] Even though the double-bind of racism and sexism is a source of pressure, it is also a source of strength in that it conditions some women to survive persistent assaults to self-esteem with considerable resiliency. Others, however, do not recover so easily and endure these assaults at great expense.

Even though the women's and the civil rights movements have made a valuable difference in the African-American woman's quest for equality, the racism documented in Davis's historical overview of the Women's Movement[9] and the sexism noted in Turner's perspective of the Civil Rights Movement[10] suggest that even these causes have not escaped the conditions of her oppression.

Much of the prejudice and discrimination influenced by racism is associated with the undeniable reality that skin color has been used as an indicator of personal value for African-Americans since slavery. Skin color has been a symbol of pride and honor,[11] a "mark of oppression,"[12] and a source of shame. It is still a primary determinant of how members of this group are initially perceived, responded to, and valued by society. Skin color has been a symbol of pride and honor,[11] a "mark of oppression"[12] and a source of shame.

Although sexism has received brilliant attention in African-American women's literature, some women still fail to recognize its impact on their lives. Nor do they tend to be aware of how the double-bind (i.e., racism and sexism) impacts their daily experiences. Therefore, far too often, the impact of being both black and female does not receive serious consideration. This is usually influenced by too little education about the topic; the reality that, comparatively, racism is more distressing, more threatening to basic survival, and more powerful; and the failure of some African-American men to recognize that sexism is a serious obstacle for African-American women. In addition, unlike sexism, there are instances when racism produces a unique bond between African-American men and women. Although some women deny beliefs in male domination and female subordination, their behaviors suggest internalization of these perceptions. Often African-American women, like other women of color, do not recognize or feel entitled to change the ways in which they may collude in this situation because of the oppressed position of men of color in the United States.

Regrettably, racism and sexism do threaten the self-esteem of African-American women and interfere with their opportunities to engage in satisfying and fulfilling relationships with African-American men.

An Imbalance Between Achievement/Work and Family Life

African-American men and women more often prefer a gender role for women that balances achievement, work, and family life.[13] Career-oriented, never-married women who aspire to fulfill this balance often experience emotional distress when there is a prolonged delay or absence of romance, marriage, and children. This is often turned against the self. Within psychotherapy such distress is displayed as self-criticism about poor choices (e.g., "How could I have been so stupid?"), low self-esteem (e.g., "I'm worthless"), self-doubt (e.g., "I'm beginning to wonder what's wrong with me"), frustration (e.g., "Nothing I do seems to work!"), helplessness ("It [involvement in a dysfunctional relationship] just happened"), and hopelessness (e.g., "It seems like I'm always going to be alone").

Low self-esteem and dissonant expectations are sometimes masked by an overextended lifestyle that is primarily restricted to academic studies or work activity. Preoccupation with these areas of life may also mask considerable distress associated with the absence of a significant other and provide a temporary escape from related conflict and distress. Over time, however, the woman may gradually give up on the possibility of a more balanced lifestyle in response to a combination of personal adjustment issues and societal conditions that persistently challenge her capacity to create this.

Parent-Child Relationships

Parent-child relationships within the African-American family are influenced by how effectively or ineffectively the family copes with and works toward overcoming oppression. This depends on the extent to which parents internalize, project, or displace onto children pejorative myths, stereotypes, and misconceptions; the availability of empowerment-oriented support systems to the family; and its capacity to embrace them. Parent-child relationships are especially challenged by the nodal role of the African-American family in society. This concept is elaborated on later in this chapter.

Traditionally the black church has provided a primary support system in African-American communities. Yet, at times its effectiveness has been limited by day-to-day realities of oppression. For instance, recognition that hard work, extra effort, and nonviolence do not always insure a better life has occasionally challenged the faith of some parents and youth in spiritual principles that have ordinarily enhanced their relationships. Nevertheless, the black church continues to be a primary source of guidance, support (i.e., spiritual, social, educational, financial, and political), and social esteem for African-American communities.

The extended family has provided a supportive supplement to parent-child relationships since the time of slavery. However, it is presently challenged by several conditions. Among these are isolation from ethnocultural ties, influenced by urbanization, suburbanization, and immigration, and social problems that influence fear, social isolation, and ineffective parenting.

Clinical interviews suggest that as early as childhood, interactions between women who manifest this syndrome and their parents support the gradual development of the underlying conflict in dissonant expectations: a desire for love versus an inability to feel deserving of this experience. This is reinforced by the societal role of women of color described in chapter three along with the systemic nature of racism, sexism, and other societal disorders that inhibit self-esteem development. It is this conflict that underlies self-perceptions of unworthiness and unlovability. This conflict also influences the tendencies of these women to become involved with men who are unavailable (e.g., due to marriage, other commitments, workaholism, emotional inaccessibility) or abusive.

The societal role of families of color offers insight into parent-child relationships experienced by women with dissonant expectations.

The Societal Role of Families of Color

The societal role of families of color is similar to the relationship of communities plagued by hazardous waste to the establishments that discard it. Media reports have made us painfully aware that some companies, factories, and nuclear sites systematically leak, dump, or emit these substances into human water supplies, landfills, or the air near densely populated communities. These communities are often plagued by exceedingly high rates of miscarriage, birth defects, cancer, and other life-threatening maladies. Predictably, many of the victims are people of color and the poor. Such exploitation has incited charges of environmental racism and classism by African-American and Latino activists and advocates for the poor. Just as these environmentally threatened communities are exploited in being forced to function as disposal receptacles for powerful establishments, families of color and the poor are forced to stabilize society by absorbing its social toxins manifested by anxiety about difference, hostility, and aggression. The cumulative impact poses serious threats to the well-being of these populations. Pinderhughes elaborates on this dynamic elsewhere.[14]

What Impact Does the Societal Role Have on Parent-Child Relationships?

Under the most ideal conditions, parenting can be stressful. The societal role of the African-American family engenders considerable distress and challenges the strengths of even the most capable parents to instill and nurture self-esteem. This may be apparent through parenting styles that involve overly rigid and/or enmeshed boundaries, a lack of balance in family roles (e.g., underfunctioning or overfunctioning),[15] ineffective interpersonal and conflict management skills, and little guidance or direction for youth in some areas of life.

Hines and Franklin contend that prolonged exposure to racism and the stress that accompanies it may increase tolerance for dysfunctional relationships.[16] As children and adolescents, women with dissonant expectations have often endured various manifestations of powerlessness such as the emotional inaccessibility of parents, family secrecy rooted in shame and pain, and early parentification. These conditions are elaborated on later in this chapter.

In an effort to simply survive oppression, some parents become entrapped by lifestyles that isolate them from vital support systems. For instance, some hold two or three jobs just "to make ends meet." This is sometimes a source of estrangement from their children despite a genuine desire to offer them the very best in life. Several factors influence this estrangement in African-American families: (1) the earning power of African-Americans is lower than that of white Americans; (2) the earning power of African-American women is lower than their male counterparts, white women, and white men; and (3) parents' attempt to disprove images of African-Americans conveyed through myths, stereotypes, and other misconceptions.

While sons are sometimes expected to satisfy the unmet emotional needs of parents, daughters more often bear the brunt of these expectations. Firstborns or only daughters seem to be particularly vulnerable, but middle and youngest daughters have also reported this experience. The dual standard that operates here seems to be influenced by the traditional caretaking role of girls and women in this society. Although some parents separate their own needs from those of their children quite early in the parenting process, others never achieve this differentiation. Often this results in the parentification of a young daughter. This powerful deselfing process involves the reliance of parents and others on the daughter for caretaking that exceeds her age-appropriate cognitive and emotional capacities and age-appropriate economic responsibilities. As one woman put it, "I had to make adult decisions with a child's mind." This dynamic is apparent in the following excerpts from case examples:

A twenty-one-year-old art student with a splendid record of achievement entered psychotherapy due to fear of losing her boyfriend who expressed an interest in dating other young women. This was her first romance. Her life had been centered around holding on to this relationship for two years even though her boyfriend had assured her repeatedly that he did not intend to abandon her. While the student took her art talent for granted, her low self-esteem was apparent in the belief that her boyfriend or no other man could ever genuinely love her.

The young woman had always tried to please her parents. The parents had grown up in poverty-stricken areas of the rural south and relocated to the same city, as young single adults, to actualize work and education aspirations. They later married and had a family. The woman had two younger siblings.

From the time she showed promise for becoming an artist, her parents told her what they wanted her to buy them when she grew up. Although stated humorously, over time it became clear that their requests were serious. Their requests were also extravagant. After the young woman was granted a scholarship to art school, her parents believed she had income to spare even though the money was automatically applied to her tuition. In reality she had very little cash. She worked part-time just to cover the costs of phone bills and toiletries. Although her parents granted her occasional requests for help with small expenses, they did so reluctantly with an agenda of their own that was most obvious. Eventually the young woman only solicited their help when there was no other alternative.

The art student's parents were in an "at-risk" credit status. By her last year of art school, she felt overwhelmed by their requests which, among other things, included opening a major credit card account in her own name that was actually to be used by them. When the student agreed to do so they assured her that payments would be made each month by the due date. However, this did not happen. She became "fair game" for bill collectors. The young woman found it difficult to set limits. Her parents' requests continued long after she graduated from art school.

A thirty-one-year-old financial analyst complained that she felt insecure in romantic relationships with men. Although she was successful in her field she derived no pleasure from her work or little else in life. The focus of her sessions almost immediately became the relationship with her boyfriend, a manipulative and exploitative man. Dissonant expectations gradually surfaced in expressed anticipation of success at work, markedly contrasted by the anticipation of failure at romance or love.

An eldest daughter, the financial analyst was from a poor family. Due to their necessity to work as children, neither of her parents graduated from high school. Her parents divorced when she was nine. By then she had already begun to do errands and chores for neighbors on a fee-for-service basis. She had also begun to take care of her young sister who had been rejected by their mother even during the pregnancy. As a child and adolescent, the woman was a surrogate mother for her sister for several years. Once, after the woman had enrolled at a nearby college and moved into a dormitory, her mother had a tantrum because her daughter had not sent money home for family expenses.

The financial analyst did little dating until her college years. Even then she spent many weekends at home looking after her sister and taking care of other family matters.

These cases are rich in clinical material and may be examined from many perspectives. However, in accordance with the theme of this chapter, these young women display low self-esteem and express dissonant expectations. Their parents' expectations of them have very needy and demanding qualities that surfaced while both women were children.

Although many details about the backgrounds of their parents are not included here, reviews of clinical hours spent with these women suggest that their parents' expectations of them were influenced by their own oppression. Parents of both women had no experience with managing more than modest sums of money or the nuances of higher education. Therefore, they believed their daughters' financial awards were more than adequate to meet educational costs and some family expenses. Also associated with expectations of their daughters was the exploitation (i.e., societal) the parents had suffered and the neediness that resulted from this. The urgent nature of their needs was associated with how early in life both young women became parentified and the persistence of this into adulthood.

Adherence to cultural proscriptions of dutiful obligation and respect for elders is common among some pluralistic populations in the United States. One is expected to share with or to give something back to the family or community of origin. This is commonly displayed in the Asian culture where the Confucian influence results in a strong emphasis on family obligation. Family support is routinely offered to less fortunate family members. However, at times the Confucian influence promotes abuse that is similar to that described in the above cases. Both women were forced to assume major family responsibilities prematurely in response to poverty and other reality problems, to inadequately differentiated boundaries, and to their parents' lack of empathy with their experiences as young girls and adolescents. These conditions of their upbringing should not be confused in any way with the interdependence or the strong kinship bonds that are often present in healthy African-American families.

Of course as children and adolescents, these young women had not yet developed the cognitive and emotional resources to satisfy much of what was expected of them. Their efforts to please were often met with criticism or additional responsibility. Praise was practically nonexistent. Over the years, the underlying message that "nothing is ever good enough" influenced them to begin to regard themselves as unlovable and to feel undeserving of significant love relationships.

Other Relevant Family Dynamics

Among other relevant family dynamics are the negative images of men of color projected by society and the absence of parental approval and guidance on matters that pertain to sexuality and heterosexual relationships. Sadly, Boyd-Franklin emphasizes that a common perception of African-American men is that they are "no good."[17] Furthermore, some women report that they are at a loss as to how to have a positive relationship with African-American men since they have no experience with positive male role models. Some of the reasons for this absence are defined later in this chapter.

Women with dissonant expectations have often grown up in somewhat isolated and conservative families that display a positive image to the outside world. During childhood and adolescence, these women have often received parental approval and support for skill mastery in academics, extracurricular activities, the arts, and participation in church activities. Instrumental aspects of self-reliance have also been encouraged in that they have been "taught to get an education, a job and to be able to provide for themselves."[18] Yet, parents' attitudes toward dating and other age-appropriate social behavior have been ambivalent, judgmental, or negative. During adolescence, they experienced their parents as overprotective, unaffectionate, and suspicious of their need for affiliation with male peers, whether platonic or romantic. Parental approval and guidance for dating are usually absent from their backgrounds. Therefore, as adolescents these women tended to be secretive about their interest in dating. For some, this was complicated further by the fact that obedience or compliance was equated with love.[19] All of this basically ruled out the possibility for involvement in romance without conflict. The following case example highlights some of these dynamics.

An eighteen-year-old college student with an outstanding record of achievement entered psychotherapy with the complaint that friends she knew well and trusted considered her a "social retardate" due to her awkwardness in social situations, age-inappropriate dependency on her mother, and other issues. She was an only daughter and the younger of two children. Her mother became troubled whenever she showed an interest in young men. Both parents discouraged her from dating due to the belief that it could only lead to an unwanted pregnancy. In high school she had befriended a group of girls that did not date and were very critical of others with boyfriends.

A few months before the student entered treatment she had become involved with her first boyfriend and had willingly become sexually active. This was a tremendous source of conflict and anxiety. She took considerable precaution to hide this relationship from both parents in fear of disapproval and the possibility that they would force her to leave college. In therapy, this young woman eventually revealed that she had never felt particularly worthwhile and found it hard to believe that any of her male peers could ever want a special relationship with her. This made it difficult to trust her boyfriend even though he and she cared for one another a great deal.

Several aspects of the parent-child relationships described in these case examples impede normal development by suppressing the natural quest for differentiation. As daughters mature, some parents experience discomfort about their increasingly evident sexuality and the motives of male peers. From an ethnocultural perspective, this is influenced, in part, by internalized stereotypes of African-Americans and sexuality.[20] Also, parents of these women have often assumed an overprotective stance in an effort to prepare their daughters to cope with racism and to avoid teen pregnancy and other possible setbacks that could result in social disgrace, postponed or forfeited career goals, and financial dependency. This is emphasized with an intensity that pressures daughters not to differentiate from the family but to remain enmeshed with the family. Significant intrusion by parents is often tolerated well into adulthood. Consequently women with dissonant expectations "experience greater difficulty in feeling good about themselves and in building connections to others."[21] In addition, because they have not had an opportunity to make more of their own choices, these women have grown up feeling powerless to determine the course of their lives and tend to believe that things "just happen" to them.

Just as societal disorders (e.g., racism, ethnocentrism, sexism) influence the development of adaptive behaviors, at times they also engender maladaptive ones. The parents of the art student and those of the financial analyst nurtured their daughters' achievement to prevent entrapment by social problems. Yet, neither had begun to view their own experiences and needs as different from those of their daughters. As indicated by these cases, over time such lack of differentiation may influence the development of dissonant expectations by narrowing a young woman's focus to someone other than herself rather than the relationship between herself and another.[22] Therefore, during childhood and adolescence these women learn to center their reality around the lives of others. Some gradually begin to view caretaking as a threatening process, which may only involve total engulfment by needs of others. Consequently, by young adulthood they are ambivalent or adverse to future possibilities for marriage and motherhood prior to ever engaging in these experiences. Caretaking and loving become associated with exploitation and intrusion rather than trust, mutuality, and intimacy.

The Straddling of Two Worlds

Living in two cultural worlds is often stressful. Because people of color in the United States are hardly ever completely removed from the reality of straddling two worlds, some lose sight of how juggling two realities lends stress to daily experiences.

McIntosh contrasts forty-six of her own daily life experiences, based on "white privilege," with those of her African-American colleagues.[23] Among those she cites are the following:

Whether I use checks, credit cards, or cash, I can count on my skin color not to work against the appearance of financial liability.

I am never asked to speak for all the people of my racial group.

I can remain oblivious of the language and customs of persons of color who constitute the world's majority without feeling in my culture any penalty for such oblivion.

My culture gives me little fear about ignoring the perspective and powers of people of other races.

Over time, being on the unempowered side of such realities is costly to self-esteem.

From a relational perspective, some women with dissonant expectations who grew up in suburban communities recall that straddling two worlds involved coping with the transition from acceptance by whites during childhood to rejection during adolescence and thereafter due to prejudice and anxiety about difference. Furthermore, some had few opportunities to develop relationships with other African-American youth or felt rejected by those who were their peers due to deliberate distancing that seemed to be associated with conflict about racial identity. For others, the straddling of two worlds has meant: (1) enduring the contrast of living in a poor or modest community of color while being educated in affluent, predominantly white schools; (2) enduring the marginality of being one of few or the only African-American suburbanite in a predominantly white suburban school setting attended by a few other African-Americans from less affluent, inner-city neighborhoods; or (3) the culture shock associated with living and being educated in poor, predominantly segregated communities of color prior to studying at affluent, predominantly white universities. Finally, straddling two worlds during adolescence and young adulthood has permitted some women few opportunities to date. This has been particularly true for those from backgrounds where there has been no deliberate and positive effort to integrate the African-American experience or ethnocultural diversity into educational and social experience from childhood and beyond. Self-esteem is diminished by this process while dissonant expectations are fostered.

Limited Availability of African-American Males

The "endangered" status of the African-American male seriously challenges the African-American woman's possibilities to have him as a partner in love and marriage. Threats to the existence of the African-American male are greater at present than at any period since the Vietnam War. The neglect of this population by the power structures of society accounts, in part, for the absence of positive African-American male role models from the early lives of women referred to earlier in this chapter. Some men, who have also experienced this absence earlier in their lives, feel unsure of how to related to women appropriately.

Disproportionately higher school dropout rates and under- and unemployment rates are reported for African-American men. Consequently, thousands are illiterate and homeless. Many lack aspirations for the future, competitive job skills, and, therefore, access to "the American dream."

The shift from an industrial to a high-tech economy has influenced African-American women to outnumber their male counterparts in the labor force by approximately 10 percent.[24] This transition reinforces preexistent insecurities between some African-American men and women. Some men are confused about how to provide for the African-American woman. Others risk rejection due to low earning power and an inability to measure up to other essential standards. On the other hand, some women tolerate dissatisfying relationships with African-American men because the availability of potential partners is limited.

Early death by violence, alcohol and substance abuse, HIV infection, AIDS, and incarceration rates are at an all-time high among African-American men. Furthermore, interracial and gay relationships and other alternative lifestyles diminish the availability of this population to African-American women. While some women respond by becoming involved with men from other racial and ethnic groups, others are immobilized by dissonant expectations.

A woman's sense of self becomes organized around her ability to make and to maintain affiliations and relationships.[25] Therefore, the limited availability of African-American men for relationships challenges the self-esteem and reinforces dissonant expectations of women who experience this syndrome.

IMPLICATIONS FOR PSYCHOTHERAPY

Empowerment through Self-Activity

To have low self-esteem is to lack appreciation for one's worth, capacity to be loved, and overall sense of competence and personal power. In order to effect change in this condition, psychotherapy needs to be ethnoculturally embedded and oriented toward empowerment. This is particularly relevant in view of the oppression African-American women experience due to inequities in power based on race and gender.[26] Self-activity needs to be at the core of the treatment process since the necessity to cope with racism, ethnocentrism, sexism, and elitism often deprives African-Americans and other pluralistic populations of the energy and skills to attend to critical self-processes.[27] Self-activity involves "attentiveness to the dynamics of the self in the transference" and is essential to the building and enhancement of self-esteem.[28] In order to facilitate self-activity, the therapist needs to be informed about ethnocultural variables such as the ones described earlier, their impact on the client's reality, and the social history of the group.

The early stages of treatment are the most critical for engaging the African-American client. Therefore, the building of rapport must involve active intervention by the therapist in the first two or three sessions. "The therapist cannot sit back passively and simply expect a commitment to evolve."[29] Therapists must also recognize early in the treatment process that what might appear to be passivity, guardedness, undertalkativeness, or hostility are not always forms of resistance or intellectual dullness. At times, these are adaptive postures that have evolved out of centuries of oppression.

Facilitation of self-activity involves:

1. helping the woman with dissonant expectations to strengthen or repair vulnerable aspects of the self influenced by societal disorders; this may involve modifying a negative self-image, building self-esteem, and improving the body image, particularly the valuing of indigenous or race-specific physical traits;

2. the therapist's use of self as a symbol of others' capacity to support the client's self-development, not only as a person, but as an African-American woman and a person of color;

3. acknowledging and supporting struggles to change rather than to be overcome by societal disorders; and

4. openness to acknowledge whatever differences may exist between the client and therapist, which conveys the unconditional acceptance that is essential to building rapport and a positive therapeutic alliance.

Self-activity lends a tone to the therapeutic environment that feels "real" to the client and facilitates attainment of the following objectives: (1) acknowledgment and reinforcement of personal strengths; (2) self-differentiation; (3) validation of social identity; and (4) nurturance of effective social and problem-solving skills.

Acknowledgment of Personal Strengths

In view of the tendency of women with dissonant expectations to identify more positively with their academic or career endeavors, it is important to acknowledge their personal strengths (e.g., warmth, resilience, appearance, determination, loyalty) in therapy. Yet, academic or career-related strengths need not be ignored. The emphasis on personal strengths instills the sense of personal significance that is basic to self-esteem development. Such significance tends to be absent in this population and is manifested by both their vascillation between overly dependent and overly dominant roles in significant love relationships. An underlying motive of women's involvement in dysfunctional relationships is to capture this longed-for significance. In a discussion on the conflict between women's relational self and societal and familial social norms, Jack emphasizes that some women "lose themselves in the process of trying to establish an intimacy they never attained [earlier in life]."[30] Women with dissonant expectations often experience this reality. Furthermore, an appreciation of how personal strengths may be gained from helping the woman to recognize how those self-defeating behaviors that limit personal effectiveness at present were once adaptive at a time in her life when she had fewer choices. This empowers her to recognize that she has reached a stage in life where she has options and, therefore, greater control over her destiny.

Self-Differentation

Achieving a differentiated sense of self is an essential task in the process of building self-esteem. This process defines the self as a distinct entity. More specifically, self-differentiation involves identifying, examining, experiencing, and accepting one's internal experience (e.g., perceptions, feelings, needs, values). This is particularly valuable for the women described here in view of their tendencies to be more attuned to the internal experiences of others than their own and to confuse their own internal experiences with those of others. Some women find that keeping a journal as an adjunct to psychotherapy facilitates the process of self-differentiation.

Therapists' understandings of clinical issues often do not encompass a clear understanding of underlying societal and political forces. African-American women and other people of color cannot be treated effectively if these forces are ignored, overlooked, or denied. Therefore, an integrative approach based on relevant components of relational feminist, psychodynamic, supportive, social, and systems frameworks is useful for facilitating self-differentiation. As a precaution, however, it is important to recognize limitations of traditional theories and strategies encompassed by this approach, particularly in relation to any sexist, biased, and negative valuations of female qualities they may embody.[31] It is also important to recognize that some of the merits of feminist therapy for Latinas can be generalized to African-American women.[32] Among these are its commitment to social change, active acknowledgment of sociopolitical forces that impinge on their experiences, and the effects of elitism in their lives.

Attention to persistent anxiety, anger, and impulsivity is a critical component of self-differentiation. Cognitive restructuring is useful for confronting distortions that impair reality testing.[33] Psychodynamic and supportive strategies are valuable for strengthening vulnerable ego functions. Finally, a detailed family history with attention to distinct racial and ethnocultural variables (e.g., attitudes toward skin color, paternity) is certain to enrich the therapist's understanding of the client and, in turn, the client's self-understanding. It is important to be aware that many African-American clients feel uncomfortable with revealing details about their families in the early stages of treatment due to strong family loyalties and because throughout history personal data has systematically been used against them. Inquiries about the family are found less intrusive thereafter once positive rapport and adequate trust have been established.

Validation of Social Identity through Social Awareness

A vital component of social therapy is psychoeducation. Acknowledgment of cultural, historical, and sociopolitical realities through psychoeducation is useful for expanding the woman's awareness of how societal disorders and systems (e.g., politics, the media, the economy) isolate and alienate people of color from their inner experiences, one another, and society at large. This minimizes the impact of persistent assaults to self-esteem and enhances ethnocultural pride and interpersonal effectiveness. In addition, validation lessens the self-blame and male bashing that commonly result from the internalization of negative stereotypes applied to people of color by the dominant culture. Social awareness is also vital to good reality testing and the experience of the self as part of a historical continuum. Fulani contends that "deprivation of a sense of oneself as historical is a major cause of all varieties of psychopathology" and influences alienation.[34] The historical role of the woman of color has been to foster ethnocultural and historical identity development. In this role she has facilitated the empowerment of people of color to confront and to change the conditions that perpetuate their oppression. Yet, fulfillment of this role has required an affinity for her own culture and history. Therefore, it is incumbent on the therapist to be attuned to historical and sociopolitical determinants of the African-American woman's experience to promote such affinity. Clinical assessment of her images of self, African-Americans as a reference group, and daily functioning must be embedded in an understanding of historical and ethnocultural factors.

Appropriate integration of the genogram[35] and ethnoculturally relevant material (e.g., African-American history, metaphors or proverbs, literature, art, music, films, current events) with treatment enhances social awareness and identity development by empowering women to change the conditions "which produce their societal understandings of themselves as 'failed superwomen'—a social role in which they cannot survive, [prosper] and grow." Individual or group formats may be useful as indicated.[36]

Finally, women with the esteem and relational issues defined here often benefit from learning to value basic friendship founded on trust, effective communication, mutual caring, common interests or values, and interpersonal compatibility. Too often they fail to recognize that friendship is a type of relationship that sometimes leads to romance, love, and commitment. Also, these women tend to enter most relationships (with people generally) with unrealistic expectations.

Nurturance of Interpersonal and Problem-Solving Skills

While women with dissonant expectations are often viewed as friendly by their peers, they tend not to reveal much of themselves to others. Although poor self-concepts bear upon this, often they also lack the interpersonal skills and the problem-solving skills to engage with others more intimately and actively. Attention to communication processes can enhance development of effective interpersonal skills by facilitating clear expression of needs, feelings, and other aspects of the self. Learning to care for the self while caring for others is of tremendous value to this population.

Women with dissonant expectations also tend to feel helpless in relationships because of inadequate problem-solving skills. Some also feel isolated and estranged from others due to the absence of a meaningful relational connection. Psychotherapy (individual or group) can free them from this position by providing a safe and supportive forum for reality testing, risk taking, and skill building in the following areas: assertiveness, limit setting, conflict resolution and anger management, personal goal setting, and decision making. Assertiveness training is particularly valuable for women of color because it mobilizes personal power.

CONCLUSION

There is considerable heterogeneity within visible racial and ethnocultural groups. Even though clients from various groups may present with similar issues in psychotherapy, an understanding of the cultural, historical, and sociopolitical contexts in which their difficulties have developed is essential to their empowerment through psychotherapy.

NOTES

1. L. W. Myers (1980). *Black women. Do they cope better?* Englewood Cliffs, NJ: Prentice-Hall; G. J. Powell & M. Fuller (1973). *Black Monday's children: A study of the effect of school desegregation on self-concepts of southern children.* New York: Appleton-Century-Crofts; M. Rosenberg & R. G. Simmons (1972). *Black and white self-esteem: The urban school child.* Washington, DC: American Sociological Association.

2. R. G. Simmons, L. Brown, D. M. Bush & D. A. Blyth (1978). Self-esteem and achievement of black and white adolescents. *Social Problems*, 26, 86–96.

3. A. H. Jenkins (1985). Attending to self-activity in the Afro-American client. *Psychotherapy*, 22(2S), 335–41.

4. W. Schofield (1964). *Psychotherapy: The Purchase of friendship.* Englewood Cliffs, NJ: Prentice-Hall.

5. Y. M. Jenkins (1982). Dissonant expectations: Professional competency vs. personal incompetency. *Aware*, 1(1), 6–13.

6. C. Turner (1987). *Clinical application of the Stone Center theoretical approach to minority women.* Works in Progress. Wellesley, MA: Wellesley College, Stone Center Working Papers Series, 28.

7. L. Fulani (1988). Poor women of color do great therapy. In L. Fulani (Ed.), *The psychopathology of everyday racism and sexism.* New York: Harrington Press, 111–20.

8. A. Smith (1990). Racism and sexism in black women's lives. Unpublished manuscript.

9. A. Davis (1981). *Women, race and class.* New York: Random House.

10. Turner (1987), *Clinical application.*

11. N. Boyd-Franklin (Ed.) (1989). *Black families in therapy.* New York: Guilford Press.

12. A. Kardiner & L. Oversey (1951). *The mark of oppression.* Cleveland: World Publishing.

13. A. Steinmann & D. J. Fox (1970). Attitudes toward women's family role among black and white undergraduates. *The Family Coordinator,* 19, 363–68.

14. E. B. Pinderhughes (1982). Afro-American families and the victim system. In M. McGoldrick, J. K. Pearce, & J. Giordano (Eds.), *Ethnicity and family therapy.* New York: Guilford Press, 108–22.

15. H. G. Lerner (1985). *The dance of anger.* New York: Harper & Row.

16. P. Hines & H. Franklin (1982). Black families. In M. McGoldrick, J. K. Pearce, & J. Giordano (Eds.), *Ethnicity and family therapy.* New York: Guilford Press, 84–107.

17. Boyd-Franklin (1989), *Black families.*

18. *Ibid.,* 225.

19. M. Peters (1981). Parenting in black families with young children: A historical perspective. Quoted in N. Boyd-Franklin (Ed.) (1989), *Black families in therapy.* New York: Guilford Press, 118–19.

20. G. E. Wyatt (1982). Identifying stereotypes of Afro-American sexuality and their impact upon sexual behavior. In B. A. Bass, G. E. Wyatt, & G. J. Powell (Eds.), *The Afro-American family: Assessment, treatment and research issues.* New York: Grune & Stratton, 333–46.

21. Turner (1987), *Clinical application.*

22. I. Stiver (1990). *Dysfunctional families and wounded relationships—Part II.* Works in Progress. Wellesley, MA: Wellesley College, Stone Center Working Papers Series, 44.

23. P. McIntosh (1988). *White privilege and male privilege: A personal account of coming to see correspondences through work in women's studies.* Working Paper. Wellesley, MA: Wellesley College, Center for Research on Women, 189.

24. A. Chapman (1988). Male-female relations: How the past affects the present. In H. McAdoo (Ed.), *Black families.* Newbury Park, CA: Sage Publications, 190–200.

25. J. B. Miller (1976). *Toward a new psychology of women.* Boston: Beacon Press.

26. V. W. Hammond (1988). "Conscious subjectivity" or use of one's self in therapeutic process. In L. Fulani (Ed.), *The psychopathology of everyday racism and sexism,* 75–82.

27. Jenkins (1985), Attending to self-activity.

28. *Ibid.,* 335.

29. *Ibid.*

30. D. Jack (1987). Silencing the self: The power of social imperatives in female depression. In R. Formanek & A. Gurian (Eds.), *Women and depression: A lifetime perspective.* New York: Springer Press, 161–81.

31. Hammond (1988), "Conscious subjectivity."

32. L. Comas-Díaz (1988). Feminist therapy with Hispanic/Latina women: Myth or reality? In L. Fulani (Ed.), *The psychopathology of everyday racism and sexism.* New York: Harrington Press, 39–62.

33. A. T. Beck (1976). *Cognitive therapy and the emotional disorders*. New York: International Universities Press.

34. L. Fulani (1988). All power to the people! But how? In L. Fulani (Ed.), *The psychopathology of everyday racism and sexism*. New York: Harrington Press, xi–xix.

35. M. McGoldrick & R. Gerson (1985). *Genograms in family assessment*. New York: W. W. Norton.

36. Fulani (1988), Poor women of color, 115.

REFERENCE

Pinderhughes, E. B. (1982). Minority women: A nodal position in the functioning of the social system. In M. Ault-Riche (Ed.), *Women and family therapy*, 51–63.

PART THREE

Deborah Ridley Brome

In embracing culturally competent frameworks, both the neophyte and experienced therapist struggle with how to incorporate a diversity perspective into their work with others. They question how one goes about implementing a diversity perspective, in both the practice and interpretation of psychotherapy. Key questions asked include: How does understanding diversity shape the process and outcome of psychotherapy for both the therapist and the client? How does diversity impact the meaning of psychotherapy for the client and therapists' interpretation of client behavior? How does one know when one is practicing from a diversity framework? Is there a right or wrong way to embrace diversity?

At a simplistic level psychotherapists wish to have a cookbook of "dos and don'ts" to define their behavior in creating a meaningful human exchange with those who are different. What Chin, De La Cancela, and Jenkins have emphasized in previous chapters is that to embrace diversity in psychotherapy is to engage in a process that can be guided by overarching principles but requires the creative energy of the therapist to explore multiple levels of understanding. It is a process in which the therapist is engaged in a perspective that requires empathic cultural, historical, systemic, and sociopolitical perspective taking.

Part three provides case examples of how one grapples with the overarching guidelines presented in parts one and two. Part three also provided the authors' analyses of the ways in which their different perspectives address common themes. What is important in this section is that the authors respect each other's voices by acknowledging their differences, yet they find common ground. This process replicates what a diversity framework wishes to achieve between therapist and client.

In chapter seven, Chin provides an example of culturally competent therapy by using the difference framework. She uses a case example of a Chinese couple to demonstrate how one uses the difference framework in conducting psychotherapy. What is highlighted is how the difference framework provides corrective guidelines in interpreting: (1) the meaning of the therapy for the clients; and (2) the way in which the clients come to understand themselves, interpret the world, and work with the therapist within this framework.

For Chin the difference framework allows the therapist to empower the client through reframing the client's behavior and emotions in ways that are culturally compatible and that address bicultural experiences. In essence the client is exposed to cultural/world view dilemmas as he or she comes to better understand the origin of these dilemmas and analyze the merits of possible solutions to them.

Whereas Chin provides an example of how culture informs self-understanding and development, De La Cancela's chapter eight emphasizes how sociopolitical realities interface with racial, cultural, and gender issues to create self-understanding for the client and therapist and how this self-understanding impacts therapy. He uses the case of a Puerto Rican male to do so. More important, he uses this case to discuss the role of social activism and political awareness on the part of the therapist as an important intervention in therapy. Specifically, he shows that a crucial area of discourse in therapy is providing a systemic interpretation of the client's development of self-understanding as a consequence of the client's cultural, historical, and sociopolitical legacies.

This discourse is psychoeducational and empowers the client with a perspective of self that matches his or her social reality. It also requires that the therapist expand his or her notions about the role of therapist.

Chapter nine culminates this part and the volume with the authors' analysis of those themes that are embodied in each of their perspectives. Collectively Chin, De La Cancela, and Jenkins's perspectives converge on the following themes: (1) each possesses a systemic perspective of human development and psychopathology; (2) each acknowledges the therapist's use of his or her ethnicity as a vehicle to promote change; (3) each advocates the use of direct and indirect approaches; and (4) each advocates the use of psychoeducational approaches. The authors also feel that gender and a group's legacy (historical and cultural) significantly shape client and therapist world views, the definition of empowerment, and the tasks of empowering.

In this last section, the authors bring together those ways in which therapists utilize diversity frameworks in creating human exchanges that acknowledge all aspects of the social and political realities of pluralistic populations. The authors call for therapists to think about diversity issues as vehicles for change and as vehicles to increase their ability to empathize with clients. The client's response to the therapist and the therapist's response to the client are better understood within a diversity framework since such a paradigm discourages deficit hypothesis thinking and allows for the coexistence of disparate world views.

CHAPTER SEVEN

THE THERAPIST-CLIENT DYAD WITH A CHINESE-AMERICAN COUPLE

Jean Lau Chin

As our society becomes increasingly diverse, we find more people of color entering psychotherapy. In order for us to practice in a culturally competent manner, we need to understand what works in psychotherapy with different racial/ethnic groups. The literature on psychotherapy with Asian-Americans has been sparse. Frequently, it is suggested that Asian-Americans are poor candidates for psychodynamic psychotherapy given their "nonverbal" styles and emphasis on "concrete issues."[1] Clinical work with Asian-American clients generally emphasizes differences in culture and family,[2] contrasting values,[3] and underutilization,[4] that is, how they present in psychotherapy. The need for sensitivity to ethnic and cultural heritage is often recommended for psychotherapy with Asian-American clients.[5]

This chapter takes a different approach. Instead of examining how Asian-American clients differ, it uses a case presentation approach involving a Chinese-American couple to illustrate several principles important in practicing culturally competent psychotherapy. First, the use of a difference framework is important to acknowledge the diversity presented by this couple. Second, examination of the therapeutic process illustrates the importance of ethnicity, gender, and race within the therapist-client dyad. These issues are integral to understanding transference issues with Asian-American clients. Third, the use of therapeutic interventions that value differences, empower the client, and reframe issues using the client's world views illustrates how psychodynamic psychotherapy can be useful with Asian-American clients.

Organization of this case by the phases that emerge over a three-year period illustrates the nature of the therapeutic process. These phases in psychotherapy parallel those in the couple's marriage and developmental life cycles. Contrasting differences were prominent within the couple's relationship and within the therapist-client dyad. These differences emerged in the couple's personality styles, world views, biculturality, behavior patterns, gender roles, and cultural practices. While many themes emerged that reflect Asian values, beliefs, and practices common among Asian-American clients, the use of a difference framework in psychotherapy was key to empowering the couple in resolving their problems. The identities of the couple have been disguised and altered to protect confidentiality.

MR. AND MRS. A: A CHINESE-AMERICAN COUPLE

Mr. and Mrs. A are a Chinese-American immigrant couple who presented for psychotherapy upon the urging of their divorce attorney. The couple had met in school and married hastily after Mr. A decided to immigrate to the United States from Taiwan for further academic studies. While their courtship had been pleasant, differences emerged almost immediately after arriving in the United States. The marriage became polarized and dysfunctional as each faced the burden of culturally prescribed expectations for family and marriage, appropriate gender roles, obligations to parents, expectations for achievement, valued character traits, and so on. Ambivalence about getting a divorce was strong given their adherence to cultural taboos. The couple had become polarized in their differences, which pervaded their behavior and values. Despite their apparent accomplishments, they felt ashamed, alienated, and inadequate; that is, each experienced considerable personal dissonance and lacked a positive sense of self.

THE THERAPIST-PATIENT DYAD: ETHNICITY, GENDER, AND RACE

Contrasting differences was an underlying theme for this couple. These differences highlight many gender, racial, and ethnic dilemmas faced by racial/ethnic individuals in developing a positive sense of self. Mr. and Mrs. A disagreed over everything including sex, marriage, career, children, family, dress code, and friends. Their differences reflected the contrast of Asian versus western values, male versus female roles, and adaptation to U.S. society versus maintaining an affiliation with their culture of origin.

As Chinese immigrants seen by a Chinese-American therapist, ethnic, gender, and racial themes were intensified within the therapeutic relationship. The therapist facilitated the projection of many roles within the therapist-patient dyad for both husband and wife.

Mrs. A's identification with the therapist as a Chinese-American female professional facilitated her projection of multiple roles—wife, mother, career woman, and female—dictated by the Chinese culture but dystonic with her own sense of self. The therapist's pregnancy intensified further transference phenomena related to these gender and ethnic roles. The transference helped Mrs. A come to terms with her dilemma about these roles. Ultimately, she was able to establish a mature relationship with her parents, gain respect for herself, and consolidate her sense of self. While adjustment to U.S. society set the context for these problems, her dynamic was not one of acculturation but rather development of a bicultural self.

Mr. A perceived the dictates of the Asian culture as harsh and demanding, that is, the prescribed roles of dominant husband, obedient son, and pursuit of intellectual excellence. This was embodied in explicit pressures from his wife and father. The therapist, as a Chinese-American female, intensified transference phenomena related to Mr. A's views of women, expectations of authority figures, and views of Asian and western culture. The therapist-client dyad enabled Mr. A to work through his conflicting relationship with a domineering father and weak mother, his struggles with adjusting to U.S. society, and his idealized views of the roles of husband, son, and scholar.

The contrast between Asian and western cultures impacted Mr. and Mrs. A differently because of their genders. For Mrs. A, it was empowering because western culture offered an opportunity to choose. For Mr. A, it was emasculating. While the roles prescribed by the Asian culture were perceived as harsh and demanding, they offered status, security, and respect. Although western culture was perceived as offering sexual and cultural freedom, it was experienced as alienating and disempowering.

DYNAMICS OF DIFFERENCE: THE MARITAL RELATIONSHIP

Contrasting differences characterized the marital relationship. They argued constantly and were engaged in many dysfunctional modes of relating. Mr. A had episodes of physical violence; he often set intellectual traps in an attempt to force Mrs. A to admit wrongdoing and to change. Mrs. A would withdraw into passive aggressive silence while Mr. A would escalate his verbal and physical abuse in an attempt to engage her. Although the couple had agreed to divorce, they were unable to proceed with it. Both perceived marriage as a permanent arrangement, and divorce as shameful and unacceptable within the Asian culture.

Character was a prominent issue in the couple's differences. Mrs. A complained of her husband's demanding behavior and volatile temper.

Mr. A acknowledged and apologized for his temper but complained of his wife's dependency and moodiness. Each saw the other's character as unbecoming of an ideal mate in marriage. Within the Asian culture, a man's temper is considered his shortcoming but is often tolerated as characteristic of his maleness. These complaints reflect perceptions within the Asian culture that character traits related to gender—male tempers and female moodiness—are immutable and to be tolerated within a marital relationship.

The couple had opposing attitudes about sex. Mrs. A viewed sex as an obligation. She saw sex as dirty, experienced it as painful, and viewed her husband's sex drive as excessive. Mr. A, on the other hand, viewed sex as a physiological need. He considered his expectations toward sex healthy and his wife's attitudes toward sex as abnormal. While Mr. A's views of sex are not uncommon within western cultures, some subtle differences are important to highlight. Western cultures emphasize sex as fulfilling the pleasure principle while Asian cultures emphasize sex as functional for physical and mental vitality. Despite the couple's complaints, each viewed the other's behavior as culturally appropriate and gender determined.

Public and private displays of sexuality were also a point of difference reflective of the classic description of the "madonna versus whore" complex some men have; they want a "lady" in the parlor and a "sex object'" in the bedroom. Mr. A had strong and "conservative" views (by western standards) about Mrs. A's dressing too seductively in public; yet, he complained vigorously about her sexual unresponsiveness in the bedroom. Mrs. A disagreed, using western standards as the guide. The different standards of western and Asian culture about proper dress codes, sexual behavior, and so on became a focal point of the couple's differences.

Mr. A's expectations of marriage included children, sex, a house, and a wife to provide for these needs as defined by Asian values. Up until very recently, these values were also the U.S./western norm. That is, marriage enabled a man to become the patriarch, to carry on the family name, and to get his needs ministered. Mrs. A objected to these culturally prescribed roles; she felt inadequate because she did not enjoy these "wifely" duties. Her expectations of marriage included only companionship and nurturance from her husband. These differing expectations of marriage reflect differences noted in many cultures between men and women, that is, emphasis on the concrete by males and on connectedness by females. Since Mrs. A often stood her ground, Mr. A, by default, often did the cooking and cleaning. However, he resented Mrs. A's failure to do her share; he also felt emasculated in his inability to control her behavior. At the same time, he often catered to her dependency needs as he felt males ought to do; he would go out of his way to accompany her so as to protect her and because she did not like to travel alone.

Intellectual achievement, highly valued within the Asian culture, was a priority for both Mr. and Mrs. A. They both had graduate-level educations and were gainfully employed as professionals. Despite these impressive achievements, Mr. A was made to feel inadequate by both his father and his wife. Mrs. A frequently devalued Mr. A's accomplishments through her exacting standards for being the best.

Family obligation was another source of difference. Mr. A often acquiesced to his father's demands to send money home because he viewed it as part of being a dutiful son. Mrs. A, on the other hand, objected to this symbolic gesture; she felt their own financial status was modest compared to his parents. Mr. A viewed his wife's behavior as selfish while Mrs. A saw her husband's behavior as self-denigrating. Underlying these differences are strong cultural dictates about the dutiful son, the positive value of other-orientation, filial piety, and so on. Within Asian cultures, selfishness is negatively valued, especially for females, whereas self-denigration tends to be viewed negatively within western cultures.

Mr. and Mrs. A also differed on the issue of family relationships. Mr. A's father was a military man with a domineering and punitive style. Mr. A was always closer to his mother and was her favorite. As the oldest son, he was always expected to excel. The family relationship was characterized by Mr. A as close but tempestuous. Mrs. A, on the other hand, recalled contradictory messages from her father about educational achievement. While she excelled in school, she recalls being chided by her father for being too proud as a female and not giving others a chance to excel over her. She, too, was the oldest in the family. Mrs. A was closer to her father. However, she recalls his work separating him from the family. As a result, her mother often played a more dominant role in the family. She characterized her family relationship as close but aloof. Both Mr. and Mrs. A's dynamic issues were tied to their fathers. The strong mother-son bond, the strong patriarchal overtones, and the emphasis on the eldest son (or its absence for Mrs. A) are dynamics that play out uniquely within Asian families.

Social and interpersonal relationships were another point of difference. Mrs. A preferred to have few friends and cherished her privacy. Mr. A, on the other hand, preferred to have many friends and defined his boundaries of space and privacy loosely. Mr. A would go out of his way to help his friends out. He emphasized doing favors for one's friends as an expression of politeness, and attending to their needs even if it meant an inconvenience to himself. While these are common social and interpersonal behaviors within Chinese culture, Mrs. A experienced this as intrusive. She viewed social activities as obligations, not as means to build friendships. While Mrs. A found support for her views within western culture, this polarity between Mr. and Mrs. A reflected their struggle with gender roles as defined by the Asian culture. Women within Asian cultures are often expected to sustain social and family relationships within an extended family network. As a result, sharing of physical space is often not viewed as violating psychological boundaries of privacy as it is within western cultures.

These differences between Mr. and Mrs. A played out through the many gender, ethnic, and racial themes within the therapeutic process. While these dynamics occurred within the context of U.S. society, acculturation provided an easy explanation for these contrasts; it is a greater challenge to understand them in the context of a bicultural environment. Asian immigrants often use these contrasts to resolve intrapsychic dynamic issues. Asian women often feel empowered by the "more liberal" western culture in its views of sexuality, women, and codes of social behavior. Asian males, on the other hand, must adjust to a loss of power and dominance within this "more liberal" western culture and, therefore, often experience the shift as emasculating, alienating, and disempowering. From a non-Asian vantage point, this often results in Asian females being viewed as flexible, more able to "acculturate," and more willing to change, while Asian males are viewed as holding on to tradition and resistant to change. From a bicultural vantage point, these differences reflect attempts to grapple with self-identity in a context that poses different cultural values; how each individual evolves a positive sense of self within a bicultural context becomes the therapeutic task.

DIAGNOSTIC FORMULATION: A DIFFERENCE FRAMEWORK

Using a difference framework with Asian-American clients warrants as examination of conceptual principles in formulating clinical diagnoses. While resolution of conflict as a principle of psychotherapy derives from western cultures, the principle of restoring harmony is more syntonic within Asian culture. Consequently, the identification of conflict for diagnostic formulation may result in therapeutic interventions that are dystonic with Asian cultures. While the uncovering of repressed emotions becomes a focus for therapeutic intervention, the emphasis on catharsis based in western tradition may in fact violate the emphasis on regulation of emotions based in Asian tradition. These differences became important in the diagnostic formulations of Mr. and Mrs. A.

The theme of loss played prominently in the dynamics of the couple. As a child, Mrs. A's objective was to become a nun. She received strong but conflicting expectations from her father; while she was encouraged to pursue academic excellence, she was also coached on the proper virtue of women as subservient and modest, that is, to be second, not first. Her marriage and immigration to the United States represented the loss of her virginity, the need to give up religion, the loss of her childhood, the failure to continue her academic achievements, and the leaving of her homeland—in essence, the acceptance of a secondary role to her husband. For Mr. A, marriage and immigration to the United States represented an attempt to achieve actualization of his lifetime goals. His faltering marriage represented the loss of social status, an inability to establish himself as a patriarch, inability to carry on the family name, and parental disapproval—in essence, he viewed himself as a failure. His losses were struggles to give up his mythical ideals about marriage, family obligations, and the perfect wife.

Consequently, the marriage needed to work at all costs for both Mr. and Mrs. A. The marriage symbolized the continued sacrifice of their own needs by both. In addition to mourning their losses in therapy, they needed to give up their idealized expectations of marriage, recognize their dilemmas of self-sacrifice, and come to terms with their inability to conform to culturally prescribed roles before they could move on with their lives.

It was easier to blame each other for these losses than to admit defeat. It was easier to control one another than to admit their lack of control over their own lives and fate. Control issues, therefore, dominated the marriage. The couple resorted to negative and volatile interactions in their attempts at problem solving. They often used semantics to prove one another wrong. The intense polarity in their marital relationship signified their struggle to maintain their sense of self—to control and resist being controlled.

Mr. A was diagnosed as a narcissistic personality with obsessional features. He communicated his issues indirectly by criticizing Mrs. A's "deficiencies." These criticisms reflected his anxiety, anger, and disapproval of Mrs. A's failure to uphold Asian cultural values; that is, she dressed too seductively, she behaved too brashly, she did not cook, and she would not fulfill social, wifely, and family obligations. He felt rejected and his masculinity challenged by Mrs. A's disinterest in sex. As a result, he resorted to intellectualization and projection as defenses. He would obsess about fine points in his arguments with Mrs. A; he often became mistrustful of her. In psychotherapy, he needed to mourn the losses, come to terms with his masculine roles, and achieve maturity in his father-son relationship.

Mrs. A was diagnosed as having an identity disorder with dependency and depressive features. In therapy, she was initially aloof and unemotional. When badgered by Mr. A, she withdrew in angry silence. When supported, she expressed feelings more readily. While she enjoyed and encouraged her husband's dominance and protectiveness in the marital relationship, she also struggled with her poor self-esteem and resistance against being controlled. For Mrs. A, marriage was a struggle between symbiotic and individuation wishes, between rebellion and conformity to culturally prescribed female roles. In psychotherapy, she also needed to mourn the losses, come to terms with feminine roles, and achieve maturity in her father-daughter relationship.

These diagnostic features characterize common differences observed between males and females in the expression of emotions not only within Asian cultures but also in other cultures. Mrs. A presented with histrionic features, that is, emotionally labile, while Mr. A presented with obsessional ones, that is, logical. Both expected Mrs. A to be nurturing, affectionate, and emotional and Mr. A to be the protector and provider in the marriage.

Both Mr. and Mrs. A colluded to maintain the status quo, tension, and differences in the marital relationship to the point of reversing positions when this status quo was threatened. Both enjoyed and valued Mr. A's dominance as protective while objecting to Mrs. A's dependency. Both accepted Mrs. A's devalued opinion of herself. Both denied wanting to control the other but did so in their obstinance. Overtly, Mr. A was more obsessional and Mrs. A more histrionic, thereby fitting with culturally prescribed sex roles; covertly, it was the reverse. While Mr. A criticized Mrs. A's attitudes toward sex, he had strong taboos against her being even remotely sensual. While he overtly expressed the stronger commitment to the marriage, he ultimately expressed the stronger wish to leave. Despite their many differences, the marriage served the couple's dependency and nurturing needs.

TREATMENT PROCESS: REFRAMING IN THE CLIENT'S WORLD VIEW AND EMPOWERMENT

The couple was seen once a week over a three-year period. Initial short-term goals were getting the couple to listen to one another and to accept one another's differences. This was accomplished by reframing these differences so that they could be heard. Long-term goals were getting the couple to decide whether or not to stay married, resolving their ambivalence about gender and ethnic roles, and developing a positive sense of self. Therapeutic outcome was empowering the couple to choose roles syntonic with their needs while fostering a sense of belongingness within a bicultural environment.

The phases of therapy capture prominent themes at particular points during the therapeutic process. These themes reflect how an Asian perspective influences gender, ethnic, and racial themes.

Phase One: Help Seeking

During this initial phase, the establishment of a therapeutic alliance was premised on Mr. and Mrs. A testing the parameters of the therapeutic relationship. The couple was seen together. The couple's disagreements and opposing viewpoints characterized this phase with attempts to make the therapist an arbitrator and advice giver—to determine who was right. At the same time, their behavior was a challenge to the therapist's authority. Each expected the therapist to make the spouse change his or her behavior; the therapist's unwillingness to do so was viewed as her inability to exercise her authority.

During the sessions, Mr. A would badger Mrs. A as she withdrew into passive aggressive silence. Mr. A would criticize and contradict everything Mrs. A said. He wanted her to be an "obedient" wife, yet he disliked her dependency. He prided himself on his independence and openness, yet he was often rigid and dogmatic. He saw the therapist as an authority figure from whom to seek advice and structure, yet his opinions were firm, and he would split hairs over therapeutic interventions. He pressed for communication and cooperation. He would emphasize logic and facts, not effect. Some claim that this is a typical male communication that occurs across many cultures.[6]

Therapeutic intervention was analogous to that of a benevolent authority figure. The therapist openly supported both parties. Without threatening Mr. A's masculinity or undermining his authoritative role as husband, he was listened to and respected. Instead of asking Mr. A to describe his feelings, examples were given or guesses were made to be confirmed or disconfirmed. This approach was also used to draw Mrs. A out of her silence. Instead of challenging Mr. A's somewhat overbearing and dominating behavior, they were reframed to convey a different, more nurturing intent. This enabled Mr. A to become less defensive and more introspective.

Mrs. A became more "open" and rapidly began to appreciate the support in the therapy. She began to talk of her need for privacy and trust. She asked Mr. A to respect her opinion; she objected to Mr. A's dogmatism and failure to consult her about decisions.

Phase Two: Asian Themes

During phase two, Mr. and Mrs. A were generally seen individually. This phase was more tempestuous and crisis oriented. Mrs. A became suicidal and Mr. A had episodes of physical violence. Their anger toward one another escalated and was acted out. The couple needed to distance from one another during this phase. Each needed the individual sessions to explore thoughts considered taboo in the spouse's presence.

The couple's differences were explored in great depth during this phase. Asian values, behaviors, and gender roles were dilemmas and prominent therapeutic themes. As they struggled with their differences, western culture provided a context that offered alternative choices. For example, Mr. A could see that sending money home to his parents to demonstrate his obedience as a son was not something others in western cultures did.

During this phase, Mrs. A was less aloof and more easily engaged. She became more introspective while Mr. A remained focused on day-to-day issues in the marital relationship. She began to work through concerns about lifestyle, education, and achievement goals. With "permission," she became more able to assert her needs and grapple with how those needs differed from parental expectations and cultural prescriptions. Mrs. A liked living in the United States because it offered choices, while Mr. A wanted to return home to reclaim an idealized status. It became apparent that her exacting standards of Mr. A paralleled those common within the Asian culture. She became more able to criticize her own father's exacting standards and her mother's "mediocre" strivings. She acknowledged her unconscious attempts to underachieve in order to please her father's definition of femininity, that is, modesty and being second. The conflicting messages became apparent. While she rebelled against being like her mother, she revealed that her father had only made it to being second best. She became suicidal as a solution to end her pain. She saw suicide as a way to punish her husband and let people know how much she had suffered, a common view of suicide within the Asian culture.

Mr. A was able to be less obsessional and to show more emotional insight and dynamic introspection. As he discussed concrete concerns about women, marriage, and sex within therapy, he actively experimented with these choices in his daily life. For example, he began dating white women during a trial separation from Mrs. A. Mr. A's somatic concerns emerged at this time; he began to use herbal medicine to restore physiological vitality. His volatile temper escalated at this time; he admitted to feeling provoked by Mrs. A's withdrawals into silence. These concerns reflect his holistic views of health and his emphasis on restoring harmony as a method of cure.

A trial separation agreed upon during this phase was more difficult for Mr. A, who became preoccupied with his shame and fear of social ostracism. He found it difficult to give up his "rights" as a husband. Fearing rejection, he became more indirect in his requests for sex and wishes for reconciliation; this came across to Mrs. A as intrusive, demanding, and paranoid. His initial optimism about therapy reverted to extreme negativism, which played itself out in the transference. He became angry in therapy and began to provoke struggles with the therapist.

Therapeutic interventions emphasized reframing issues in the world view of the couple. The therapist was acutely aware of the choices she had made as a Chinese-American female and that this intensified transference feelings. It was clear that Mrs. A's transference feelings reflected her need for support from a "competent" female figure while Mr. A's transference feelings reflected his need to work through his anger toward Mrs. A, females, and authority figures and to test the benevolence of the therapist as an authority figure.

Phase Three: Idealized Mother

During this phase, the couple decided to reconcile and agreed to pay more attention to one another's needs. Mrs. A's transference feelings intensified as she struggled to model the therapist while maintaining her individuality. Mrs. A became more supportive of Mr. A. She had been able to gain distance and discuss her dilemma between cultural dictates and personal aims. She resented her dependency but realized how she, as a female, had been socialized to need others and seek protection from men.

Transference feelings were also intensified by the therapist's pregnancy and delivery during this time. While Mrs. A was adamant about not wanting children, she identified positively with the therapist's delivery. While she viewed the therapist as an idealized mother, the pregnancy reinforced her feelings of inadequacy as a woman. She became more interested in the therapist's academic credentials, that is, dilemmas about career and maternal roles. She admired the therapist's patience, caring, and listening while expressing disappointment with her mother's failure to enjoy parenthood. Since she did not experience rejection from an idealized mother nor inadequacy in not meeting up to standards, this experience was therapeutic for Mrs. A. She became less critical and more nurturing in the marriage. She made concrete efforts to "be a better wife."

Phase Four: Mourning

As the couple began to work through transference feelings, the marriage was emotionally over. Their differences were characterized by reversal of roles. Mr. A became more regressed and withdrawn. His social "humiliation" because of the trial separation isolated him from his friends. His therapeutic alliance strengthened. Therapeutic content consisted of his rage toward Mrs. A and feelings of self-pity. He began to describe his feelings of helplessness in the marriage, which resulted in his controlling behavior. As Mrs. A became more independent, assertive, and less devaluing, Mr. A became rejecting and less able to respond to Mrs. A's attempts to be more generous and nurturing. Much of these feelings occurred in response to perceived losses of the many idealized expectations from his marriage.

Mr. A's negative views toward women emerged during this phase. He acknowledged his dependent relationship with his mother and his tendency to sexualize all relationships with women. He experimented with dating and acting single in a way that objectified women. He tried to exercise sexual freedom in the "western way." Whereas earlier transference projections involved the therapist as an authority figure, these involved her as a female. He was able to recognize the emotional barrier he often created between himself and his wife as he struggled against his dependency needs.

Phase Five: Ambivalence

After about a year and a half, the couple again decided to work things out. Mr. A became less obsessional but more indecisive. As he projected less, he began to feel more inadequate and question his own accomplishments. His yearnings intensified to return home, where he felt he would be valued as a scholar.

Mrs. A, on the other hand, was more able to compromise and felt more committed to the marriage. She felt less trapped and more able to see marriage as a choice, not an obligation. She began to relate the sexual myths she had learned from her mother about how all men were cold and ruthless.

This was a time in which differences between the couple attenuated. They became more introspective and began to face their own ambivalence about gender and cultural roles.

Phase Six: Identity—Race, Culture, Gender

During year two, therapeutic content emphasized Mr. A's fear of failure, lack of confidence, and career ambivalence. At this point, his issues mirrored Mrs. A's initial presentation in therapy. He struggled with his obligations as oldest son, the wish to return home, and pressures to excel. Therapy for Mrs. A emphasized boundary issues. She did not like people doing special things for her. She worried about being nurturing because it was too feminine.

Both Mr. and Mrs. A began to grapple with career choices. This reflected their ability to distance from one another and symbolized their struggles with separation/individuation. As the couple negotiated geographic location for their career choice, they struggled to compromise while maintaining their individual identities. Mrs. A struggled to assert her autonomy, while Mr. A struggled to maintain his status. Their compromise was to move to a neutral location where neither one had professional ties, in order to make a new start.

Phase Seven: Achieving Maturity

At two and a half years, the tension in the marriage had attenuated. Following a return visit to their homeland and parents, the couple experienced a major turning point, which enabled them to separate from a psychological bond that had proved dysfunctional to their achievement of maturity.

During their return visit, the couple had a major confrontation with Mr. A's father. Father-in-law had blamed Mrs. A for not having a baby, causing the couple's marital dissolution, and the father-in-law to lose face. Father-in-law threatened to disown Mr. A unless he divorced Mrs. A. Mr. A's inability to follow this face-saving gesture and exercise of patriarchal authority made him realize how much he had changed. He was able to separate from his father by taking Mrs. A's side. Rather than challenge his father, he chose to appease his father by asking Mrs. A to apologize to him. Mrs. A did this willingly, in accordance with Asian tradition.

This return visit represented a major turning point in the couple's dynamics. An acquiescent son, Mr. A became enraged with his father's unreasonableness. With great difficulty, he acknowledged his disappointment that his father would sacrifice their father-son relationship to save face. He regretted his inability to be a dutiful son. The trip had dashed his idealized hopes of returning home as an accomplished and respected scholar.

This trip facilitated Mr. A's ability to work on the father-son relationship in therapy. He recalled his position of favor among the women in his family and his position of disfavor with his father. He no longer felt torn by the excessive demands of his father, that is, to please and to rebel. He began to develop different outlooks toward life in the United States, toward women, and toward the demands of culture. He also began to examine his attitudes toward sex and his double standard toward women: that a wife could be sexual only in the bedroom, sisters and mothers can be friends because they are not sexual objects, and contact with all other women is taboo because they are sexual objects.

During this phase, positive transference reactions from Mr. A intensified. He identified with the role of the therapist, was more inquisitive about her as a female, and became intrigued with becoming a counselor.

He began dating white women as a way to experiment with his new identity.

The trip was also corrective for Mrs. A in her relationship with her parents. She reexperienced a sense of togetherness with her father and nurturance from her mother. She had been able to negotiate a reunion with her parents. She was no longer resentful about cultural prescriptions. She became more thoughtful about how to become more dutiful as a daughter. She began to make plans for her parents' retirement.

Phase Eight: Termination

The couple was now ready to terminate. Concretely, the couple decided to make a new start by moving to a new and neutral location. They were no longer polarized in their differences; they had agreed to some constructive steps to make the marriage work. While the couple ultimately decided to divorce, the split was amiable. The marriage had symbolized many unresolved issues about gender and cultural roles in the couple's search for a positive identity. Their differences mirrored their ambivalence about cultural prescriptions and their fit with personal circumstance. Their immigration to the United States merely heightened this contrast as they were exposed to a bicultural environment.

SIGNIFICANCE FOR PSYCHOTHERAPY WITH DIVERSE POPULATIONS

The use of a case presentation is illustrative of the therapeutic process with diverse populations. Only as the therapy valued the differences between Mr. and Mrs. A were they empowered to make those choices most fitting of their needs. Only as the therapist modelled choices within an Asian-American context could Mr. and Mrs. A evolve a positive sense of self that validated their cultural origins. Only as issues were reframed within the world view of the couple was the therapy facilitative in resolving issues brought to therapy.

This case is significant because it dispels some common myths about psychotherapy with Chinese-Americans. First, a psychodynamic approach can be effective if the therapeutic process is sensitive to racial, cultural, and gender issues. Second, the therapeutic relationship can facilitate the expression of emotions by males when they do not feel emasculated and do feel validated in their mode of presentation. Third, transference issues must attend to race, ethnicity, and gender with clients from communities of color.

The nuances of world views illustrated many polarities between males and females and between Asian and western cultures. These world views were polarized in the couple's differences and were reflected in their behavior and attitudes toward marriage, interpersonal relationships, sex, and career. These differences would have been less intense had the couple not immigrated to the United States. It was their very awareness of difference between the Asian and western cultures that intensified their ambivalence about culturally prescribed roles that compromised their development of identity and achievement of maturity within a bicultural context. How to work with these individual dynamic issues in transference while preserving the integrity of the couple's culture was the challenge to psychotherapy.

NOTES

1. E. Toupin (1980). Counseling Asians: Psychotherapy in the context of racism and Asian-American history. *American Journal of Orthopsychiatry*, 50(1), 75–86; J. Yamamoto (1978). Therapy for Asian-Americans. *Journal of the National Medical Association*, 70, 267–70.

2. S. Shon & D. Ja (1982). Asian families. In M. McGoldrick, J. K. Pearce, & J. Giordano (Eds.), *Ethnicity and family therapy*. New York: Guilford Press, 208–28.

3. M. Tinloy (1978). Counseling Asian-Americans: A contrast in values. *Journal of Non-White Concerns in Personnel and Guidance*, 6(2), 71–77.

4. S. Sue & H. McKinney (1975). Asian Americans in the community mental health care system. *American Journal of Orthopsychiatry*, 45(1), 111–18.

5. M.P.P. Root (1985). Guidelines for facilitating therapy with Asian American clients. *Psychotherapy*, 22(2), 349–56.

6. R. Bly & D. Tannen (1992). Where are women and men today? *New Age Journal*, January/February, 28–32, 92–97.

CHAPTER EIGHT

AFFIRMATIVE THERAPY WITH A SEVERELY DISTURBED PUERTO RICAN MALE

Victor De La Cancela

What follows is a case history selected from a practice composed of Latino male clients who are seriously emotionally disturbed or severely psychiatrically labeled. This chapter is meant to illustrate emergent therapeutic approaches that are useful with some members of this population. The primary intent is to demonstrate that an empowering profeminist and male-affirmative approach can be utilized in therapy with certain persistently troubled Puerto Rican male patients.

The emergent therapy described is one that progressively integrates psychodynamic, systemic, and feminist understanding with a social, cultural, political, and historical analysis of the individual client's life history. Given the clients' language preferences, therapy was conducted either primarily in Spanish or English or in whatever combination the clients were most comfortable with.

CASELOAD CHARACTERISTICS

Some problems that these men presented as a group included: poor marital communication leading to recurrent threats of or attempts at separation; suicidal ideation; paranoid delusions; and verbal abuse of family members. These men were from twenty-six to forty-two years old, and all were Puerto Ricans who had resided on the mainland from thirteen to seventeen years. They had been married from seven to seventeen years and had two to four children. Upon initial interview, all were oriented to person, place, and time and were of average intellectual functioning.

They all had depressive affect and somatic concerns and reported being treated as "less than men" by their families and society at large. Their subjective reports included being slighted, disrespected, discounted, and invalidated. A common complaint was that people treated them as *locos* (crazies) who were not to be taken seriously. Their Diagnostic Statistical Manual (DSM III-R) diagnostic labels included: schizophrenia, paranoid type; brief reactive psychoses; bipolar disorder, manic; and paranoid personality disorder. Generally, the treatment plan called for psychotherapy lasting from one to two and a half years. Weekly sessions were scheduled with movement to biweekly and monthly sessions after agreed upon changes in the service plan.

In considering the selected case history, bear in mind that this is a treatment summary in which the highlighted themes, sequence of issues, dynamic content, interventions, and reported progress focus on conducting empowering ethnic- and gender-competent psychotherapy. It presents application of such a perspective to a long-term psychiatric survivor since most clinicians have neglected the racial, ethnic, gender, and class diversity of this consumer population.

Therefore, this report does not emphasize aspects of the treatment process that are of diagnostic interest, that is, the client's primitive oral dependency issues; his use of reaction formation and denial as defenses; and his pre-Oedipal and Oedipal fears. These aspects of the therapeutic work are deemed important, but in the interest of brevity and the present focus they are not further developed here.

COMPADRE JACINTO

Jacinto Bonito is a thirty-four-year-old Puerto Rican man who has resided on the U.S. mainland for thirteen years. His marriage of nine years to Maria del Carmen has borne two children: a girl, age nine, and a boy, age eight. Mr. Bonito has intermittently worked as a security guard for several years. His previous substance use history included cocaine, heroin, and marijuana. His current drug of choice is alcohol, and he abuses it episodically, such as weekend binging.

Jacinto complains of being irritable especially with his wife, sister, and mother. Significantly, he reports an adolescent history of conduct disturbance and a self-perception of being rejected and punished by others without reason. In particular, Jacinto reports feeling abandoned from his preadolescent years on. His family members and some past therapists question how truthful his report of maternal neglect is. Interestingly, he also reports having been a sometimes parentified and favored child.

Jacinto has explosive and assaultive propensities; in fact he was incarcerated for stabbing a man that questioned his heterosexuality. At different times, he has threatened his mother, struck his siblings, and battered his wife. Jacinto has had at least three involuntary psychiatric hospitalizations. Two were precipitated by his suicide attempts (one was a psychotropic medication overdose while the other was pouring gasoline on himself).

Jacinto is a person of color whose racial characteristics reflect the legacy of European Caucasian and African influences in Puerto Rico. Though he does not identify as a black man, he is the darkest skinned member of his family. His siblings manifest the diversified "success" that Puerto Ricans on the mainland achieve; one is a respected Latino community leader, and others are *barrio* dealers and users of illicit drugs. Jacinto's ambivalence toward his family is manifested in cycles of seeking his siblings out and then disparaging them. It is of note that his extended family was heavily involved in similarly ambivalent contact with Jacinto and his wife. These approach-avoidance patterns are particularly distressing to his spouse who finds comfort through church activities. Though Roman Catholic in name, the Bonitos avail themselves of Pentecostal ministers and spiritist practices in times of crisis.

Many of the couple's troubles are related to financial concerns. Mr. Bonito is angry that the irregular jobs, psychiatric hospitalizations, and low wages he experiences make his family depend on public assistance. Their arguments over money often lead to difficulties with intimacy. Jacinto has occasionally been impotent, a symptom related to unemployment in other clinical accounts.[1] Additionally, given the development of a strong mother-child alliance, Jacinto at times is cast as an ogre around money issues. Thus divorce threats are constantly surfacing, leading to chronic tension among all family members. Mrs. Bonito's response to Jacinto's threats vacillate between fearing abandonment and a longed-for release from "this disappointing man" who reminds her of her physically abusive father.

CONTEXTUALIZING THROUGH THERAPY

Jacinto was referred for therapy following a psychiatric hospitalization. At the start of therapy he was on an antipsychotic drug used in the treatment of both acute and chronic schizophrenia (Loxapine, 5 mg) and generally compensated except for pronounced paranoiac thoughts. Believing a nonthreatening approach would engender trust in Jacinto, the therapist first focused on his employment status. Sessions explored how, in a capital-dominated society, being employed is connected with masculinity;[2] how being denied a job interacts with a welfare system that compensates female heads of household more highly if fathers/husbands are not around, thus further marginalizing males; and how both racism and classism limit many fathers of color in helping children reach better futures.

These discussions explored with Jacinto the social roots of his family conflicts. Many of his marital difficulties were a result of emotions engendered by their joint socioeconomic oppression. Social contextualizing of Jacinto's male-female issues and his personal history led to offering him the following interpretations. Since his father was relatively emotionally absent during his childhood, it was to be expected that he would have some difficulty in relating to a spouse. His wife was socioculturally primed to expect him to play his "required role in the economy"[3] while she also struggled with vestiges of an individual history of paternal domination and a collective legacy of patriarchy. Given such experiences, a negotiated goal of therapy became discovering more flexible family roles for each of them.

CREATING MALE-FEMALE ROLE AWARENESS

Jacinto's psychopathology (paranoia) and social pathology (patriarchal male chauvinism and wife battering) understandably made him fearful of any potential "emasculation" by a therapy that encouraged changes to his male self-view. Additionally, given experiences of discrimination related to his racial, ethnic, and psychiatric labels, he maintained a healthy "cultural paranoia."[4] Considering these dynamics, the therapist engaged in self-disclosure to prevent Jacinto's flight from therapy, thereby sharing feelings and fears as a man, a person of color, and a heterosexual.[5]

Jacinto was encouraged to consider couples therapy aimed at increased understanding of himself, his wife, and their relationship. Since his spouse Maria del Carmen was also in therapy with a Latina clinician at the same center, it was relatively easy to arrange couples sessions on a biweekly basis for Jacinto and his wife. The therapy was structured to model nonsexist interactions and was conducted by male and female cotherapists. Each therapist was respectful of the other's authority and communication in the session, being careful to convey kinship with both partners to allay any fears that interventions were negatively gender biased.

Hence, the therapists pointed out when the clients' reactions were stereotyped attitudes toward men or women rather than individualized reactions to each other. Since they too were living in this sexist society, the therapists recognized that they partook of certain nonegalitarian views, and, thus, they respectfully challenged each other when these views influenced particular interventions. For example, the male therapist confronted the female therapist when she unfairly pathologized males by claiming that *all* men were emotional babies.[6]

As Jacinto and Maria del Carmen progressed in their role awareness, they sought out further counseling through telephone calls. Rather than discourage these out-of-session contacts as "traditional" therapies might have, the therapists responded favorably toward building further trust and reinforcing behavioral assignments made in the sessions.

Significant issues that emerged in the couple's phone contacts and intrasession work included: Jacinto's conflict with ambivalence toward his mother and the Puerto Rican "cultural" idealization of mothers; Jacinto's going on "medication holidays" to binge on alcohol or to avoid the side effects of erection and ejaculation difficulties; Maria del Carmen's infantilizing Jacinto while criticizing his male role "failures" as a sexual and economic provider; and the mother-child alliances that intentionally or unconsciously disempowered or protected Jacinto.

Attention was paid to how Jacinto's contacts with his brothers were not as destructive as Maria thought, given the satisfaction he got from playing an "older male" advisor role. Maria del Carmen's nearly exclusive control of the children was discussed in terms of Puerto Rican culture and socioeconomic influences on the "mother's role."[7] Also, her going "on strike" sexually as a method of punishing/controlling Jacinto was also addressed.

This gender role awareness focus led to questioning who in their family of origin most influenced their sex-role identity and how Puerto Rican male-female roles differed from other ethnic groups. For example, unlike the alleged obsolescence of the "male as breadwinner role" among U.S. Caucasian middle-class men,[8] this role is still valued and sought after by Puerto Rican and other males and females of color who feel they have been denied it. Thus, the therapists demonstrated how both partners were in transitional male-female roles and relationships. The clients' individual personal histories were used to illustrate circumstances in which the man was allegedly in charge, yet which showed the often hidden and unacknowledged force of women in the family. The couple was encouraged to assume participant-observer stances to their difficulties. This was framed as going beyond the content of their fights and observing as much as possible the process of their struggles, that is, what is happening here and now.

Emphasizing the process of their interactions allowed examination of the structure of their communication. It was seen that whatever they discussed, whether it was money, a trip to Puerto Rico, sexuality, or child discipline, they did not listen to each other. Their communication attempts were restructure to set aside a one-hour-per-week "homework" session in which Maria del Carmen did not collapse into hostile silences and Jacinto did not dominate the talk. Building this communication in the couple's office-based therapy allowed for practice of these new behaviors at home. Homework assignments were as innocuous as possible to avoid issues that might lead to physical violence. Hence, they were asked to negotiate around food such as what flavor ice cream they should have for dessert or whether to go out for pizza or have Chinese food delivered. Through practice, the couple recognized that their whole family had internalized barriers to family unity, such as the acting out of one of the children whenever they planned a family activity or one parent's tendency to see only the negative.

In the center-based work, more emotionally charged issues were addressed, such as: inconsistent maternal discipline, at times bordering on child abuse; Maria del Carmen's anger at Jacinto and fear of reprisal; Jacinto's provocative sexualizing of relationships; divorce and separation considerations; Jacinto's suicidality; and the legal consequences of his spousal abuse.

Maria del Carmen was made aware of women's shelters and referred to advocates in getting restraint orders as needed. Jacinto was encouraged to voluntarily remove himself from the home when he feared abusing his wife. This resulted in his staying with male friends or renting single-room occupancy apartments on a short-term basis. A meeting between Jacinto and a police community relations officer was held as a preventive measure since Jacinto had "done time" for assaulting other people during his domestic conflicts. This resulted in the police officer proactively intervening in a landlord-tenant dispute Jacinto was engaged in before it escalated to violence. Jacinto agreed to this meeting after arriving at a session with a stiletto that he had purchased to "protect" himself from the "abusive" landlord.

It was discovered that in-laws and rumors figured prominently in the couple's disputes. They were advised to ignore innuendoes and to appropriately confront family members who persisted in being destructive to their relationship. Similarly, Jacinto was encouraged to support Maria del Carmen in her dealing with the children rather than always casting himself as the lenient, permissive father.

THERAPY FOR THE WHOLE MAN

Jacinto's individual issues included frequent somatic complaints—gastric disturbances, weight fluctuations, breathing difficulties, and chronic back problems. His therapist inquired about these, given that many men express their psychological discomfort through physical complaints.[9] Additionally, the Puerto Rican culture's reported lack of mind-body dualism made such communications of distress particularly meaningful.[10] The health status of Latinos in the United States includes high rates of cardiovascular disease, stomach cancer, and excess mortality leading to a need for all health providers to take seriously the Latino client's reported physical complaints.[11]

For example, given Jacinto's previous history of IV-drug use and incarceration, his impaired judgment, and the nature of his symptoms (gastric, weight loss, respiratory), HIV risk counseling was included in the therapy. He was also given a referral to a local health center for a checkup at which it was confirmed that his respiratory symptoms were related to asbestos exposure in earlier employment. Jacinto's response revealed that he truly expected to die within a few years given his poor health—a belief that significantly impacted his interactions with his wife and children, that is, doing what he could to secure his son's future and a sense of resignation to his marital difficulties. As a method of joining with Jacinto in his efforts to provide for his family, the therapist advocated and brokered on his behalf to secure legal assistance in filing an occupational health lawsuit against the employer that had knowingly exposed workers like him to asbestos.

Equally important was the attention paid to Jacinto's psychiatric complaints; rather than seeing these as uncontrollable symptoms, Jacinto was educated to recognize the "distress call" nature of these symptoms. Concretely this translated into linking symptoms with emotional precipitants. It also meant confronting him on what was not psychiatric symptomatology but social pathology—that is, those attitudes, beliefs, and behaviors that could be related to external causes for which he had to take full responsibility.

For example, Jacinto asserted that he battered his wife because he was mentally ill, unemployed, or lost control. The therapist countered such allegations with interventions that highlighted how Jacinto selectively lost control—for example, he punched her rather than kicked her.[12] These social "reality checks" included the fact that many males living with mental illness feel frustrated, but they do not assault their spouses; that other Puerto Rican men are unemployed or have had abusive parents, yet they themselves are not abusive adults. The consistent message was that Jacinto's issues as a batterer were not the result of his personal pathology but more a result of his benefitting from the social control it gave him over a woman.[13]

To curb his domestic violence, a therapeutic contract was drawn up which allowed the therapist regular telephone contact with Maria del Carmen to check up on Jacinto's progress in this regard.[14] Confrontation of both Jacinto's and his wife's denial of alcohol as a problem was facilitated by these contacts. Thus a trial of disulfiram, a drug creating a physically adverse reaction to alcohol, was initiated as an adjunct in Jacinto's therapy. Related analyses involved helping Jacinto recognize the societal, cultural, and "masculine" pressures that "demanded" an instrumental role of him.

Male socialization that focused him on performance—on doing something—which led him to internalize feelings of failure when he could not easily meet the breadwinner-provider role. Acknowledging these dynamics and his own personal history allowed Jacinto to view himself and his father as "good-enough fathers": ones that more often than not did the best they could under the circumstances.[15] The approach also included the use of humor, a coping mechanism which Vazquez Erazo suggests might be more useful for Puerto Rican working-class males.[16] She states that irony and satire may be of service to men because it permits them to tell their life stories without having to be "particularly self-revealing."

The symbolic meaning of playing dominoes among Puerto Rican men led to its use as a therapeutic adjunct.[17] Through such "play therapy," Jacinto safely dealt with "issues of power, cooperation and antagonism." Playing dominoes appeared to be particularly useful when he was unable to openly express feelings because it allowed "talking through" the concrete moves of the game and commentary on its process. Yet another method of indirect self-disclosure was having Jacinto write a letter to his father as a cathartic and clarification exercise. This has been found to be an effective technique even when the letters are not mailed since they give men a feeling of control over their past.[18]

Given that racial and ethnic background, economic oppression, low educational opportunities, and the stigmatization of mental illness appear to increase the posthospitalization difficulties of discharged long-term psychiatric survivors, therapy focused on how these factors operated in Jacinto's life. He reported that previously received mental health services were maintenance oriented rather than focused on rehabilitation. Many low-income, schizophrenic, and culturally/linguistically diverse patients are often seen as needing only medication and as incapable of engaging in or benefiting from "talking therapy."[19] Indeed Jacinto's medical record amply documented this view. As a corrective intervention, the therapist aggressively reached out to Jacinto whenever he missed sessions and made therapy accessible through flexible scheduling and locations, as well as referral to other community resources. This approach has been demonstrated to positively impact on aftercare services to Latinos.[20]

A psychoeducational component was also integrated into Jacinto's treatment plan.[21] This intervention addresses the patients' concerns about mental illness and encourages them and their families to take an active part in rehabilitation,[22] in such matters as, for example, attending to personal grooming. Further assessments of Jacinto's needs led to inclusion of additional behavioral and didactic approaches such as: sex education; anger management training; social skills training; and teaching him how to be an "expert on feelings" by identifying and labelling physiological emotional states in himself and others.[23]

COUNTERTRANSFERENCE, EMPATHY AND EMPOWERMENT

Since Jacinto's therapist was a Puerto Rican man, he was, as Liebert phrases it, "also a child of the culture."[24] As such, hearing Jacinto engage in homophobic, sexist, classist, racist, or ethnocentric stereotyping was not a neutral event to which the therapist could be inured. Rather it stirred countertransference feelings related to: tolerating the expression of negative feelings about being Puerto Rican; acknowledging that as a male the therapist profited from masculine hegemony and institutional and personal patriarchy;[25] and recognizing that at times clinical practice was phallocentric, for it made him uncomfortable with wanting to express nurturance by hugging Jacinto or allowing tears as an empathic response to Jacinto's pain.[26]

It became clear how the male therapist was helping Jacinto to define how men are supposed to act, while at the same time the therapist was learning from Jacinto.[27] Thus, both therapist and patient struggled to understand and accept their own sentimentality, an emotion which is often stereotypically related to weakness and femininity.[28] The countertransferential challenge was to avoid identifying "too much or too little with one side or the other" of Jacinto's views or feelings.[29] Of aid in the therapeutic work was the therapist's supervision session, which included both individual and group supervision from both male and female supervisors who focused on the dynamics of conducting sociocultural and gender-competent therapy.

Thus, the therapist was advised that to address Jacinto's homophobia, the challenge was to appear neither seductive nor castrating and to sensitively allay transference anxiety about being infantilized or made effeminate by a male therapist.[30] Since at a more basic level Jacinto had a regressed self-identity, the task of keeping the transference nonintimidating was more compelling. This meant never losing sight of the expectations and stress that Jacinto underwent in trying to meet both his .cultural and personal definition of being "macho."[31] Helpful in this regard was Závala-Martínez's reminders of the life-stress-mediating function of "traditional" antifeminist gender roles—that is, those aspects that help men and women survive changing sociohistoric and economic conditions.[32] When therapists bear in mind the patient's difficulties in coming to terms with external cultural and social demands on his or her personal self-definition as a man or a woman, the use of transference and countertransference takes on new meanings.

Traditionally, psychodynamic theory views countertransference both as a pitfall for therapists and as an indicator of the client's experience. In a progressive therapy, utilization of countertransference as a reflection of the client's affective state can also signal when the client feels disempowered and thus provide clues to making the therapy an empowerment process. Hammond's definition of the therapist's "conscious subjectivity" or use of oneself in therapy becomes important.[33] This involves sharing common experiences related to gender, race, or group oppression. It teaches the skill of appropriate self-disclosure through modeling as well as openness, empathy, action orientation, and moving from the status of a victim to an empowered identification.

Obviously, an empowering therapy does not subscribe to the dictum of therapeutic neutrality, a standard of traditional practice that one of the most prominent psychoanalysts in Latin America, Marie Langer, believes is untenable given that all therapeutic interventions contain unconscious or conscious ideological baggage.[34]

CASE SYNOPSIS

The therapy conducted with Jacinto was sensitive to the triple health care legacy that he and other people of color have: folk healing, "colonial" medical interventions in his country of origin, and modern western medicine. This legacy, combined with his socioeconomic situation and psychiatric history, required modification of therapeutic techniques so that the therapy could respond to his needs in those areas to which he had acculturated within the dominant culture, as well as those to which he had not. This biopsychosocially competent and empowering approach required both contextualizing his issues within ethnic, racial, gender, and political currents and respecting his personhood and uniqueness.

The acknowledgment of his "self" was accomplished by soliciting his participation in making decisions about his care, advocating for protection of his rights, and modeling how to make the system work on his behalf. Given his previous disenfranchisement by custodial care and provider attitudes toward him, a proactive-affirmative therapy approach was used. This approach "teamed up" with him to enhance his support network, learn new communication skills, mediate conflict, and honestly encourage his power over the process of treatment.[35] This led to increased possibilities for him to change his behavior and to recognize where he could exercise his responsibilities.

FUTURE DIRECTIONS

There remain many unanswered questions in working with Puerto Rican men who are oppressed "from without and from within."[36] Specifically, their roles as workers, motivations to be employed, preferences as family members, views of their lover or domestic partner's participation in the labor force (be these male or female), and child care practices are of interest insofar as their attitudes and perceptions impact on their interpersonal behaviors. Their present socioeconomic standing as a primarily poor and working-class group necessitates a strong emphasis on the psychology of labor and unemployment.

A pro-male-of-color therapeutic focus may lead to discovery of how Puerto Rican males "resist indignity and oppression and create a meaningful existence for themselves and their families on a day-to-day basis."[37] It may answer such questions as "How are Puerto Rican males, as persons of color, involved in sociohistoric and cultural arrangements that include "an equal relationship of authority between men and women"? How do they benefit from a Caucasian, male-dominated society even when they are not as privileged as Caucasian men are in U.S. society?[38]

Though the clinical interventions presented here focus on the individual case of a Puerto Rican male, they can be adapted for use with other Latino, African-American, and Asian-American males with psychiatric illness who share similar problems in living and histories of oppression and who may be viewed anxiously by therapists unfamiliar with them. It is often true that these three groups of males, along with Native Americans, are viewed by therapists as emasculated, overly aggressive toward women, and thus underdeveloped or deviant when compared to their Caucasian counterparts. However, few of the mental health workers who so label these men have explored the contextual situations of men of color.

Each group has experienced some form of dehumanization at the hands of powerful others, whether it was the enslavement of African men, the colonization of Latino men, the indentured servitude of Asians, or the decimation of the Indian. Each has experienced Euro-American oppression and authoritarianism in a manner that begets long-standing and strongly felt emotions. For example, they have experienced historical devaluation of their cultural products, religions, and spiritual beliefs and exploitation of their labor force in the United States.

Their masculine cultural values, in particular, have been misperceived, so that Latino males, for example, are often thought to be "too" connected to their mothers and thus Oedipally involved. Such views on the part of therapists combine with the internalized negative stereotypes that men of color have, and serve as obstacles to effective therapy with them. Male-affirmative therapy approaches hold promise for developing challenges to these barriers.

Future empirical study of the applicability of this model to different diagnostic types of the long-term psychiatric survivor spectrum and therapeutic outcome would be of further utility.[39] For example, clinical experience has indicated that the electively mute, medication-noncompliant, delusional, violence prone, and highly regressed male client may experience this approach as seductive, go into a "homosexual panic" or transference psychosis, and become assaultive.

Even as attempts are made to empower the Puerto Rican male living with psychiatric illness through psychotherapeutic interventions, these approaches by themselves are not enough. In the case of Jacinto, it is expected that long-term followup will reveal continuing economic instability and conflicts of a racial, ethnic, or cultural nature with the dominant society. As Luepnitz states in reference to the political impact of a feminist family psychotherapy on an African-American adolescent male: "Even the best therapy cannot bring about radical social change."[40]

However, Loo suggests that because social movements and legislative redress "lead to an undoing of harm unmatched by individual psychotherapy, we should seriously consider involvement in social action both as part of our professional training and of the therapeutic process."[41] Hence, the disempowered in therapy may need to "work through" how past oppression has been internalized, made subjective, and personalized, as well as how they might radically restructure power relationships at a macrolevel. The concomitant process for the empowering therapist is one of discovering how to promote personal and political consciousness through new therapeutic praxis responsive to a professional self-definition as an "agent of change."[42]

NOTES

1. J. Brecher (1977). Sex, stress and health. *International Journal of Health Services*, 7, 89–101; H. S. Kaplan (1974). *The new sex therapy*. New York: Brunner/Mazel.

2. R. Staples (1971). The myth of the impotent black male. *The Black Scholar*, June, 2–9.

3. J. H. Pleck (1984). Men's power with women, other men and society: A men's movement analysis. In P. Rieker & E. Carmen (Eds.), *The gender gap in psychotherapy*. New York: Plenum, 79–89.

4. W. Grier & P. Cobbs (1968). *Black rage*. New York: Bantam Books.

5. J. C. Sternbach (1977). Men's awareness. *State and mind*, 6(1), 28–31.

6. G. R. Brooks (1989). Status of the men's movement within the professions. *National Organization of Changing Men: Men and Mental Health Task Group Newsletter*, 1(1), 5–7.

7. O. Ramirez (1983). Book review: Ethnicity and family therapy. *La Red/The Net: Newsletter of the National Chicano Council on Higher Education*, 66(March), 28–30.

8. J. M. Eichler (1989). What are men's issues? Paper presented at Men's Issues course, Cambridge Hospital Department of Psychiatry, January 21. Cambridge, MA.

9. M. Rappaport (1974). Treating the whole man: Integrating mental health into the mainstream of service. *Hospital & Community Psychiatry*, 25(4), 245–46.

10. R. A. Ruiz (1982). Mental health, Hispanics, and service. *La Red/The Net: Newsletter of the National Chicano Council on Higher Education*, 61(November), 3–7.

11. Report of the Secretary's Task Force on Black and Minority Health (1986). *Volume VIII: Hispanic health/inventory survey.* Washington, DC: U.S. Department of Health and Human Services.

12. D. Adams (1983). Men unlearning violence: A group approach for abusive husbands. Paper presented at the annual meeting of the American Orthopsychiatric Association, April 1. Boston.

13. F. Mederos (1987). Patriarchy and the psychology of men. Unpublished manuscript.

14. D. Adams (1984). Stages of anti-sexist awareness and change for men who batter. Paper presented at the 92nd Annual Convention of the American Psychological Association, August 24. Toronto.

15. S. Osherson (1986). *Finding our fathers: The unfinished business of manhood.* New York: Free Press.

16. B. Vazquez Erazo (1987). The stories our mothers tell: Projections-of-self in the stories of Puerto Rican garment workers. In R. Benmayor, A. Juarabe, C. Alvarez, & B. Vazquez (Eds.), *Stories to live by: Continuity and change in three generations of Puerto Rican women.* New York: Centro de Estudios Puertorriquenos.

17. J. Inclan (1982). Interpersonal relations among Puerto Rican men: Or, why so much dominoes? Paper presented at the 59th annual meeting of the American Orthospychiatric Association, March 29. San Francisco.

18. Osherson (1986), *Finding our fathers.*

19. C. Rivera (1986). Research issues: Posthospitalization adjustment of chronically mentally ill Hispanic patients. *Research Bulletin: Hispanic Research Center*, 9(1), 1–9.

20. *Ibid.*; O. Rodriguez (1985). Overcoming barriers to clinical services among chronically mentally ill Hispanics: Lessons from the evaluation of the project COPA demonstration. *Research Bulletin: Hispanic Research Center*, 9(1), 9–15.

21. O. Rodriguez (1983). Barriers to clinical services among chronically mentally ill Hispanics. *Research Bulletin: Hispanic Research Center*, 3(4), 2–14.

22. *Ibid.*

23. S. Ludwig & D. Hingsburger (1989). Preparation for counseling and psychotherapy: Teaching about feelings. *Psychiatric Aspects of Mental Retardation Reviews*, 8(1), 1–7.

24. R. S. Liebert (1986). The history of male homosexuality from ancient Greece through the Renaissance: Implications for psychoanalytic theory. In G. I. Fogel, F. M. Lane, & R. S. Liebert (Eds.), *The psychology of men: New psychoanalytic perspectives.* New York: Basic Books, 181–210.

25. Mederos (1987), *Patriarchy.*

26. J. Munder Ross (1986). Beyond the phallic illusion: Notes on man's heterosexuality. In G. I. Fogel, F. M. Lane, & R. S. Liebert (Eds.), *The psychology of men: New psychoanalytic perspectives.* New York: Basic Books, 49–70.

27. G. Stade (1986). Dracula's women, and why men love to hate them. In G. I. Fogel, F. M. Lane, & R. S. Liebert (Eds.), *The psychology of men: New psychoanalytic perspectives.* New York: Basic Books, 25–48.

28. R. Schafer (1986). Men who struggle against sentimentality. In G. I. Fogel,

F. M. Lane, & R. S. Liebert (Eds.), *The psychology of men: New psychoanalytic perspectives*. New York: Basic Books, 95–110.

29. *Ibid.*

30. *Ibid.*

31. J. Reyes (1987). Treatment modalities and the Puerto Rican migrant. Unpublished manuscript.

32. I. Závala-Martínez (1987). *En la lucha*: The economic and socioemotional struggles of Puerto Rican women. *Women & Therapy*, 6(4), 3–24.

33. V. W. Hammond (1987). "Conscious subjectivity" or use of one's self in therapeutic process. *Women & Therapy*, 6(4), 75–81.

34. N. Caro Hollander (1987). Marxism, psychoanalysis and feminism: A view from Latin America. *Women & Therapy*, 6(4), 87–108.

35. V. De La Cancela & A. McDowell (1992). AIDS: Health care intervention models for communities of color. *Journal of Multi-Cultural Social Work*, 2(3), 107–22.

36. J. Espinoza (n.d.). Untitled poem.

37. Vazquez Erazo (1987), The stories, 50.

38. S. Parker (1988). Why "women of color." In *National Institute for Women of Color Network News*. Washington, DC: National Institute for Women of Color, 1–2.

39. J. C. Sternbach (1989). The men's seminar: An educational and support group for men. Unpublished manuscript.

40. D. A. Luepnitz (1988). *The family interpreted: Feminist theory in clinical practice*. New York: Basic Books, 315.

41. C. Loo (1989). Eliminating the harm of racism: An analysis of the Civil Liberties Act (HR 442) and the presidential campaign of the Reverend Jesse Jackson. *Focus on Ethnic Minority Psychology*, 3(1), 5.

42. V. De La Cancela (1985). Psychotherapy: A political act. *Practice: The Journal of Politics, Economics, Psychology, Sociology and Culture*, 3(3), 48–52; V. De La Cancela (1985). Towards a sociocultural psychotherapy for low-income ethnic minorities. *Psychotherapy*, 22(2S), 427–35; V. De La Cancela, P. J. Guarnaccia, & E. Carrillo (1986). Psychosocial distress among Latinos: A critical analysis of *Ataques de Nervios*. *Humanity and Society*, 10, 431–47; I. Závala-Martínez (1986). Praxis in psychology: Integrating clinical and community orientation with Latinos. *The Community Psychologist*, 19(2), 11.

CHAPTER NINE

THEMES IN PSYCHOTHERAPY WITH DIVERSE POPULATIONS

Jean Lau Chin, Victor De La Cancela, and Yvonne M. Jenkins

THE AUTHORS' PERSPECTIVES

As authors, we came together from different theoretical and cultural perspectives. It is important to highlight these differences as reflective of the theme of diversity intended in this book. There are also common themes that are important to highlight in this concluding chapter. These themes can serve as the basis for developing principles of practice in psychotherapy with diverse populations. In particular, they illustrate the special importance of different principles of practice that must be a part of "general" theory and practice to be relevant to diverse racial and ethnic groups in the United States.

As African-American, Latino/Puerto Rican, and Asian-American, we share the common experience of people of color in the United States. This includes the experiences of oppression and differentness within a white majority society. As female and male, we share the views of a profeminist and male-affirmative approach. Each of us starts from a different theoretical perspective; each shares the common goals of diversity and empowerment in psychotherapy. Jenkins focuses on how society's responses to ethnocultural diversity impact on social and self-esteem of clients. De La Cancela focuses on the importance of a sociopolitical perspective in psychotherapy. Chin focuses on the assumptive frameworks used by clients and therapists to organize life experiences. Together, we communicate the power of diversity in influencing the therapeutic process. Jenkins emphasizes that contexts for presenting problems, dynamic content, and the relational process of psychotherapy often involve racial, sociohistorical, and gender themes. De La Cancela emphasizes the socioeconomic context and sociopolitical factors that influence the practice and outcomes of psychotherapy. Chin emphasizes cultural themes and world views that provide the context for ethnic differences in the practice of psychotherapy. Despite these differences, or perhaps because of them, variations in the clinical perspectives reflect an approach that is racially, ethnically, gender, and politically conscious. It is the comprehensiveness of this more "authentic" emphasis that empowers the individual and promotes positive identity development among diverse ethnocultural groups.

COMPARISON OF THEORETICAL PERSPECTIVES

In chapter three, Jenkins discusses diversity, social esteem, and self-esteem from ethnocultural and historical perspectives. The prominent influence of race on the social and self-esteem of African-Americans is highlighted. The intricate relationship between race and power creates an oppressive sociopolitical context reinforced by racism and discrimination that has historically been negative and damaging to self-esteem. The intolerance for difference has perpetuated a mainstream focus that has negatively influenced development of self-esteem, diverted gender and ethnic identity, and disenfranchised people of color. Jenkins argues that one of the main principles of the diversity movement is to promote social esteem through group acceptance and pride in belongingness. She asserts that greater tolerance for difference may enhance the connectedness between people that nurtures and protects self-esteem and social esteem.

In chapter four, Chin discusses troublesome concepts common in our repertoire that mitigate against dealing competently with diverse racial and ethnic groups. These concepts underlie assumptive frameworks that reflect an emphasis on sameness and intolerance for difference. In applying these concepts to people of color and diverse groups—that is, racial, ethnic, and gender differences—we undermine the very basis of self-identity essential to optimal psychological growth. Chin proposes some culturally competent concepts. Use of these alternative concepts acknowledges the diversity among our clients—cultural, racial, gender, and sociopolitical differences—and their importance as contexts of psychotherapy.

In chapter five, De La Cancela discusses two areas that reflect a progressive perspective to examine political, professional, and personal issues as an important context for practicing psychotherapy. De La Cancela discusses leading social issues such as HIV/AIDS and men of color, and the need to review and critique underlying principles and models of practice. He illustrates the negative impact of capitalist principles—that is, the predominant U.S. sociopolitical context—and their use in perpetuating a mainstream society. De La Cancela argues for psychotherapists to review the values upheld by governing principles of practice and to question whether they, in effect, mitigate against diversity.

The three authors underscore similar concepts of diversity and empowerment while coming from different perspectives. All three authors emphasize the importance of context in the practice of psychotherapy. De La Cancela emphasizes the sociopolitical context while Jenkins emphasizes the social context and Chin emphasizes the world view of the client. In psychotherapy, Jenkins promotes the development of social and self-esteem while De La Cancela advocates for the examination of values and Chin for the acknowledgment of difference.

COMPARISON OF CLINICAL PERSPECTIVES

In chapter six, Jenkins describes how ethnocultural history has influenced a self-defeating mode of coping among some African-American women—that is, low self-esteem and dissonant expectations. Given the tradition of racism that has oppressed African-Americans since the slavery era, Jenkins contends that dissonant expectations among a subset of African-American women are an outcome of fragile self-esteem development influenced by social and psychological factors.[1] Women with dissonant expectations subscribe to the belief that they are unlovable despite otherwise successful academic and professional careers. Drawn to men who are unavailable to them, these women assume an extremely self-defeating approach to love relationships that almost always validates this belief. Dissonant expectations emanate from their cultural cutoff from the past that commenced as early as the slavery era. Slavery disconnected African slaves from their cultural roots. Although African-Americans have developed strong adaptive mechanisms despite this cultural cutoff, slavery, and subsequent forms of oppression, this has not been without significant sacrifice. For example, during slavery, a woman's capacity for work and her breeding were valued highly, while her intellectual and emotional well-being were grossly disregarded. One consequence has been the reinforcement of the "nodal role," a societal role in which African-Americans and other ethnocultural groups of color have internalized much of the anxiety, hostility, and sense of inferiority projected onto them by the white majority in response to their differences. In some situations, this has adversely affected parenting styles and family systems and has, therefore, precluded healthy psychological development and personality integration.

Women with dissonant expectations often tend to be selfless caretakers who have had excessive demands made of them since childhood. Caretaking is a gender-based role that is sanctioned to an extent by the culture, such as in the form of demands for financial support. Jenkins also emphasizes that oppression frustrates satisfaction of basic human needs, resulting in desperation. Desperation resulting from traditional sociopolitical factors and cultural proscriptions in the African-American culture have, at times, impaired parental effectiveness, created parent-child role reversals, and engendered pressures among some African-American women to stay in the family and out of relationships.

In chapter seven, Chin presents a clinical case with a Chinese-American immigrant couple. Their marital discord and struggle to define roles within their marriage and families of origin speak to the significance of cultural and gender issues. Family obligations and gender role expectations prescribed by Asian culture engendered a tension that played out in the polar differences between the couple. The use of a valuing differences framework, as presented in chapter four, is illustrated through this clinical material. When tolerance for the differences among character, gender, and culture is permitted and valued within psychotherapy, the individuals are empowered to achieve self-actualization and self-differentiation. The use of an intrapsychic approach is syntonic with an emphasis on the external reality context—that is, on race, ethnic, and gender differences.

For Asian-Americans, race heightens the awareness of difference from and a sense of fit with the white majority. Some experience this difference with a sense of superiority while others experience a sense of alienation and inferiority. While African-Americans often feel a cultural cutoff from their ethnocultural and historical roots, Asian-Americans feel intensely the demands to adhere to prescriptions of culture; both feel the wish to link with the past. The contrasts between Asian and western values merely mirrored the intrapsychic dilemma felt by the couple. While choices made by the couple were inconsistent with some Asian values, they did not reject their culture. The therapist framed these choices, therefore, not as adopting "more liberal" western values, as is commonly done, but rather as a resolution of personal dilemma entrapped by cultural and family expectations.

In chapter eight, De La Cancela presents a case with a seriously disturbed, Puerto Rican male client. The case illustrates the use of an empowering profeminist and male-affirmative approach with persistently troubled Puerto Rican males. Common problems presented by these clients typically include poor marital communication, threats of separation, suicidal ideation, paranoid delusions, and verbal abuse of family members.[2] Presenting symptoms typically include depressive affect, somatic concerns, and concerns about masculinity. The client was frequently explosive and assaultive and made several suicide attempts. De La Cancela's therapeutic approach emphasized the progressive integration of psychodynamic and systemic theory with an examination of the external sociopolitical context. The emergence of gender and ethnic themes and how they related to the client's dysfunctional behavior became important in guiding De La Cancela's therapeutic approach; in other words, the client felt his dark skin color was devalued in society and that his unemployment in a capitalist society reinforced his feelings of emasculation.

In applying their theoretical perspectives to clinical material, each of the authors emphasizes the importance of race, culture, and gender variables in the dynamics, therapeutic relationship, and interventions of psychotherapy. While Jenkins emphasizes that awareness of the ethnocultural context, including history, is crucial for understanding behavior, Chin focuses on how to reframe psychotherapy interventions that value individual choices without devaluing cultural values. De La Cancela focuses on reality testing with the client those societal values that disempower or disenfranchise people of color. Each of these approaches underscores the importance of acknowledging diversity in our practice and empowering our clients to promote optimal development.

CLINICAL PRACTICE WITH DIVERSE ETHNOCULTURAL INDIVIDUALS

Given the historical racial and cultural context of people of color, all three authors recommend active intervention by the therapist to build rapport in the initial phases of psychotherapy. African-American clients are often initially misconstrued as passive, guarded, suspicious, or awkward, when their response is often an adaptive response to a history of subjugation and racism within the United States. Clients from all three ethnic groups often respond similarly because of cultural values governing relationships with authority figures, a history of racism, and reactions to colonization within their countries of origin.

All three authors support involvement of the ethnic self by the therapist—that is, self-activity, self-disclosure, and countertransference—as essential to prompting empathy within the therapeutic relationship. For many people of color, it is more difficult to experience the therapy as real without relating to the ethnic identity of the therapist. Jenkins supports Fulani's view that "deprivation of a sense of oneself as historical is a major cause of all varieties of psychopathology."[3] Consequently, the therapist's use of self is facilitative to supporting fragile self-esteem and promoting self-differentiation. Chin emphasizes the bias therapists bring in world views to the therapeutic relationship and the countertransference feelings stirred by ethnic stereotyping. De La Cancela emphasizes the ethnic therapist as role model and the therapist's measured self-disclosure as promoting a corrective therapeutic experience.

All three authors support the use of a systems approach. As Chin states, this acknowledges psychotherapy as rooted in the cultural context of society and the client.[4] As Jenkins states, this acknowledgment minimizes the effects of institutionalized assaults to social and self-esteem, supports healthy family dynamics, and strives generally to attain a connectedness to cultural roots. As De La Cancela states, this attention to the external context helps clients to test reality, to differentiate between stereotypic attitudes and individual reactions, and to recognize the distress call of psychiatric symptoms.

The use of indirectedness is advocated by the authors as syntonic with cultural values. In so doing, this draws on the symbolism within cultures and the nonverbal communications that often are more crucial to therapeutic outcomes, establishment of meaning, and the formation of therapeutic alliances than the verbal elaborations. For example, De La Cancela played dominoes with his client to communicate an alliance based on cultural similarity and directed his client to write a letter to his father as a means of indirect self-disclosure.

The use of cognitive and psychoeducational interventions was described by all three authors as perhaps tempering the balance on catharsis, "letting it all hang out," and other practice prescriptions commonly used for handling feelings in psychotherapy. Whether it is the anger against racism within African-American communities, the importance of regulating feelings together with their expression in Asian-American communities, or the perception of uncontrolled emotional expression within Latino cultures, the emphasis on cognitive and psychoeducational interventions is deemed important to teach a client to be an expert on his or her feelings. De La Cancela taught a client to regulate feelings, and Chin emphasized ways for the client to buy into the cultural mores of psychotherapy.

RACIAL AND ETHNIC THEMES

All three authors subscribe to the importance of race and ethnicity in the practice of psychotherapy. These are reflected in the authors' personal, theoretical, and clinical perspectives. How the issues of race and ethnicity emerge as therapeutic content and in therapeutic relationship are yet other dimensions. Whereas race and ethnicity are prominent self-defining characteristics for people of color, these themes inevitably emerge in relation to social and self-esteem, self-identity, and the nature of the therapist-client dyad. However, the complexity of race and ethnic themes is multi-determined.

Race is commonly associated with skin color, that is, black versus white. Valuations negatively correlating with degree of melanin in the skin influence many aspects of psychotherapy practice, that is, therapeutic content, self-esteem, social esteem, transference, and countertransference reactions. Race as self-identity and skin color in relation to self-esteem are most dominant for African-Americans since these criteria have been used by the white majority to define this group. Given the racial heterogeneity of Latinos within the United States, they are often perceived as belonging to various racial groups (Caucasian, Negroid, and Mongoloid). Yet ethnically, they feel affiliation to none since self-identity within their countries of origin is often subordinate to cultural identity. Among Puerto Ricans, for example, racial classification interacts with class such that having economic power means being white even when one is dark.[5] Puerto Ricans and Mexican-Americans are also distinguished from all other persons of color in the United States by their preponderance in the lowest socioeconomic strata of society.[6] For Asians, ethnicity interacts strongly with race in defining self-identity. Characteristics of Asians have more often been attributed to ethnic and national origin rather than skin color. For example, the internment of Japanese during World War II differentiated Chinese, as desirable, from Japanese, as undesirable. Asians and Latinos place great emphasis on their ancestry and the sociopolitical significance of nationality such that a major concern is political identity—that is, colonized versus free and independent.

Other physical attributes associated with race, such as hair color and texture, eye shape, body build, height, and lip size, often become important in defining self-esteem and self-identity because they are defined as attractive or unattractive according to white majority ideals. As the clinical material illustrates, none of the clients were immune to these comparisons and valuations within the larger sociopolitical context irrespective of their affiliations and self-valuations with their own culture and race.

Ethnicity and culture are more elusive as they emerge in therapeutic content. When these themes are manifest and explicit, it is not uncommon for therapists to assume and diagnose pathology based on problems of self-identity, alienation, or cultural conflict. When they go unnoticed, it is not uncommon to assume the client is just like any other client—that is, white. Consequently, the approaches of all three authors take a culturally affirmative approach of using ethnic and cultural themes to reinforce self-identity and self-esteem and to use psychotherapy to bring about a cultural, racial, and ethnic consciousness that supports and strengthens racial and cultural identity. Jenkins illustrates this with her conceptualization of dissonant expectations while Chin illustrates it with her work on family obligation (filial piety).

GENDER THEMES

For people of color, gender roles are often viewed as secondary or intricately related to culture and race. While this does not diminish the importance of gender themes in psychotherapy, it makes for differences within clinical practice when working with people of color.

Male and female roles dictated by culture influence the behavior of both therapist and client. Given the sociopolitical context of present-day society, the male therapist often struggles to accept his own sentimentality while the female therapist struggles to define multiple roles, that is, as wife and professional. Consequently, appropriate self-disclosure by the therapist, not neutrality, is viewed by De La Cancela as empowering because it models and shares strategies for ending sexism and heterosexism.

While the caretaking roles of women described by all three authors would appear to be a universal phenomenon, the subtle differences across race and cultures are important to underscore. Racial definition of the self takes precedence over gender identity for many African-American women due to the prominence of race in their oppression according to Jenkins. African-American women, as well as other women of color, are often expected to be the system balancers and tension reducers in their families despite limited economic resources. Selfless caretaking is commonly an experience of women of color due to the constraints imposed on their families by society. African-American men, on the other hand, often feel inadequate, disenfranchised, and disempowered in their prescribed roles as providers. The selfless caretaking role of African-American daughters, the cultural idealization of Puerto Rican mothers, and the self-sacrificing of Asian women are prominent images in each of these cultures and speak to the prominence of women's roles in the social systems of all three cultures. The male is alledgedly in charge, yet there is a hidden and unacknowledged force of women in these families.

In response to these gender roles, all three authors focus on the psychological price that fosters the marginalization of males and self-sacrifice of women among people of color. When masculinity is only related to employment status, society defines and emasculates. For men of color, this is especially true when low socioeconomic status is involved. Consequently, many men are fearful of losing their masculinity in psychotherapy. Fathers are often emotionally absent. The use of physical force and domestic violence to demonstrate control over women is illustrated within all three cultures by the authors.

While these socialization patterns for gender roles that focus on performance result in feelings of failure for men of color, they are often a source of competence for women of color. All three authors talk of the career and socioeconomic accomplishments experienced by women of color as a measure of success while paying an emotional price for roles associated with nurturance and caretaking.

Therapeutic interventions advocated by all three authors focus on gender awareness and reality testing. While all three authors cite problems commonly discussed in the literature—physical violence, in-law complaints, somatic complaints—each reframes them in ways that do not further marginalize males or undermine cultural values of extended family. All three authors emphasize empowering the clients in their respective gender roles. As De La Cancela describes it, a male-affirmative and profeminist approach is important to empower clients.

SOCIOPOLITICAL THEMES

Sociopolitical themes pervade the ethnic and gender themes for all three authors. All three authors speak to some aspect of oppression that influences the personal and psychological experience of people of color. This includes the history of racism that has disempowered people of color, the bias in world views that has devalued the cultures of people of color, and the political system that legislates behaviors and resources and continues to oppress people of color.

Whereas psychotherapy is frequently emphasized as an internal or intrapsychic process, all three authors focus on the external context as unavoidably part of the therapeutic process. Consequently, the role of therapist is key to reality testing for the client. This reality testing, moreover, is viewed not from a perspective of psychotherapy in which the client distorts, but rather as one of external reality in which society distorts.

While De La Cancela clearly takes a more sociopolitical approach, the authors differ in their points of emphasis. The theme of empowerment is prominent among all three authors as a way to correct the injustices of the past and their negative impact on current psychological functioning in the present. Chin emphasizes reframing from the vantage point of the client's culture while De La Cancela points to the therapist's responsibility in not reinforcing oppressive practices when providing clinical services. Jenkins emphasizes the importance of helping the client to recognize the overwhelming effects of oppression on the family and to let go of feeling responsible for correcting these.

In recommending a therapeutic approach, Jenkins emphasizes the importance of exploring sociopolitical roots of family conflicts in an effort to restore social esteem and self-esteem and to recognize the social context as damaging to the self-concept, personal identity, and competence. Chin emphasizes the sociopolitical context as an intricate part of the therapeutic relationship; this results in qualitative differences in the experience of psychotherapy for people of color, which must be understood in the therapeutic formulations and interventions used. De La Cancela asserts that the empowering therapist will engage the client in a process to discover how to promote personal and political consciousness. In the context of psychotherapy, he describes empowerment as a therapeutic partnership where the coparticipants transfer knowledge toward self-care.[7] He emphasizes the need for clients to work through how past oppression has been internalized, made subjective, and personalized. He also encourages therapists to contribute to the development of a therapeutic approach that merges with social action toward building caring societies and "people making" based on true equality and social justice.

IMPLICATIONS FOR THE FUTURE

As we look at the changing face of the U.S. population, diversity takes on greater prominence in all aspects of society. This will and must influence ways in which we deliver services to people of color and other diverse groups. "Standard practice" is no longer relevant when it is insensitive or not applicable to significant groups of people. In looking at implications for the future, we support the following general recommendations to therapists working with diverse populations and people of color:

1. Value differences and acknowledge the importance of diversity in the psychotherapeutic process.

2. Empower the client, taking into consideration racial, ethnic, and gender themes. Redefine your role as therapist to be healer, teacher, and facilitator.[8]

3. Acknowledge the sociopolitical context—past, present, and possible future—and learn to integrate its significance into the therapeutic context. At the most basic level, integrate provision of information about legal and health services, make referrals and linkages, and build social supports into the therapy.[9]

4. Operationalize how diversity influences your interventions, formation of therapeutic alliances, diagnoses of psychopathology, and so on. For example, diversity means that most people of color have, at the very least, a bicultural identity that includes the identity that was forced upon them by their exclusion from mainstream U.S. society, and the identity they have forged to maintain their heritage, strengths, and values.[10]

5. Acknowledge the positive as well as negative bias of cultural world views of both client and therapist. Explore cultural strengths, values, attitudes, and beliefs that enhance mental health maintenance or define the experience of being different.

6. Develop a male-affirmative/profeminist approach.

7. Use the "prescription warning label" approach, that is, that generic prescriptions for psychotherapy really do not exist.

CONCLUSION

Our hope is that, at this point, readers will be convinced of the need to develop less sexist, Eurocentric, or victim-blaming psychotherapeutic theory and approaches. Diversity in practice will hopefully be followed by practitioners attending to how experiences of difference contribute to such psychological tasks as developing social and self-esteem. The culturally competent clinician will recognize the difficulties that people of color have in not only developing adequate self-esteem but in preserving and maintaining it in the face of sociopolitical obstacles to their individual and collective success.

We have clearly favored a social-change-oriented practice as contributing to therapeutic "authenticity" wherein the dyad can acknowledge, confront, and work together to remedy the "historical cutoff," internalized oppression, and self-alienation many disenfranchised people of color experience. The therapist's or counselor's task is, therefore, to engage clients in an ethnoculturally inclusive examination of their life histories and potential. We strongly believe that contextualizing the patient's possibilities guards against the raising of expectations for a self-actualization that, though humanistically idealized, is unrealistic and may actually be antitherapeutic or unethical given a client's external reality.

Some of us experience a tension as we bring this book to a close in that we have failed to include an appreciation of people of color as spiritual. Certainly, this is a major critique that we make as therapists and citizens interested in human rights and, therefore, committed to the elimination and prevention of discrimination due to creed and religion. Though we did not give much attention to the topic, we encourage others more adept in this area to discuss how diversity in race, culture, class, and gender is inextricably connected to how we value and believe in cultural legends and myths, religious traditions, mystical symbols, and spirituality. Indeed, we would argue, as Chin exemplifies in her discussion of the Ajase complex versus the Oedipus complex, that there are models of male and female behaviors and mythopoetic images that are more relevant to persons of color than the Greek mythology that has been held as a standard from which universal western myths have evolved.

Certainly, Jungian therapists and others have pointed to the empowering aspects of symbols, and even before the holistic New Age era therapists were aware of their cultural similarities to gurus, shamans, medicine men, and so-called witch doctors. In addition, for indigenous peoples, African-Americans, and Latinos, the spiritual and religious have merged with folk healing and therapy as remedial for individual problems,[11] as well as with organized social action for collective justice, such as liberation theology and the southern Christian leadership conference. Therefore, there is a vast area for progressive exploration of the value of rituals and ceremonies in fashioning healing approaches. We welcome others to teach us all how to become competent in this regard.

NOTES

1. Y. M. Jenkins (1982). Dissonant expectations: Professional competency vs. personal competency. *Aware*, 1(1), 6–13.

2. V. De La Cancela (1990). Latino CMI males: Social therapy approaches. *The Clinical Psychologist*, 43(5), 74–77.

3. L. Fulani (1988). Poor women of color do great therapy. In L. Fulani (Ed.), *The psychotherapy of everyday racism and sexism*. New York: Harrington Press, 115.

4. J. L. Chin (1991). Transference. In J. L. Chin, J. H. Liem, M. Domokos-Cheng Ham, & G. K. Hong (Eds.), *The use of transference and empathy in psychotherapy with Asian Americans*. Manuscript submitted for publication.

5. C. E. Rodriguez (1980). Puerto Ricans: Between black and white. In C. E. Rodriguez, V. Sanchez Korrol, & J. O. Alers (Eds.), *The Puerto Rican struggle: Essays on survival in the U.S.* New York: Puerto Rican Migration Research Consortium, 20–30.

6. P. Y. Guzman (1980). Puerto Rican barrio politics in the United States. In C. E. Rodriguez, V. Sanchez Korrol, & J. O. Alers (Eds.), *The Puerto Rican struggle: Essays on survival in the U.S.* New York: Puerto Rican Migration Research Consortium, 121–28.

7. J. S. Gordon (1990). Holistic medicine and mental health practice: Towards a new synthesis. *American Journal of Orthopsychiatry*, 60(3), 357–70.

8. V. De La Cancela & L. P. Guzman (1991). Latino mental health service needs: Implications for training psychologists. In H. F. Myers, P. Wohlford, L. P. Guzman, & R. J. Echemendia (Eds.), *Ethnic minority perspectives on clinical training and services in psychology*. Washington, DC: American Psychological Association, 559–64.

9. V. De La Cancela (1991). Progressive counseling with Latino refugees and families. *Journal of Progressive Human Services*, 2(2), 19–34.

10. V. De La Cancela (1991). Salsa and control: An AmeRican response to Latino health care needs. *Journal of Multi-Cultural Community Health*, 1(2), 23–29.

11. V. L. De La Cancela & I. Závala-Martínez (1983). An analysis of culturalism in Latino mental health: Folk medicine as a case in point. *Hispanic Journal of Behavioral Sciences*, 5(3), 251–74; L. Zuchman, O. Crespo, V. De La Cancela & A. Spielman (1987). A study of Puerto Rican espiritismo as a counseling adjunct in an East Harlem child welfare agency. *El Boletin: Newsletter of the National Hispanic Psychological Association*, 4(3), 5–7.

AFTERWORD

L. Philip Guzman

The importance of culture as a variable that impacts a clinician's intervention with clients is gaining greater acceptance in psychology and other related disciplines. In part, this is due to the growth of populations of color within the United States. From 1980 to 1990 the census of African-Americans increased 13.2 percent; Latinos, 53 percent; and Asian-Americans, 107.8 percent (U.S. Department of Commerce News, 1991). As impressive as these percentages may be, it is widely believed that they represent an underestimation of the true number of ethnically diverse populations in the United States. Nevertheless, these percentages reflect the changing composition of our society, which is forcing both private and public segments of the country to reevaluate themselves in relationship to culturally diverse groups. The buzzword of the 1990s is "diversity." Large corporations are training their staffs to be able to effectively manage a diverse workforce. The private business sector realizes that its future workforce and consumer market will comprise greater numbers of ethnically diverse group members than in the past (Copeland, 1988). The human service arena, unfortunately, has lagged behind in its commitment to fully embrace cultural diversity. There continues to exist the assumption that generic clinical training is sufficiently broad in scope to be applicable to all groups, regardless of ethnicity. This is quite evident in the training of psychologists where a great proportion of students receive little or no exposure to working with culturally different individuals. In 1982 Bernal and Padilla (1982) found that of 106 clinical psychology programs only 41 percent reported offering courses on multiculturalism. More currently, the Office of Ethnic Minority Affairs of the American Psychological Association (APA) con-

,d an analysis of 570 psychology programs that reported, according
.e data in the *1990 Graduate Study in Psychology and Associated Fields*,
ring multicultural courses or curricula. The findings indicated that
6U percent of the doctoral psychology programs and 76 percent of the
master's programs offered no training on multicultural issues.

With the projection that ethnically diverse groups will encompass a
third of this nation by the turn of the century, it seems most prudent
that culturally different individuals should be aggressively recruited to
enter mental health professions to meet the needs of this changing society. Unfortunately, data have indicated that cultural diversity representation within psychology and other related fields has not increased
significantly within the past decade (Kohout & Pion, 1990; Sanchez,
Demmler, & Davis, 1990). With the outlook that there will not be sufficient numbers of ethnically diverse therapists to work within ethnocultural communities, there is the need for all therapists to be
competently trained to conduct therapy with people of different cultures.

The APA has attempted to foster cultural diversity training within its
profession. It adopted, in 1978, criteria on individual and cultural differences by which all clinical, counseling, and school psychology programs are to be evaluated for accreditation. Unfortunately, these criteria
have had minimum effect on increasing the percentage of ethnically
different students or faculty, or on producing culturally relevant training
curricula. More recently, in 1990 the APA approved *Guidelines for Providers of Psychological Services to Ethnic, Linguistic, and Culturally Diverse
Populations*. These guidelines, consisting of nine general principles, were
established to help practitioners in their work with culturally and linguistically different clients. The guidelines, presented here in an abbre-
viated form, cover a broad range of issues that must be attended to in
order to provide culturally appropriate and competent services to ethnic,
linguistic, and culturally diverse individuals.

1. Psychologists educate their clients to the processes of psychological intervention, such as goals and expectations; the scope and, where appropriate,
   legal limits of confidentiality; and the psychologists' orientation.

2. Psychologists are cognizant of relevant research and practice issues as related
   to the population being served.

3. Psychologists recognize ethnicity and culture as significant parameters in
   understanding psychological processes.

4. Psychologists respect the roles of family members and community structures,
   hierarchies, values, and beliefs within the client's culture.

5. Psychologists respect client's religious and/or spiritual beliefs and values,
   including attributions and taboos, since they affect world view, psychosocial
   functioning, and expressions of distress.

6. Psychologists interact in the language requested by the client and, if this is not feasible, make an appropriate referral.

7. Psychologists consider the impact of adverse social, environmental, and political factors in assessing problems and designing interventions.

8. Psychologists attend to as well as work to eliminate biases, prejudices, and discriminatory practices.

9. Psychologists working with culturally diverse populations should document culturally and sociopolitically relevant factors in the records. These may include, but are not limited to:

   a. number of generations in the country

   b. number of years in the country

   c. fluency in English

   d. extent of family support

   e. community resources

   f. level of education

   g. change in social status as a result of coming to this country (for immigrants or refugee)

   h. intimate relationship with people of different backgrounds

   i. level of stress related to acculturation. (APA, 1990)

These guidelines provide an outline of areas that are important to consider when working with ethnically and linguistically diverse individuals. They require therapists to recognize and respect the values, beliefs, and mores of a client's culture. The authors, throughout the book, demonstrate many of the principles embodied in the APA guidelines. They recognize the importance that culture and ethnicity have on the therapeutic process. As clearly illustrated in their case examples, the strategic interventions utilized by the authors incorporate social, environmental, and political factors relevant to the client. The authors recognize that prejudice and discrimination have had a tremendous impact on the world view of their clients, and they implement psychological interventions to address these issues.

The APA guidelines are important in that they provide the necessary components and building blocks toward developing cultural competency. As with any competency, the process is developmental. The therapist must first have an understanding of his or her own ethnicity and the values and beliefs of his or her culture. From this vantage point the therapist can then proceed to the stage of becoming culturally aware. This is achieved by acquiring a level of factual knowledge about the ethnic group one is working with. From the level of cultural awareness, a therapist can then evolve to the next level, which is cultural sensitivity. At this stage, a therapist effectively and intuitively understands the perspective of the client who is culturally different. The final step to becoming culturally competent is when a clinician is able to intervene effectively and appropriately with the clients, once having achieved and integrated cultural awareness and sensitivity. The process of cultural competency, thus, involves three factors. The first is the acknowledgement that a therapist enters the therapeutic process with his or her own cultural values, beliefs, and assumptions, and that this, in turn, influences the therapeutic process. Likewise, the client also comes into treatment with his or her own cultural orientation that has impacted on his or her psychological and behavioral perspective. The client's cultural background is the second variable that a therapist must become cognizant of. Finally, the therapist must understand the influence of the sociopolitical environment in which both the client and the therapist live. Incorporating these three factors—the therapist's awareness of his or her own cultural upbringing, the cultural upbringing of the client, and the social context in which they live—into the clinical training of therapists will create greater numbers of clinicians that are culturally aware, culturally sensitive, and culturally competent.

The need for cultural competency is what the authors demonstrate throughout this book. Each in his or her own style relates appropriate intervention strategies that are culturally competent yet distinct from one another. The authors' diverse perspectives on clinical interventions with clients illustrate that there is no singular approach to working with people who are culturally and ethnically different. Each author presents a theoretical and practical perspective to therapy that is reflective of his or her own cultural orientation. Jenkins provides a sociohistorical perspective toward treatment with African-Americans. The historical legacy of African-Americans is extremely important to the development of the social esteem, self-esteem, and identity of African-Americans. Therefore, an awareness of and sensitivity to the historical aspects of the African-American experience provide the necessary contextual framework from which to intervene diagnostically and therapeutically.

From a different vantage point, De La Cancela approaches treatment intervention from a sociopolitical orientation. For Latinos, the issues of colonization and imperialism have greater significance. Latinos from Central and South America as well as from the Caribbean have an extensive history of oppression under foreign rule. Thus, the realities surrounding political domination influence the psychological perspective of both the therapist and the client who come from a Latino culture.

As an Asian-American, Chin also provides a cultural framework for treatment that is in keeping with her cultural orientation. The desire for harmony and equilibrium in life is a cultural value esteemed within the Asian community. Chin's approach is to understand the cultural clashes that are encountered by ethnically different group members within this country and to find ways to achieve homeostasis. The concept of world view holds that people possess different perspectives due to their cultural upbringing and that these differences need to be honored and can coexist in harmony with one another.

All the authors propose distinct yet culturally appropriate interventions with their respective ethnic groups. They demonstrate a number of important and relevant concerns. First, it is not ethically appropriate to assume that the therapeutic approaches designed for European-American clients will meet the needs of other ethnically different group members. Utilization and dropout studies clearly show that people of color discontinue or do not access those services that are not culturally appropriate (Cheung, 1991). It is imperative that therapists realize that culture and ethnicity are variables that impact our lives and determine, to varying extent, how people think, feel, and behave. Second, there is no singular theoretical approach to working with people of different cultural backgrounds. However, it is important that therapists become culturally aware, culturally sensitive, and culturally competent. Third, cultural competence requires that a therapist reflect on the impact of his or her culture on the therapeutic process, the impact of the client's culture, as well as the impact of the sociopolitical environment that both parties share.

The demands on the knowledge and skills of a therapist are changing. This change is being ushered in by the reconfiguration of the demographic composition taking place in the United States. As greater numbers of ethnically diverse groups enter the workplace and assume greater economic influence within the United States, the therapeutic marketplace will turn its attention to the needs of these individuals. This will result in an increased awareness and appreciation of cultural differences. Currently, society is undergoing this transition. There is a growing desire and need to recruit more ethnically distinct group members into the mental health fields. Unfortunately, mental health professions have not been proactive in achieving cultural diversity representation within their ranks. Psychology, for example, has not increased its percentage of African-American, Latino, and Asian-American professionals in over fifteen years (Guzman, 1991; Guzman, Schiavo, & Puente, in press). With a growing ethnically diverse population and an inadequate supply of mental health professionals representative of these groups, there will be a need to train all therapists to become culturally competent. The manner in which we are training our clinicians will have to change. Not only must our training programs develop therapists that are clinically competent but they must also be culturally competent. In fact, given our changing society, it will be difficult to be clinically competent without being culturally competent.

As the twenty-first century approaches, the sheer numbers in society of those who are ethnically, culturally, and linguistically different will necessitate greater attention to their needs and concerns. The result will be the provision of mental health services that are culturally appropriate. Theoretical orientations for working with ethnically different clients will flourish. Jenkins, De La Cancela, and Chin provide an excellent example of a variety of theoretical approaches that are effective in providing culturally competent interventions with ethnically diverse clients. This book presents the direction that needs to be taken in the future in order to develop culturally competent therapists to work in a multicultural and pluralistic society.

REFERENCES

American Psychological Association (APA) (1990). *Guidelines for providers of psychological services to ethnic, linguistic, and culturally diverse populations.* Washington, DC: APA.

Bernal, M. E., & Padilla, A. M. (1982). Status of minority curricula and training in clinical psychology. *American Psychologist*, 37(7), 780–87.

Cheung, F. K. (1991). The use of mental health services by ethnic minorities. In H. F. Myers, P. Wohlford, L. P. Guzman, & R. J. Echemendia (Eds.), *Ethnic minority perspectives on clinical training and services in psychology.* Washington, DC: American Psychological Association, 23–31.

Copeland, L. (1988). Valuing workplace diversity. *Personnel Administrator*, 33(11), 38–40.

Guzman, L. P. (1991). Incorporating cultural diversity into psychology training programs. In H. F. Myers, P. Wohlford, L. P. Guzman, & R. J. Echemendia (Eds.), *Ethnic minority perspectives on clinical training and services in psychology.* Washington, DC: American Psychological Association, 67–70.

Guzman, L. P., Schiavo, R. S., & Puente, A. E. (in press). Ethnic minorities in the teaching of psychology. In A. E. Puente, J. R. Matthews, C. L. Brewer (Eds.), *Teaching psychology in America: A history.* Washington, DC: American Psychological Association.

Kohout, J., & Pion, G. (1990). Participation of ethnic minorities in psychology: Where do we stand today? In G. Stricker, E. Davis-Russell, E. Bourg, E. Duran, W. R. Hammond, J. McHolland, K. Polite, & B. E. Vaughn (Eds.), *Toward ethnic diversification in psychology education and training.* Washington, DC: American Psychological Association, 153–65.

Sanchez, A. M., Demmler, J., & Davis, M. (1990). *Toward pluralism in the mental health disciplines: Status of minority student recruitment and retention in the western states.* Boulder, CO: Western Interstate Commission for Higher Education.

U.S. Department of Commerce News (1991). *Census Bureau releases 1990 census count on specific racial groups* (Released June 12: CB91–215). Washington, DC: U.S. Government Printing Office.

BIBLIOGRAPHY

Acosta, F. X., Yamamoto, J., & Evans, L. (1982). *Effective psychotherapy with low income and minority patients.* New York: Plenum.

Adams, D. (1983). Men unlearning violence: A group approach for abusive husbands. Paper presented at the annual meeting of the American Orthopsychiatric Association, April 1. Boston.

Adams, D. (1984). Stages of anti-sexist awareness and change for men who batter. Paper presented at the 92nd Annual Convention of the American Psychological Association, August 24. Toronto.

Ahuna, C., Cornell, G., Fong, J., Tanaka, C. A., & Yang, J. (1991). Graduate students' perspective on cultural diversity. *Focus: Notes from the Society for the Psychological Study of Ethnic Minority Issues,* 5(2), 9–10.

Albee, G. (1977). Does including psychotherapy in health insurance represent a subsidy to the rich from the poor? *American Psychologist,* 32, 719–21.

Albee, G. (1986). Toward a just society: Lessons from observations on the primary prevention of psychopathology. *American Psychologist,* 41, 891–98.

Alvarado, R. (1976). *Racism, elitism, professionalism: Barriers to community mental health.* New York: Aronson, Inc.

American Psychiatric Association (1989). *Treatments of psychiatric disorders: A task force report of the American Psychiatric Association.* Washington, DC: APA.

American Psychological Association (1990). *Guidelines for providers of psychological services to ethnic, linguistic, and culturally diverse populations.* Washington, DC: APA.

Aponte, H. (1971). The family school interview: An ecostructural approach. *Family Process,* 15(3), 303–11.

Aponte, H. (1976). Under-organization in the poor family. *Family therapy: Theory and practice.* New York: Gardner Press, 432–48.

Arce, A. (1982). Cultural aspects of mental health care for Hispanic Americans. In A. Gaw (Ed.), *Cross cultural psychiatry.* Littleton, MA: Wright-PSG, 137–48.

Arenas, S., Cross, H., & Willard, W. (1980). Curanderos and mental health professionals: A comparative study on perception of psychopathology. *Hispanic Journal of Behavioral Sciences*, 2, 345–64.

Atkinson, D. R., Morten, G., & Sue, D. W. (1989). A minority identity development model. In D. R. Atkinson, G. Morten, & D. W. Sue (Eds.), *Counseling American minorities: A cross-cultural perspective*. Dubuque, IA: W. C. Brown, 35–52.

Axelson, J. A. (1985). *Counseling and development in a multicultural society*. Belmont, CA: Brooks/Cole.

Bass, B. A., Wyatt, G. E., & Powell, G. J. (1982). *The Afro-American family: Assessment, treatment and research issues*. New York: Grune & Stratton.

Beck, A. T. (1976). *Cognitive therapy and the emotional disorders*. New York: International Universities Press.

Becker, D., Lira, E., Castillo, M. I., Gome, E., & Kovalskys, J. (1990). Therapy with victims of political repression in Chile: The challenge of social reparation. *Journal of Social Issues*, 46(3), 133–49.

Bednar, R. L., Wells, M. G., & Peterson, S. R. (1989). *Self-esteem: Paradoxes and innovations in clinical theory and practice*. Washington, DC: American Psychological Association.

Bergin, A. E., & Garfield, S. L. (1971). *Psychotherapy and behavior change: An empirical analysis*. New York: John Wiley & Sons.

Bernal, M. E., & Padilla, A. M. (1982). Status of minority curricula and training in clinical psychology. *American Psychologist*, 37(7), 780–87.

Bieliauskas, V. J. (1977). Mental health care in the USSR. *American Psychologist*, 32(5), 374–79.

Bly, R., & Tannen, D. (1992). Where are women and men today? *New Age Journal*, January/February, 28–32, 92–97.

Boyd-Franklin, N. (Ed.) (1989). *Black families in therapy*. New York: Guilford Press.

Brecher, J. (1977). Sex, stress and health. *International Journal of Health Services*, 7, 89–101.

Brooks, G. R. (1989). Status of the men's movement within the professions. *National Organization of Changing Men: Men and Mental Health Task Group Newsletter*, 1(1), 5–7.

Buhler, C. (1962). *Values in psychotherapy*. New York: The Free Press.

Camayd-Freixas, Y., & Uriarte, M. (1980). The organization of mental health services in Cuba. *Hispanic Journal of Behavioral Sciences*, 2, 337–54.

Canino, I., et al. (1991). Letter to the editor. *American Journal of Psychiatry*, 148(4), 543–44.

Carabajal, J. (1991). Mentoring and the collective experience: A case in point. *Focus: Notes from the Society for the Psychological Study of Ethnic Minority Issues*, 5(1), 3–5.

Caro Hollander, N. (1987). Marxism, psychoanalysis and feminism: A view from Latin-America. *Women & Therapy*, 6(4), 87–108.

Carrillo, J. E. (1988). AIDS and the Latino community. *Centro de Estudios Puertorriquenos Bulletin*, 2(4), 7–14.

Carrillo, J. E., & De La Cancela, V. (1992). The Cambridge Hospital Latino health clinic: A model for interagency integration of health services for Latinos at the provider level. *Journal of the National Medical Association*, 84(6), 178–82.

Chan, C. S. (1988). Asian-American women: Psychological responses to sexual exploitation and cultural stereotypes. In L. Fulani (Ed.), *The psychopathology of everyday racism and sexism*. New York: Harrington Press, 33–38.

Chapman, A. (1988). Male-female relations: How the past affects the present. In H. McAdoo (Ed.), *Black families*. Newbury Park, CA: Sage Publications, 190–200.

Cheung, F. K. (1991). The use of mental health services by ethnic minorities. In H. F. Myers, P. Wohlford, L. P. Guzman, & R. J. Echemendia (Eds.), *Ethnic minority perspectives on clinical training and services in psychology*. Washington, DC: American Psychological Association, 23–31.

Chin, J. L. (1981). Institutional racism and mental health: An Asian American perspective. In O. A. Barbarin, P. R. Good, O. M. Pharr, & J. A. Siskind (Eds.), *Institutional racism and community competence*. Washington, DC: U.S. Government Printing Office, 44–55.

Chin, J. L. (in press). Transference. In J. L. Chin, J. H. Liem, M. Domokos-Cheng Ham, & G. K. Hong, (Eds.), *Transference and empathy in Asian-American psychotherapy*. Westport, CT: Praeger.

Comas-Díaz, L. (1988). Feminist therapy with Hispanic/Latina women: Myth or reality? In L. Fulani (Ed.), *The psychopathology of everyday racism and sexism*. New York: Harrington Press, 39–62.

Comas-Díaz, L. (1990). Hispanic/Latino communities: Psychological implications. *Journal of Training & Practice in Professional Psychology*, 4(1), 14–35.

Comas-Díaz, L. (1982). Mental health needs of mainland Puerto Rican women. In R. E. Zambrana (Ed.), *Work, family and health: Latina women in transition*. New York: Hispanic Research Center, Fordham University, 1–10.

Comas-Díaz, L., & Griffith, E.E.H. (Eds.) (1988). *Clinical guidelines in cross-cultural mental health*. New York: John Wiley & Sons.

Comas-Díaz, L., & Minrath, M. (1985). Psychotherapy with ethnic minority borderline clients. *Psychotherapy*, 22(2S), 416–18.

Commissioner's Task Force (CTF) (1991). *The Commissioner's Task Force report on mental health services for children and adolescents*. New York: Department of Mental Health, Mental Retardation and Alcoholism Services.

Copeland, L. (1988). Valuing workplace diversity. *Personnel Administrator*, 33(11), 38–40.

Cross, T. L., Bazron, B. J., Dennis, K. W., and Isaacs, M. R. (1989). *Towards a culturally competent system of care*. Washington, DC: CASSP Technical Assistance Center, Georgetown University Child Development Center.

Cross, W. E., Jr. (1971). The negro-to-black conversion experience: Towards a psychology of black liberation. *Black World*, 20, 13–27.

Dana, R. H. (Ed.) (1993). *Multicultural assessment perspectives for professional psychology*. Needham Heights, MA: Allyn & Bacon.

Davis, A. (1981). *Women, race and class*. New York: Random House.

DeFour, D. C. (1991). Issues in mentoring ethnic minority students. *Focus: Notes from the Society for the Psychological Study of Ethnic Minority Issues*, 5(1), 1–2.

De La Cancela, E., & De La Cancela, V. (1989). "La Bodega": A natural support system in mainland Puerto Rican communities. *El Boletin: Newsletter of the National Hispanic Psychological Association*, 6(2), 3–6.

De La Cancela, V. (1993). "Coolin' ": The psychosocial communication of African and Latino men. *Urban League Review*, 16(12).

De La Cancela, V. (1991). The endangered black male: Reversing the trend for African-American and Latino males. *Journal of Multi-Cultural Community Health*, 1(1), 16–19.

De La Cancela, V. (1992). Keeping African-American & Latino males alive: Policy and program initiatives in health. *Journal of Multi-Cultural Community Health*, 2(1), 31–39.

De La Cancela, V. (1988). Labor pains: Puerto Rican males in transition. *Centro de Estudios Puertorriquenos Bulletin*, 2(4), 40–55.

De La Cancela, V. (1990). Latino CMI males: Social therapy approaches. *The Clinical Psychologist*, 43(5), 74–77.

De La Cancela, V. (1990). Letter to the editor. Unpublished manuscript.

De La Cancela, V. (1989). Minority AIDS prevention: Moving beyond cultural perspectives towards sociopolitical empowerment. *AIDS Education and Prevention*, 1(2), 89–95.

De La Cancela, V. L. (1978). On being a minority student in clinical psychology. *Journal of Contemporary Psychotherapy*, 9(2), 178–82.

De La Cancela, V. (1991). Progressive counseling with Latino refugees and families. *Journal of Progressive Human Services*, 2(2), 19–34.

De La Cancela, V. (1985). Psychotherapy: A political act. *Practice: The Journal of Politics, Economics, Psychology, Sociology and Culture*, 3(3), 48–52.

De La Cancela, V. (1991). Salsa and control: An AmeRican Response to Latino health care needs. *Journal of Multi-Cultural Community Health*, 1(2), 23–29.

De La Cancela, V. (1989). Salud, dinero, y amor: Beyond wishing Latinos good health. *Practice: The Journal of Politics, Economics, Psychology, Sociology and Culture*, 6(3) & 7(1), 81–94.

De La Cancela, V. (1985). Towards a sociocultural psychotherapy for low-income ethnic minorities. *Psychotherapy*, 22(2S), 427–35.

De La Cancela, V. (1991). Working affirmatively with Puerto Rican men: Professional and personal reflections. *Journal of Feminist Family Therapy*, 2(3/4), 195–211.

De La Cancela, V., Guarnaccia, P. J., & Carrillo, E. (1986). Psychosocial distress among Latinos: A critical analysis of *Ataques de Nervios*. *Humanity and Society*, 10, 431–47.

De La Cancela, V., & Guzman, L. P. (1991). Latino mental health service needs: Implications for training psychologists. In H. F. Myers, P. Wohlford, L. P. Guzman, & R. J. Echemendia (Eds.), *Ethnic minority perspectives on clinical training and services in psychology*. Washington, DC: American Psychological Association, 59–64.

De La Cancela, V., & McDowell, A. (1992). AIDS: Health care intervention models for communities of color. *Journal of Multi-Cultural Social Work*, 2(3), 107–22.

De La Cancela, V., & Sotomayor, G. M. (1992). Rainbow warriors: Reducing institutional racism in mental health. *Journal of Mental Health Counseling*, 15(1), 55–71.

De La Cancela, V. L., & Závala-Martínez, I. (1983). As analysis of culturalism in Latino mental health: Folk medicine as a case in point. *Hispanic Journal of Behavioral Sciences*, 5(3), 251–74.

de la Vega, E. (1990). Considerations for reaching the Latino population with sexuality and HIV/AIDS information and education. *SIECUS Report*, 18(3), 1–8.

Delgado, M. (1983). Hispanic and psychotherapeutic groups. *International Journal of Group Psychotherapy*, 33, 507–20.

Derbort, J. (1992). Racism, bias, and barriers in psychotherapy: The white therapist-client of color experience. *Journal of Multi-Cultural Community Health*, 2(1), 22–25.

Dudley, G. R., & Rawlins, M. R. (1985). Special issue: Psychotherapy with ethnic minorities. *Psychotherapy*, 22(2S).

Eichler, J. M. (1989). What are men's issues? Paper presented at Men's Issues Course, Cambridge Hospital Department of Psychiatry, January 21. Cambridge, MA.

Espinoza, J. (n.d.). Untitled poem.

Franklin, J. H., & Moss, A. A., Jr. (1988). *From slavery to freedom*. New York: Alfred A. Knopf.

Fulani, L. (1988). All power to the people! But how? In L. Fulani (Ed.), *The psychopathology of everyday racism and sexism*. New York: Harrington Press, xi–xix.

Fulani, L. (Ed.) (1987). *The politics of race and gender in therapy*. New York: Haworth Press.

Fulani, L. (1988). Poor women of color do great therapy. In L. Fulani (Ed.), *The psychopathology of everyday racism and sexism*. New York: Harrington Press, 111–20.

Garcia-Preto, N. (1982). Puerto Rican families. In M. McGoldrick, J. K. Pearce, & J. Giordano (Eds.), *Ethnicity and family therapy*. New York: Guilford Press, 164–86.

Gardner, L. (1980). Racial, ethnic and social class considerations in psychotherapy supervision. In A. Hess (Ed.), *Psychotherapy supervision: Theory, research and practice*. New York: John Wiley, 474–508.

Gibbs, J. T. (1987). Identity and marginality: Issues in the treatment of biracial adolescents. *American Journal of Orthopsychiatry*, 57, 265–78.

Gil, D. (1978). Clinical practice and the politics of human liberation. *Catalyst: A Socialist Journal of the Social Services*, 2, 61–69.

Gordon, J. S. (1990). Holistic medicine and mental health practice: Towards a new synthesis. *American Journal of Orthopsychiatry*, 60(3), 357–70.

Grier, W., & Cobbs, P. (1968). *Black rage*. New York: Bantam Books.

Guarnaccia, P. J., De La Cancela V., and Carillo, E. The multiple meanings of *ataques de nervios* in the Latino community. *Medical Anthropology*, 2, 47–62.

Guzman, L. P. (1991). Incorporating cultural diversity into psychology training programs. In H. F. Myers, P. Wohlford, L. P. Guzman, & R. J. Echemendia (Eds.), *Ethnic minority perspectives on clinical training and services in psychology*. Washington, DC: American Psychological Association, 67–70.

Guzman, L. P., Schiavo, R. S., & Puente, A. E. (in press). Ethnic minorities in the teaching of psychology. In A. E. Puente, J. R. Matthews, & C. L.

Brewer (Eds.), *Teaching psychology in America: A history*. Washington, DC: American Psychological Association.

Guzman, P. Y. (1980). Puerto Rican barrio politics in the United States. In C. E. Rodriguez, V. Sanchez Korrol, & J. O. Alers (Eds.), *The Puerto Rican struggle: Essays on survival in the U.S.* New York: Puerto Rican Migration Research Consortium, 121–28.

Habach, E. (1972). *Ni machismo, ni hembrismo (Neither machismo nor hembrismo)*. Coleccion: Protesta. Caracas: Publicaciones EPLA.

Haley, A. (1976). *Roots*. New York: Doubleday.

Hall, E. T. (1976). How cultures collide. *Psychology Today*, July, 66–97.

Hall, R., & Sandler, B. (1983). *Academic mentoring for women students and faculty: 65A new look at an old way to get ahead*. Washington, DC: Project on the Status and Education of Women.

Hammond, V. W. (1988). "Conscious subjectivity" or use of one's self in therapeutic process. In L. Fulani (Ed.), *The psychopathology of everyday racism and sexism*. New York: Harrington Press, 75–82.

Hammond, V. W. (1987). "Conscious subjectivity" or use of one's self in therapeutic process. *Women & Therapy*, 6(4), 75–81.

Heine, J., & Garcia-Passalacqua, J. M. (1983). *The Puerto Rican question*. New York: Foreign Policy Association.

Hines, P., & Franklin, H. (1982). Black families. In M. McGoldrick, J. K. Pearce, and J. Giordano (Eds.), *Ethnicity and family therapy*. New York: Guilford Press, 84–107.

Hopps, J. (1982). Oppression based on color. *Social Work*, 27(1), 3–5.

Howard, G. S. (1991). A narrative approach to thinking, cross-cultural psychology, and psychotherapy. *American Psychologist*, 46(3), 187–97.

Howell, R. M. (1990). Native Americans, stereotypes and HIV/AIDS: Our continuing struggle for survival. *SIECUS Report*, 18(3), 9–15.

Ibrahim, F. A. (1985). Effectiveness in cross-cultural counseling and psychotherapy: A framework. *Psychotherapy*, 22(2S), 321–23.

Inclan, J. (1982). Interpersonal relations among Puerto Rican men: Or, why so much dominoes? Paper presented at the 59th annual meeting of the American Orthopsychiatric Association, March 29. San Francisco.

Inclan, J. (1985). Variations in value orientations in mental health work with Puerto Ricans. *Psychotherapy*, 22(2S), 324–34.

Iwasaki, T. (1971). Discussion, cultural aspects of transference and countertransference by G. Ticho. *Bulletin of the Menninger Clinic*, 35(5), 330–34.

Jack, D. (1987). Silencing the self: The power of social imperatives in female depression. In R. Formanek & A. Gurian (Eds.), *Women and depression: A lifetime perspective*. New York: Springer Press, 161–81.

Jenkins, A. H. (1985). Attending to self-activity in the Afro-American client. *Psychotherapy*, 22(2S), 335–41.

Jenkins, Y. M. (1983). Dissonant expectations: Professional competency vs. personal incompetency. *Aware*, 1(1), 6–13.

Jones, A. C. (1985). Psychological functioning in black Americans: A conceptual guide for use in psychotherapy. *Psychotherapy*, 22(2), 363–69.

Jones, E. E., & Korchin, S. (1982). *Minority mental health*. New York: Praeger.

Jones, F. (1980). The black psychologist as consultant and therapist. In R. L. Jones (Ed.), *Black psychology*. New York: Harper & Row.

Jones, H. (1981). *Bad blood: The Tuskegee syphilis experiment*. New York: Free Press. Quoted in H. Bulhan (1985). *Frantz Fanon and the psychology of oppression*. New York: Plenum Press, 87.

Kaplan, H. S. (1974). *The new sex therapy*. New York: Brunner/Mazel.

Kardiner, A., & Ovesey, L. (1951). *The mark of oppression*. Cleveland: World Publishing.

Karsau, T. B. (1991). Letter to the editor. *American Journal of Psychiatry*, 148(4), 544.

Keefe, S. W., Padilla, A. M., & Carlos, M. L. (1978). *Emotional support systems in two cultures: A comparison of Mexican-Americans and Anglo-Americans*. Occasional Paper no. 7. Los Angeles: University of California, Spanish Speaking Mental Health Research Center.

Kluckhohn, F. R., & Strodbeck, F. L. (1961). *Variations in value orientations*. Evanston, IL: Row, Peterson.

Kohout, J., & Pion, G. (1990). Participation of ethnic minorities in psychology: Where do we stand today? In G. Stricker, E. Davis-Russell, E. Bourg, E. Duran, W. R. Hammond, J. McHolland, K. Polite, & B. E. Vaughn (Eds.), *Toward ethnic diversification in psychology education and training*. Washington, DC: American Psychological Association, 153–65.

Kuhn, T. (1970). *The structure of scientific revolutions*. Chicago: University of Chicago Press.

La Due, R. (1991). Coyote returns: Lessons from the trickster. *Focus: Notes from the Society for the Psychological Study of Ethnic Minority Issues*, 5(1), 10–11.

La Due, R. (1990). An Indian by any other name or don't "Kemo Sabe" me, Tonto. *Focus: Notes from the Society for the Psychological Study of Ethnic Minority Issues*, 4(2), 10–11.

La Franiere, S. (1992). U.S. court overrules return of Haitians. *The Boston Globe*, July 30, 1, 5.

La Viera, T. (1985). *AmeRican*. Houston: Arte Publico.

Lefley, H. (1986). Why cross-cultural training? Applies issues in culture and mental health service delivery. In H. Lefley & P. Pedersen (Eds.), *Cross-cultural training for mental health professionals*. Springfield, IL: Charles C. Thomas, 11–37.

Lerner, H. G. (1985). *The dance of anger*. New York: Harper & Row.

LeVine, E. S., & Padilla, A. M. (1980). *Crossing cultures in therapy: Pluralistic counseling for the Hispanic*. Monterey, CA: Brooks/Cole.

Liebert, R. S. (1986). The history of male homosexuality from ancient Greece through the Renaissance: Implications for psychoanalytic theory. In G. I. Fogel, F. M. Lane, & R. S. Liebert (Eds.), *The psychology of men: New psychoanalytic perspectives*. New York: Basic Books, 181–210.

London, P. (1986). *The modes and morals of psychotherapy*, 2nd ed. Washington, DC: Hemisphere.

Loo, C. (1989). Eliminating the harm of racism: An analysis of the Civil Liberties Act (HR 442) and the presidential campaign of the Reverend Jesse Jackson. *Focus on Ethnic Minority Psychology*, 3(1), 5.

Lowe, C. M. (1976). *Value orientations in counseling and psychotherapy: The meanings of mental health*, 2nd ed. Cranston, RI: Carroll Press.

Ludwig, S., & Hingsburger, D. (1989). Preparation for counseling and psychotherapy: Teaching about feelings. *Psychiatric Aspects of Mental Retardation Reviews*, 8(1), 1–7.

Luepnitz, D. A. (1988). *The family interpreted: Feminist theory in clinical practice*. New York: Basic Books.

Lum, D. (1986). *Social work practice and people of color*. Monterey, CA: Brooks/Cole.

Lykes, M. B., & Liem, R. (1990). Human rights and mental health in the United States: Lessons from Latin America. *Journal of Social Issues*, 46(3), 151–65.

Majors, R., & Bilson, J. M. (1992). *Cool pose: The dilemmas of black manhood in America*. New York: Lexington Books.

Maldonado-Denis, M. (1972). *Puerto Rico: A social historical interpretation*. New York: Random House.

Maslow, A. (1954). *Motivation and personality*. New York: Harper & Row.

Matlin, N. (1976). *Modelos conceptuales para supervision de consejeros*. San Juan: Psicologos de Puerto Rico Asociados.

McGoldrick, M., & Gerson, R. (1985). *Genograms in family assessment*. New York: W. W. Norton.

McGoldrick, M., Pearce, J. K., & Giordano, J. (Eds.) (1982). *Ethnicity and family therapy*. New York: Guilford Press.

McIntosh, P. (1988). *White privilege and male privilege: A personal account of coming to see correspondences through work in women's studies*. Working Paper. Wellesley, MA: Wellesley College, Center for Research on Women, 189.

Mederos, F. (1987). Patriarchy and the psychology of men. Unpublished manuscript.

Meeks, K. (1992). Congressman Rangel calls for health care for all Americans at forum. *New York Amsterdam Times*, February 1, 11.

Miller, J. B. (1976). *Toward a new psychology of women*. Boston: Beacon Press.

Milville, M. (1991). Personal and professional perspectives on mentoring and the VREG graduate student. *Focus: Notes from the Society for the Psychological Study of Ethnic Minority Issues*, 5(1), 14.

Minuchin, S. (1974). *Families and family therapy*. Cambridge, MA: Harvard University Press.

Montero, M. (1990). Ideology and psychosocial research in Third World contexts. *Journal of Social Issues*, 46(3), 43–55.

Moreno Vega, M. (1992). The politics of art. *Under One Sun: News and Events of the Caribbean Cultural Center*, Winter, 1–3.

Morten, G., & Atkinson, D. R. (1983). Minority identity development and preference for counselor race. *Journal of Negro Education*, 52, 156–61.

Munder Ross, J. (1986). Beyond the phallic illusion: Notes on man's heterosexuality. In G. I. Fogel, F. M. Lane, & R. S. Liebert (Eds.), *The psychology of men: New psychoanalytic perspectives*. New York: Basic Books, 49–70.

Myers, L. W. (1980). *Black women. Do they cope better?* Englewood Cliffs, NJ: Prentice-Hall.

National Association for the Advancement of Colored People (NAACP) &

TransAfrica (1992). Letter recruiting participants for demonstration of civil disobedience to protest treatment of Haitian refugees, July 10.

Nelson, C., & Tienda, M. (1988). The structure of Hispanic ethnicity: Historical and contemporary perspectives. In. R. D. Alba (Ed.), *Ethnicity and race in the U.S.A.: Toward the twenty-first century*. New York: Routledge, 49–74.

Okazawa-Rey, M., Robinson, R., & Ward, J. V. (1988). Black women and the politics of skin color and hair. In M. Braude (Ed.), *Women, power, and therapy*. New York: Harrington Press, 89–102.

Okonogi as quoted by Tatara (1980), as cited by Yamamoto, J. (1982). *Beyond Buddhism*. Downers Grove, IL: Intervarsity Press.

Oler, C. (1989). Psychotherapy with black clients' racial identity and locus of control. *Psychotherapy*, 26(2), 233–41.

Osherson, S. (1986). *Finding our fathers: The unfinished business of manhood*. New York: Free Press.

Oskamp, S. (1990). *The editor's page. Journal of Social Issues*, 46(3), iv–v.

Padilla, A. M., & Ruiz, R. (1973). *Latino mental health: A review of literature*. Rockville, MD: National Institute of Mental Health.

Paludi, M. A., DeFour, D. C., Braithwaite, J., Chan, B., Garvey, C., Kramer, N., Lawrence, D., & Haring-Hidore, M. (1991). Academic mentoring for women: Issues of sex, power and politics. *Focus: Notes from the Society for the Psychological Study of Ethnic Minority Issues*, 5(1), 7–8.

Pares-Avile, J. (1987). AIDS in the Latino community: A call for action. *El Boletin: Newsletter of the National Hispanic Psychological Association*, 4(2), 8–9.

Parker, S. (1988). Why "women of color." In *National Institute for Women of Color Network News*. Washington, DC: National Institute for Women of Color, 1–2.

Peoples Press Puerto Rico Project (1977). *Puerto Rico: The flame of resistance*. San Juan: Peoples Press.

Peters, M. (1981). Parenting in black families with young children: A historical perspective. Quoted in N. Boyd-Franklin (Ed.) (1989), *Black families in therapy*. New York: Guilford Press, 118–19.

Peterson, W. (1978). Chinese Americans and Japanese Americans. In T. Sowell (Ed.), *American ethnic groups*. Washington, DC: Urban Institute Press, 65–106.

Pinderhughes, E. B. (1982). Afro-American families and the victim system. In M. McGoldrick, J. K. Pearce, and J. Giordano (Eds.), *Ethnicity and family therapy*. New York: Guilford Press, 108–22.

Pinderhughes, E. B. (1982). Minority women: A nodal position in the functioning of the social system. In M. Ault-Riche (Ed.), *Women and family therapy*. 51–63.

Pinderhughes, E. B. (1989). *Understanding race, ethnicity, and power*. New York: Free Press.

Pleck, J. H. (1984). Men's power with women, other men and society: A men's movement analysis. In P. Rieker & E. Carmen (Eds.), *The gender gap in psychotherapy*. New York: Plenum, 79–89.

Powell, G. J., & Fuller, M. (1973). *Black Monday's children: A study of the effect of school desegregation on self-concepts of southern children*. New York: Appleton-Century-Crofts.

Ramirez, O. (1983). Book review: Ethnicity and family therapy. *La Red/The Net: Newsletter of the National Chicano Council on Higher Education*, 66 (March), 28–30.

Ramos-McKay, J. M., Comas-Diaz, L., & Rivera, L. A. (1988). Puerto Ricans: In L. Comas-Diaz, and E.E.H. Griffith (Eds.), *Clinical guidelines in cross-cultural mental health*. New York: John Wiley & Sons, 204–32.

Rappaport, M. (1974). Treating the whole man: Integrating mental health into the mainstream of service. *Hospital & Community Psychiatry*, 25(4), 245–46.

Ratner, C. (1978). Mental illness in the People's Republic of China. *Far East Reporter*, February, 80–84.

Report of the Secretary's Task Force on Black and Minority Health (1986). *Volume VIII: Hispanic health/inventory survey*. Washington, DC: U.S. Department of Health and Human Services.

Reyes, J. (1989). A study of the mental health treatment of Puerto Rican migrants. Ph.D. dissertation, Department of Educational Foundation, University of Cincinnati.

Reyes, J. (1987). Treatment modalities and the Puerto Rican migrant. Unpublished manuscript.

Rivera, C. (1986). Research issues: Posthospitalization adjustment of chronically mentally ill Hispanic patients. *Research Bulletin: Hispanic Research Center*, 9(1), 1–9.

Rodriguez, C. E. (1991). Another way of looking at race. *The Boston Sunday Globe*, May 12, 69–70.

Rodriguez, C. E. (1980). Puerto Ricans: Between black and white. In C. E. Rodriguez, V. Sanchez Korrol, & J. O. Alers (Eds.), *The Puerto Rican struggle: Essays on survival in the U.S.* New York: Puerto Rican Migration Research Consortium, 20–30.

Rodriguez, O. (1983). Barriers to clinical services among chronically mentally ill Hispanics. *Research Bulletin: Hispanic Research Center*, 3(4), 2–14.

Rodriguez, O. (1985). Overcoming barriers to clinical services among chronically mentally ill Hispanics: Lessons from the evaluation of the project COPA demonstration. *Research Bulletin: Hispanic Research Center*, 9(1), 9–15.

Rodriguez, S. (1992). Multiculturalism: A third generation approach to managing diversity. *EAPA Exchange*, (March), 14–19.

Root, M.P.P. (1985). Guidelines for facilitating therapy with Asian American clients. *Psychotherapy*, 22(2), 349–56.

Rosenbaum, M. (Ed.) (1982). *Ethics and values in psychotherapy: A guidebook*. Riverside, NJ: The Free Press.

Rosenberg, M., & Simmons, R. G. (1972). *Black and white self-esteem: The urban school child*. Washington, DC: American Sociological Association.

Ruiz, R. A. (1982). Mental health, Hispanics and service. *La Red/The Net: Newsletter of the National Chicano Council on Higher Education*, 61(November), 3–7.

Sacks, J. L. (1992). After the riots: Counselors essential in the healing process. *Guidepost*, 34(14), 1.

Sacks, M. H. (1981). Book review, Psychotherapy supervision: Theory, research and practice. *American Journal of Psychiatry*, 138(2), 267–68.

Sanchez, A. M., Demmler, J., & Davis, M. (1990). *Toward pluralism in the mental health disciplines: Status of minority student recruitment and retention in the western states.* Boulder, CO: Western Interstate Commission for Higher Education.

Schafer, R. (1986). Men who struggle against sentimentality. In G. I. Fogel, F. M. Lane, & R. S. Liebert (Eds.), *The psychology of men: New psychoanalytic perspectives.* New York: Basic Books, 95–110.

Schofield, W. (1964). *Psychotherapy: The purchase of friendship.* Englewood Cliffs, NJ: Prentice-Hall.

Shon, S., & Ja, D. (1982). Asian families: In M. McGoldrick, J. K. Pearce, & J. Giordano (Eds.), *Ethnicity and family therapy.* New York: Guilford Press, 208–28.

Silen, J. A. (1970). *We, the Puerto Rican people: A study of oppression and resistance.* New York: Monthly Review Press.

Simmons, R. G., Brown, L., Bush, D. M., & Blyth, D. A. (1978). Self-esteem and achievement of black and white adolescents. *Social Problems, 26,* 86–96.

Sloan, T. S. (1990). Psychology for the Third World? *Journal of Social Issues, 46*(3), 1–20.

Sluzki, C. E. (1982). The Latin lover revisited. In M. McGoldrick, J. K. Pearce, & J. Giordano (Eds.), *Ethnicity and family therapy.* New York: Guilford Press, 492–98.

Smith, A. (1990). Racism and sexism in black women's lives. Unpublished manuscript.

Solomon, B. (1976). Social work in multiethnic society. In M. Sotomayer (Ed.), *Cross-cultural perspectives in social work practice and education.* Council on Social Work Education, 176.

Stade, G. (1986). Dracula's women, and why men love to hate them. In G. I. Fogel, F. M. Lane, & R. S. Liebert (Eds.), *The psychology of men: New psychoanalytic perspectives.* New York: Basic Books, 25–48.

Staples, R. (1971). The myth of the impotent black male. *The Black Scholar,* June, 2–9.

Steele, S. (1990). *The content of our character.* New York: St. Martin's Press.

Steinmann, A., & Fox, D. J. (1970). Attitudes toward women's family role among black and white undergraduates. *The Family Coordinator, 19,* 363–68.

Sternbach, J. C. (1977). Men's awareness. *State and mind, 6*(1), 28–31.

Sternbach, J. C. (1989). The men's seminar: An educational and support group for men. Unpublished manuscript.

Stevens, E. (1973). Machismo and marianismo. *Transaction-Society, 10*(6), 57–63.

Stiver, I. (1990). *Dysfunctional families and wounded relationships—Part II.* Works in progress. Wellesley, MA: Wellesley College, Stone Center Working Papers Series, 44.

Strupp, H. H. (1980). Humanism and psychotherapy: A personal statement of the therapist's essential values. *Psychotherapy: Theory, Research, and Practice, 17,* 396–400.

Sue, D. W. (1992). Multiculturalism: The road less traveled. *American Counselor, 1*(1), 6–14.

Sue, D. W. (1978). World views and counseling. *Personnel and Guidance Journal*, 56, 458–62.

Sue, D. W., Richardson, E. I., Ruiz, R. A., & Smith, E. J. (1981). *Counseling the culturally different: Theory and practice*. New York: John Wiley & Sons.

Sue, D. W., & Sue, D. (1990). *Counseling the culturally different*. New York: John Wiley & Sons.

Sue, S. (1991). Changing needs for mentoring over the life span. *Focus: Notes from the Society for the Psychological Study of Ethnic Minority Issues*, 5(1), 6.

Sue, S. (1982). Ethnic minority issues in psychology. *American Psychologist*, 38, 583–92.

Sue, S., & McKinney, H. (1975). Asian Americans in the community mental health care system. *American Journal of Orthopsychiatry*, 45(1), 111–18.

Sue, S., & Morishima, J. K. (1982). *The mental health of Asian Americans*. San Francisco: Jossey-Bass.

Tennov, D. (1976). *Psychotherapy: The hazardous cure*. New York: Anchor Books.

Thomas, A., & Sillen, S. (1972). *Racism and psychiatry*. New York: Brunner/Mazel.

Thomas, M. B., & Dansby, P. G. (1985). Family structures, therapeutic issues, and strengths. *Psychotherapy*, 22(2S), 398–407.

Thomas, P. (1987). *Down these mean streets*. New York: Alfred A. Knopf.

Tinloy, M. (1978). Counseling Asian-Americans: A contrast in values. *Journal of Non-White Concerns in Personnel and Guidance*, 6(2), 71–77.

Tjeltveit, A. C. (1989). The ubiquity of models of human beings in psychotherapy: The need for rigorous reflection. *Psychotherapy*, 26(1), 1–10.

Tong, B. R. (1990). "Ornamental Orientals" and others: Ethnic labels in review. *Focus: Notes from the Society for the Psychological Study of Ethnic Minority Issues*, 4(2), 8–9.

Toupin, E. (1980). Counseling Asians: Psychotherapy in the context of racism and Asian-American history. *American Journal of Orthopsychiatry*, 50(1), 76–86.

Trimble, J. E. (1990). Application of psychological knowledge for American Indians and Alaska Natives. *Journal of Training & Practice in Professional Psychology*, 4(1), 45–63.

Tseng, W. (1973). The concept of personality in Confucian thought. *Psychiatry*, 36, 191–202.

Turner, C. (1987). *Clinical application of the Stone Center theoretical approach to minority women*. Works in progress, Wellesley, MA: Wellesley College, Stone Center Working Papers Series, 28.

Tyler, F. B., Brome, D., & Williams, J. (1991). *Ethnic validity, ecology and psychotherapy*. New York: Plenum Press.

Tyler, F. B., Sussewell, D. R., & Williams-McCoy, J. (1985). Ethnic validity in psychotherapy. *Psychotherapy*, 22(2S), 311–20.

U.S. Department of Commerce News (1991). *Census Bureau releases 1990 census count on specific racial groups* (released June 12: CB91–215). Washington, DC: U.S. Government Printing Office.

Valvidieso, R., & Davis, C. (1988). *Hispanics: Challenging issues for the 1990's*. Washington, DC: Population Reference Bureau.

Vazquez Erazo, B. (1987). The stories our mothers tell: Projections-of-self in the stories of Puerto Rican garment workers. In R. Benmayor, A. Juarabe, C.

Alvarez, & B. Vazquez (Eds.), *Stories to live by: Continuity and change in three generations of Puerto Rican women*. New York: Centro de Estudios Puertorriquenos.

Wagenheim, K. (1970). *Puerto Rico: A profile*. New York: Praeger.

Wagenheim, K., & Wagenheim, O. J. (Eds.) (1973). *The Puerto Ricans*. New York: Anchor Books.

Ward, D. (1991). Disputing the myth: The AIDS problem in the gay community has not been solved. *Journal of Multi-Cultural Community Health*, 1(2), 30–33.

Wong, M. O. (1988). The Chinese American family. In C. Mindel & R. W. Habenstein (Eds.), *Ethnic families in America: Patterns and variations*. New York: Elsevier, 230–57.

Wyatt, G. E. (1982). Identifying stereotypes of Afro-American sexuality and their impact upon sexual behavior. In B. A. Bass, G. E. Wyatt, & G. J. Powell (Eds.), *The Afro-American family: Assessment, treatment and research issues*. New York: Grune & Stratton, 333–46.

Yamamoto, J. (1978). Therapy for Asian-Americans. *Journal of the National Medical Association*, 70, 267–70.

Závala, I. M., & Rodriguez, R. (Eds.) (1980). *The intellectual roots of independence: An anthology of Puerto Rican political essays*. New York: Monthly Review Press.

Závala-Martínez, I. (1987). *En la lucha*: The economic and socioemotional struggles of Puerto Rican women. *Women & Therapy*, 6(4), 3–24.

Závala-Martínez, I. (1981). Personal communication.

Závala-Martínez, I. (1992). Personal communication.

Závala-Martínez, I. (1986). Praxis in psychology: Integrating clinical and community orientation with Latinos. *The Community Psychologist*, 9(2), 11.

Zuchman, L., Crespo, O., De La Cancela, V., & Spielman, A. (1987). A study of Puerto Rican espiritismo as a counseling adjunct in an East Harlem child welfare agency. *El Boletin: Newsletter of the National Hispanic Psychological Association*, 4(3), 5–7.

INDEX

Acculturation: as outcome, 73–74; vs. biculturalism, 78

Affirmative therapy, Puerto Rican male, 157–68

African-American men, 8, 178; limited availability of, 129–30

African-Americans, 8; antidiscriminatory legislation, 21–22; culture meaning, 33–34; discriminatory legislation, 20; gender roles, 35–36; historical overview, 18–23; meaning of ethnicity, 32; meaning of race, 31; postsixties sociopolitical climate, 22–23; segregation, 20–21; slavery, 18–21

African-American women, 117–34, 178; acknowledgment of personal strengths, 131; and black church, 122; dissonant expectations, 118; empowerment through self-activity, 130–34; extended family structure, 122; family dynamics, 126–28; imbalance between achievement/ work and family life, 121; interpersonal and problem-solving skills, 133–34; parent-child relationships, 122, 123; racism and sexism, 120–

21; self-differentation, 132; and self-esteem, 117–18; slavery, 119–20; societal role of families of color, 123–26; validation of social identity through social awareness, 132–33

Ajase complex vs. Oedipal complex, 88

Albee, G., 10

Alternatives vs. labeling, 80

Ambivalence, Chinese-American couple, 152

American label, 7

American Psychiatric Association, 98, 183, 184

Antidiscrimination legislation, African-Americans, 21–22

Asian-American males, 8

Asian-Americans, 82–89, 174; gender roles, 36

Asian themes, Chinese-American couple, 149–51

Assumptive framework, 70–71

Belongingness, individual vs. social, 87

Biculturation vs. acculturation, 78

Browning of America, 38

Brown vs. Board of Education, 21

About the Authors

JEAN LAU CHIN is Director of the South Cove Community Health Center in Boston, Massachusetts. She is coauthor of *Transference and Empathy in Asian American Psychotherapy* (Praeger, 1993).

VICTOR DE LA CANCELA, a clinical community psychologist licensed in three states, is currently the Senior Assistant Vice President, Managed Care Education and Special Projects for the New York City Health and Hospitals Corporation, the largest municipal health care system in the United States.

YVONNE M. JENKINS, a counseling and clinical psychologist, is on the staff of Harvard University Health Services, Cambridge, Massachusetts. She is also in private practice with Moore and Frauenhofer Psychological Associates, Brookline, Massachusetts.